Not Peace but a Sword

The Great Chasm Between
Christianity and Islam

ROBERT SPENCER

Not Peace but a Sword
The Great Chasm Between
Christianity and Islam

San Diego
2013

Not Peace but a Sword
The Great Chasm Between Christianity and Islam
© 2013 by Robert Spencer

Unless otherwise noted, biblical citations are taken from the
Revised Standard Version of the Bible
(© 1971 by Division of Christian Education of the National Council
of the Churches of Christ in the United States of America).

Published by Catholic Answers, Inc.
2020 Gillespie Way
El Cajon, California 92020
1-888-291-8000 orders
619-387-0042 fax
catholic.com
Printed in the United States of America

ISBN 978-1-938983-28-3 (hardcover)
ISBN 978-1-938983-27-6 (paperback)

All italics added for emphasis in citations from Scripture and ancient texts are the author's.

In memory of the Christian martyrs of Islamic jihad,
known and unknown.

*Your martyrs, O Lord, received the crown of immortality
from you, O our God, on account of their struggle.
Armed with your strength, they have vanquished their persecutors
and crushed the powerless arrogance of demons. Through their
intercessions, O Christ God, save our souls.*

This book would not have been written were it not for Todd M. Aglialoro, who conceived of it, encouraged me to write it, smoothed out its infelicities, and ably saw it through to completion. I am grateful for his patience and his keen eye. Thanks also to Fr. Thomas P. Steinmetz, a priest of priests, and to the many Catholic and Orthodox believers from the Middle East who discussed the issues in this book with me. Though I cannot name them for unfortunate but unavoidable reasons, I am deeply grateful for their insights.

Contents

Introduction 11

1. Time for an "Ecumenical Jihad"? 15

2. Three Great Abrahamic Faiths?................... 33

3. The Same God? 53

4. The Same Jesus?............................... 79

5. Are We All Muslims Now? 103

6. A Common Desire for Justice? 115

7. A Shared Sexual Ethic? 139

8. An Honest Desire for Dialogue? 163

Conclusion: Not Peace but a Sword.................... 185

Epilogue: The Kreeft/Spencer Debate................. 189

Appendix: Fundamental Differences.................. 239

Endnotes 244

Introduction

Vile Heretics, Separated Brethren, or Something Else?

Can't we all just get along? Maybe not. And if not, what then?

A book about the differences, rather than similarities, of two religious traditions, and how in certain important ways we may *not* be able to get along, and indeed should not work closely together (even as we strive always to preserve harmonious relations), may seem at first glance to be uncharitable. It is certainly against the spirit of the age.

To those who assume that to speak of other religions in anything but a complimentary fashion is contrary to Vatican II and to the divine command to love our neighbor, it may even seem un-Christian.

It is a peculiar, albeit common, misconception of our age to think that dispensing with the truth can be an act of charity. It never truly can be. We must always, as the Apostle says, speak the truth in love—that is, enunciate the realities that we know to be true without rancor, or pride, or arrogance, or condemnation. But, we must never think our obligation to be charitable can or should overwhelm our responsibility to bear witness to the truth.

When it comes to people of other faiths, as Catholics we must always treat them with the respect they warrant as human beings made in the image of God and endowed with an immortal soul, a soul for whom Christ died. It is not, however, an act either of disrespect or lack of charity to speak honestly about what divides us, about why we have separate religious traditions in the first place, and what the prospects are, in light of these differences, for collaboration and genuine dialogue.

In fact, one of the oddities of contemporary "interfaith dialogue" is that all too often, out of overzealous irenicism, it glosses over, or ignores altogether, the disagreements between religious traditions, as if pretending that they didn't exist would make them go away. This approach may make for a pleasant afternoon coffee, but as a basis for lasting cooperation or partnership it is fraught with hazards. The most obvious of these is the possibility that the very differences of belief and outlook that have been downplayed will operate in some way to derail the collaborative effort: People act all the time on the basis of the core assumptions and beliefs they have about the world and other people, and there is no field in which core assumptions and beliefs are more likely to come into play than the religious realm.

A respectful and accurate examination of differences, then, can make cooperation between people of different faiths more fruitful, helping all parties see the parameters for dialogue clearly and guard against unrealistic expectations. This is particularly true regarding the vexing question of dialogue and cooperation with Muslims.

It is fashionable in certain sectors for Catholics in the U.S. and Europe to call upon the Church to make common cause on life issues, and other areas of apparently shared moral concern, with Muslims. After all, both Catholics and Muslims face the same radical secularist foe; it's time, or so the contention goes, for a common front of believers to defend the theistic worldview against ever more intrusive, arrogant, and assertive unbelievers. At the same time, however, this call for a common cause seems to meet an immediate obstacle in the growing Muslim aggression against Christians around the globe. For many, this raises some fundamental questions: Is cooperation with Muslims really a good idea? If so, to what extent can it be done? What are the implications of that cooperation?

Related to these questions are considerations of what might be accomplished through dialogue between Catholics and Muslims, and indeed whether, given the realities of Islam's theological view of Christians as well as present-day political realities, such dialogue (that is, a genuine, honest, mutually respectful give-and-take) is even possible.

To answer these questions properly, Catholics should have a clear understanding of what they're getting into when they enter into dialogue or make common cause with Muslims: They should know what Muslims actually believe about various issues of morality and ethics, and what they think of Catholics and of Christianity in general. Only then can they avoid pitfalls in a field that is unusually strewn with them.

★★★

Islam today presents a double aspect. On the one hand, Islamic jihadists, acting explicitly and proudly in the name of Islam and its texts and teachings, commit acts of violence and persecute Christians with increasing virulence in Egypt, Iraq, Pakistan, Nigeria, Indonesia, and elsewhere. (In such contexts it may be useful to recall that the Crusades, for all their errors and excesses, were a defensive action after 450 years of unanswered Islamic aggression.)

On the other hand, Muslims in Western countries reach out to Catholics and other non-Muslims, pointing out all the many things that we have in common. These Muslims appear to be as different from their co-religionists who are torching churches and massacring Christians as a tongues-speaking, fire-baptized Pentecostal is from a blue-blooded Episcopalian who listens to NPR in his Mercedes.

The relationship between these two groups of Muslims, and the relationship of Islam in general to Christianity and the Catholic Church, is the preoccupation of this book. We will explore how Muslims understand not only their own religion but also ours, and what that implies for the prospects of collaboration, dialogue, and more. We'll also compare the Muslim and Catholic understandings of God, Christ, revelation, salvation, and morality.

The object of these explorations is to generate more light than heat, but these are heated issues. It is our responsibility as Catholics to approach Muslims, as everyone else, with unflagging charity.

That does not, however, require that we close our eyes.

1

Time for an "Ecumenical Jihad"?

They're pious. They're pro-life. They're uncompromising. What's not to like?

Many faithful Catholics today look at Muslims and see a formidable friend and ally in the struggle against secularist efforts to drive religion out of the public square and erase all vestiges of natural law from positive law. The Qur'an, the holy book of Islam, tells Muslims that "thou wilt surely find the nearest of them in love to the believers are those who say 'We are Christians'; that, because some of them are priests and monks, and they wax not proud" (5:82).[1] And some Christians have been anxious to show that same love to the believers in Islam. The foremost popular exponent of this view is the Catholic philosopher and apologist Peter Kreeft, who engagingly articulated the need for this alliance in his 1996 book *Ecumenical Jihad* and reiterated and expanded upon his call for it in his 2010 follow-up, *Between Allah and Jesus*.

"The age of religious wars is ending," proclaimed Kreeft five years before the September 11 attacks. Kreeft continued: "The age of religious *war* is beginning: a war of all religions against none."[2] Kreeft issues a strong call for making common cause with Muslims on moral issues and questions relating to maintaining a place for religion in public life. Noting that the highly charged Arabic word *jihad* actually means simply "struggle," he maintains that "an 'ecumenical jihad' is possible and is called for, for the simple and strong reason that Muslims and Christians preach and practice the same First Commandment: *islam*, total surrender, submission of the human will to the divine will. We fight side by side not only

because we face a common enemy but above all because we
serve and worship the same divine Commander."[3]

Leaving aside for a moment the question of whether
Catholics and Muslims view the submission of the human
will to the divine will in an identical or even analogous way,
bolstering Kreeft's point is the fact that Catholics and Muslims have already fought side by side. At the United Nations
World Conference on Population and Development, held
in Cairo in 1994, the international media made a great deal
out of a Vatican alliance with Muslim nations in opposition
to anti-life initiatives. At the World Conference on Women
held the next year in Beijing, Catholics and Muslims together called upon the conference to emphasize the family's
role as society's basic unit.

These alliances were not flawless. At the Cairo conference, the Church along with Muslim leaders succeeded in
ensuring that the final document affirmed that "in no case
should abortion be promoted as a method of family planning,"[4] but the Vatican failed to strike from the document
all language suggesting that abortion was a woman's right,
leading the *New York Times* to report with obvious satisfaction that "many conference delegates said the Vatican seriously miscalculated its potential clout in the debate, especially among . . . Islamic governments to which it had
appealed for support."[5] The Muslim representatives agreed
to the language ruling out the use of abortion as a means
of family planning but opposed Vatican efforts to call for
an end to it in all circumstances. For Islamic law, unlike
Church teaching and contrary to widespread belief, does
not forbid abortion in every case.[6]

Of course, Vatican officials don't have to secure 100 percent agreement with everyone with whom they collaborate.
The limitations of such cooperation with Muslims, how-

ever, are not isolated to disagreements about various aspects of core issues. They also stem from the irreconcilability between the calls for Christian-Muslim cooperation and the trend of anti-Christian violence committed by Muslims.

The jihad against modern-day Christians

In the popular mind, even after all these centuries since the Crusades, most Westerners tend to think that if there has been any aggression between Muslims and Christians, it was the Christians' fault. And so it is that the epithet of choice that Islamic jihadists apply to their foes today is *crusaders*. Canny at public relations, the jihadists hope thereby to conjure up an image of aggressive Christian warriors forcing non-Christians to convert or expelling them from their lands and establishing a Christian theocracy.

Islamic jihadists for years called American forces in Iraq and Afghanistan "Crusaders" and claimed that they were there as part of a war being waged by Christians against Islam. Confirmation of this came from an unlikely source in January 2011, when the acclaimed journalist Seymour Hersh, speaking in Qatar, charged that retired General Stanley McChrystal and military personnel currently serving in special operations units were part of a secret cabal bent on waging a new Crusade against Muslims: "They do see what they're doing—and this is not an atypical attitude among some military—it's a crusade, literally," Hersh asserted. "They see themselves as the protectors of the Christians. They're protecting them from the Muslims [as in] the thirteenth century. And this is their function."[7]

If McChrystal and others really considered themselves to be "the protectors of the Christians" from Islamic jihad attacks, they were failing dismally at their task. There is, of course, no new Crusade, but Christians in Muslim lands are being victimized more relentlessly and brutally today than they have been for centuries.

Egyptian Catholic spokesman Fr. Rafic Greische told Vatican Radio in December 2010 that "Muslim fundamentalists . . . want the Christians to evacuate from the Middle East and leave. And this is what is happening every day."[8] From Egypt to Nigeria, from Iraq to Pakistan, Christians in majority-Muslim countries face a grimmer present and a more uncertain future than ever as Islamic jihadists step up their efforts to Islamize them, to drive them out of their lands—or to kill them outright.

Still, the world generally continues to avert its eyes. Fearful of offending Muslim sensibilities, the international community has largely ignored this persecution, allowing it to continue under the cover of darkness. Thus unchallenged, Muslim persecution of Christians has become a drearily familiar narrative, repeated with increasingly terrifying frequency in Muslim-controlled areas throughout the world.

Moreover, this religious bigotry, hatred, and violence are legitimized by holy writ: the Qur'an and other Islamic texts and teachings. Nowhere else does religious bigotry have such bloody consequences. And yet, nowhere else does such religious bigotry take place almost entirely without comment, let alone condemnation, from the human rights community.

Emblematic of how the mainstream media, and in turn human rights organizations, gloss over the harsh reality of Christian persecution is a January 2011 Associated Press story. When machete-wielding Muslims brutally murdered six Christians in Nigeria in January 2011, AP's headline was "6 dead in religion-torn central Nigerian region," as if the cause of the problem was "sectarian strife" that was the equal responsibility of both sides. The lead paragraph read: "Authorities say machete-wielding attackers have killed six people in two attacks on Christian villages in central Nigeria."[9] Although the victims were identified, the attackers were not until later in the story, and then only in the context of their retaliating against an earlier attack upon Muslims by Christians. And indeed, Christians have fought back in Nigeria, but Islamic jihadists are the aggressors and created the conflict. One would never, however, get that idea from the Associated Press.

Human rights organizations give only perfunctory recognition to such outrages, and world leaders yawn. Christians are not fashionable or politically correct victims.

Before the Gulf War, some estimates held the number of Christians in Iraq to be approaching a million or more; but since 2003, over half of Iraq's prewar Christians have fled the country. This is not to suggest that the brutal regime of Saddam Hussein was particularly hospitable to Iraqi Christians; even in the relatively secular Iraq of Saddam, where Deputy Prime Minister Tariq Aziz was a Chaldean Catholic Christian, the small Christian community faced random violence from the Muslim majority. Aside from outbreaks of actual persecution, including murder, Christians were routinely pressured to renounce their religion and to marry Muslims.[10]

But now the situation has grown exponentially worse. Saddam did not enforce the fullness of Islamic law mandating the subjugation of Christians; now, numerous armed groups are determined to do so, or to punish those Christians who do not submit. Jihadists bombed forty Iraqi churches between 2004 and 2011—seven on a single day, Orthodox Christmas Eve 2007.[11] The most notorious attack came on October 31, 2010, a Sunday, when jihadists stormed the crowded Our Lady of Salvation church in Baghdad and began murdering worshippers in cold blood. Sixty-eight people were killed.[12]

The situation of Christians in Egypt is no better. Late in 2010 Copts in Egypt experienced an unprecedented reign of terror. An Islamic suicide bomber murdered twenty-two people and wounded eighty more at the Coptic Christian Church of the Saints in Alexandria, Egypt on New Year's Eve.[13] Just days later in 2011, as Christmas (which Copts celebrate on January 7) approached, an Islamic website carried this ominous exhortation: "Blow up the churches while they are celebrating Christmas or any other time when the churches are packed."[14]

Islamic authorities in Egypt are generally disinclined to discuss the plight of Christians there. When Pope Benedict XVI spoke out in January 2011 against the persecution of Christians in Egypt and elsewhere in the Middle East, Al-Azhar University in Cairo, the world's most prestigious Sunni Muslim institution, reacted angrily, breaking off dialogue with the Vatican and accusing the Pope of interference in internal Egyptian affairs. In a statement, Al-Azhar denounced the pontiff's "repeated negative references to Islam and his claims that Muslims persecute those living among them in the Middle East."[15] This was not the first time Al-Azhar had moved against those who decried the persecution of Christians in Egypt rather than against the persecutors: Just weeks before taking issue with the Pope's statements, Al-Azhar demanded that Copts repudiate a U.S. report on Coptic persecution.[16] The Mubarak government of Egypt, meanwhile, recalled its ambassador to the Vatican.[17]

In Pakistan, Christians are physically attacked and falsely accused under the nation's blasphemy laws so frequently that a steady stream of Christians is converting to Islam simply in order to be safe from legal harassment and rampaging Islamist mobs.[18] In 2010, blasphemy charges against a Christian woman, Asia Bibi, gained international attention and widespread criticism of Pakistan's blasphemy laws. Yet, when the governor of Punjab, Salman Taseer, spoke out in favor of the repeal of such laws, he was assassinated by an Islamic supremacist who explained that he was acting in defense of the blasphemy laws.[19]

And just as Al-Azhar reacted angrily when the Pope spoke out against the persecution of Christians in Egypt, in Pakistan Islamic supremacist groups became enraged when the pontiff called for repeal of the nation's blasphemy laws. Farid Paracha, the leader of Jamaat-i-Islami, the largest pro-Sharia party in Pakistan, fumed: "The Pope's statement is an insult to Muslims across the world."[20] Islamic supremacist groups held rallies protesting the Pope's statement as "part of a conspiracy to pit the world's religions against each other," in the words of Pakistani parliamentarian Sahibzada Fazal Karim.[21]

The punishment for exercising freedom of conscience: death

Converts from Islam to Christianity are often hunted in the Muslim world, where virtually all religious authorities agree that such individuals deserve death. Muhammad himself commanded this: "Whoever changed his Islamic religion, then kill him."[22] This is still the position of all the schools of Islamic jurisprudence, although there is some disagreement over whether the law applies only to men or to women also.

At Cairo's Al-Azhar University, the most prestigious and influential institution in the Islamic world, an Islamic manual certified as a reliable guide to Sunni Muslim orthodoxy, states: "When a person who has reached puberty and is sane voluntarily apostatizes from Islam, he deserves to be killed." Although the right to kill an apostate is reserved in Islamic law to the leader of the community and theoretically other Muslims can be punished for taking this duty upon themselves, in practice a Muslim who kills an apostate needs to pay no indemnity and perform no expiatory acts (as he must in other kinds of murder cases under classic Islamic law). This accommodation is made because killing an apostate "is killing someone who deserves to die."[23]

IslamOnline, a website manned by a team of Islam scholars headed by the internationally influential Sheikh Yusuf al-Qaradawi, explains, "If a sane person who has reached puberty voluntarily apostatizes from Islam, he deserves to be punished. In such a case, it is obligatory for the caliph (or his representative) to ask him to repent and return to Islam.

If he does, it is accepted from him, but if he refuses, he is immediately killed." And what if someone doesn't wait for a caliph to appear and takes matters into his own hands? Although the killer is to be "disciplined" for "arrogating the caliph's prerogative and encroaching upon his rights," there is "no blood money for killing an apostate (or any expiation)"— in other words, no significant punishment for the killer.[24]

Two Afghans, Said Musa and Abdul Rahman, know all this well. Both were arrested for the crime of leaving Islam for Christianity.[25] The Afghan Constitution stipulates that "no law can be contrary to the beliefs and provisions of the sacred religion of Islam."[26] Even after Abdul Rahman's arrest, which took place in 2006, Western analysts seem to have had trouble grasping the import of this provision. A "human rights expert" quoted by the *Times of London* summed up confusion widespread in Western countries: "The constitution says Islam is the religion of Afghanistan, yet it also mentions the Universal Declaration of Human Rights, and Article 18 specifically forbids this kind of recourse. It really highlights the problem the judiciary faces."[27]

But, in fact, there was no contradiction. The constitution may declare its "respect" for the Universal Declaration of Human Rights, but it also says that no law can contra-dict Islamic law. The Constitution's definition of religious freedom is explicit: "The religion of the state of the Islamic Republic of Afghanistan is the sacred religion of Islam. Fol-lowers of other religions are free to exercise their faith and perform their religious rites *within the limits of the provisions of law*" (emphasis added).

The death penalty for apostasy is deeply ingrained in Is-lamic culture—which is one reason why it was Abdul Rah-man's own family that went to police to file a complaint about his conversion. Whatever triggered their action in 2006, they could be confident that the police would receive such a com-plaint with the utmost seriousness. After an international out-cry, Abdul Rahman was eventually spirited out of Afghani-stan to relative safety in Italy. Despite the publicity, his case was hardly unique, as other nearly identical cases—that of Said Musa in February 2011 and that of Youcef Nadarkhani in early 2012—attest. And yet, while international indigna-tion rained down upon the Afghan government for the arrest and trial of Abdul Rahman, the world community showed hardly any interest at all in Said Musa. Perhaps the interven-ing years had inured the world's opinion makers to Islamic atrocities against Christians, although Nadarkhani's capital trial in Iran did call new international attention to the plight of ex-Muslims in Muslim countries.

Meanwhile, in Egypt in August 2007, Mohammed Hega-zy, a convert from Islam to Christianity, was forced to go into hiding after a death sentence was pronounced against him by Islamic clerics. He refused to flee Egypt, declaring, "I know there are fatwas to shed my blood, but I will not give up and I will not leave the country."[28] Early in 2008, his father told Egyptian newspapers: "I am going to try to talk to my son and convince him to return to Islam. If he refuses, I am going to kill him with my own hands." Hegazy remains in hiding in Egypt.[29]

A tradition of persecution

The prophet of Islam set the pattern for all of this, for he himself made war against Christians. Muhammad's last military expedition was against the Christian forces of the Byzantine Empire in the northern Arabian garrison of Tabuk; and shortly after their prophet's death, Islamic jihadists conquered and Islamized the Christian lands of the Middle East, North Africa, and Spain. The jihad then pointed toward Christian Europe and continued for centuries, the high-water mark coming in 1453 with the conquest of Constantinople. After September 1683, when the Ottoman siege of Vienna was broken, the Islamic tide in Europe began to recede. But the doctrines that fueled the jihad against Christians were never reformed or rejected by any Islamic sect.

Consequently, with the renewal of jihadist sentiments among Muslims in the twentieth century came renewed persecution of Christians. This chilling story told by a woman who lived during the Ottoman Empire of the late nineteenth century captures the moment of that renewal in one household:

> Then one night, my husband came home and told me that the padisha had sent word that we were to kill all the Christians in our village, and that we would have to kill our neighbours. I was very angry, and told him that I did not care who gave such orders, they were wrong. These neighbours had always been kind to us, and if he dared to kill them Allah would pay us out. I tried all I could to stop him, but he killed them—killed them with his own hand.[30]

The Christian population in Turkey has declined from 15 percent in 1920 to 1 percent today. In Syria, it has declined from 33 percent to 10 percent in the same span. In Bethlehem, 85 percent of the population was Christian in 1948; today, 12 percent hold to the faith founded by the town's most celebrated native son.[31] The burden of the past lies heavy on the present for Christians in the Muslim world. Sheikh Omar Bakri Muhammad, a controversial pro-Osama Muslim leader who lived for years in Great Britain but is now barred from reentering that country, wrote in October 2002, "We cannot simply say that because we have no Khilafah [caliphate] we can just go ahead and kill any non-Muslim, rather, we must still fulfill their Dhimmah."[32]

The *Dhimmah* is the Islamic legal contract of protection for Jews, Christians, and some other inferiors under Islamic rule; those who accept this protection, and the concomitant deprivation of various rights, are known as *dhimmis*. In 1999, Sheikh Yussef Salameh, the Palestinian Authority's undersecretary for religious endowment, according to Jonathan Adelman and Agota Kuperman of the Foundation for the Defense of Democracies, "praised the idea that Christians should become *dhimmis* under Muslim rule, and such suggestions have become more common since the second intifada began in October 2000."[33]

In a recent Friday sermon at a mosque in Mecca, Sheikh Marzouq Salem Al-Ghamdi spelled out the Sharia's injunctions for *dhimmis*:

> If the infidels live among the Muslims, in accordance with the conditions set out by the Prophet—there is nothing wrong with it provided they pay Jizya to the Islamic treasury. Other conditions are . . . that they do not renovate a church or a monastery, do not rebuild ones that were

destroyed, that they feed for three days any Muslim who passes by their homes . . . that they rise when a Muslim wishes to sit, that they do not imitate Muslims in dress and speech, nor ride horses, nor own swords, nor arm themselves with any kind of weapon; that they do not sell wine, do not show the cross, do not ring church bells, do not raise their voices during prayer, that they shave their hair in front so as to make them easily identifiable, do not incite anyone against the Muslims, and do not strike a Muslim. . . . If they violate these conditions, they have no protection.[34]

These Sharia provisions have not been fully enforced since the mid-nineteenth century, but today's jihadists want to restore these laws along with the rest of the Sharia. The idea that Christians must "feel themselves subdued" (Qur'an 9:29) in Islamic lands is also very much alive. When the first Catholic Church in Qatar opened in March 2008, it sported no cross, no bell, no steeple, and no sign. "The idea," explained the church's pastor, Fr. Tom Veneracion, "is to be discreet because we don't want to inflame any sensitivities."[35]

In the Philippines, the church in the nation's one Islamic city, Marawi, has also done away with the cross. A Catholic priest, Fr. Teresito Soganub, explains: "To avoid arguments and to avoid further misunderstandings we just plant the cross deep in our hearts." Fr. Soganub, according to Reuters, "doesn't wear a crucifix or a clerical collar and sports a beard out of respect for his Muslim neighbors." He celebrates few weddings, since roast pork is a staple of wedding receptions for Filipino Catholics.[36]

It is easy to see the need for such discretion. Preaching in a mosque in Al-Damam, Saudi Arabia, the popular Saudi Sheikh Muhammad Saleh Al-Munajjid recommended hatred of Christians and Jews as a proper course: "Muslims must educate their children to Jihad. This is the greatest benefit of the situation: educating the children to Jihad and to hatred of the Jews, the Christians, and the infidels; educating the children to Jihad and to revival of the embers of Jihad in their souls. This is what is needed now."[37]

The silence of human rights groups

What Justus Reid Weiner, an international human rights lawyer, stated in December 2007 about Christians in Palestinian areas applies to Christians in the Islamic world generally: "The systematic persecution of Christian Arabs living in Palestinian areas is being met with nearly total silence by the international community, human rights activists, the media and NGOs." He said that if nothing were done, no Christians would be left there in fifteen years, for "Christian leaders are being forced to abandon their followers to the forces of radical Islam."[38]

The nearly total silence manifests itself in the curiously euphemistic manner in which human rights groups report on the plight of Christians, when they notice that plight at all. For example, Amnesty International's 2007 report on the human rights situation in Egypt dismisses the suffering of Coptic Christians in a single sentence so filled with euphemism and moral equivalence and so lacking in context that it almost erases the crime it describes: "There were sporadic outbreaks of sectarian violence between Muslims and Christians. In April [2006], three days of religious violence in Alexandria resulted in at least three deaths and dozens of injuries."[39] In reality, the strife began when a Muslim stabbed a Christian to death inside a church, and when armed jihadists attacked three churches in Alexandria that same month.[40]

The passive voice seems to be the rule of the day where jihad violence against Christians is concerned. The 2007 Amnesty International report on Indonesia includes this line: "Minority religious groups and church buildings continued to be attacked." By whom? AI is silent. "In Sulawesi, sporadic religious violence occurred throughout the year."[41] Who is responsible for that violence? AI doesn't say. Amnesty International seems more concerned about protecting Islam and Islamic groups from being implicated in human rights abuses than about protecting Christians from those abuses.

It appears that Christianity—even indigenous Egyptian Christianity, which of course predates the advent of Islam in that country—is too closely identified with the United States and the West for the multiculturalist tastes of the human rights elite. The situation is dire. Melkite Greek Catholic Patriarch Gregory III, who lives in Damascus, declared in April 2006 that "after 11 September, there is a plot to eliminate all the Christian minorities from the Arabic world. . . . Our simple existence ruins the equations whereby Arabs can't be other than Moslems, and Christians but be Westerners. . . . If the Chaldeans, the Assyrians, the Orthodox, the Latin Catholics leave, if the Middle East is cleansed of all the Arabic Christians, the Moslem Arab world and a so-called Christian Western world will be left face to face. It will be easier to provoke a clash and justify it with religion."[42] Several years later, Gregory III himself showed he felt the pressure to please the Muslims—or else—when he publicly blamed the Muslim persecution of Christians not on Islamic supremacists but on that ever-present bogey of Middle Eastern conspiracy theories, the Zionists.[43]

Yet some American Catholics and non-Christians are surprised to discover that there are ancient communities of Christians in Islamic lands at all and that those communities are being persecuted. Others are indifferent because of the growing movement of fashionable atheism, which sees all religions as equally repugnant and liable to lead to violence, whatever the differences in their actual teachings. And many Westerners, particularly those in the human rights elite, are wedded to a worldview in which only non-Western non-Christians can possibly fit into the human rights groups' victim paradigm: Middle Eastern Christians are identified with white Western oppressors and could not be victims. Some Westerners even indulge in a certain *schadenfreude* at the persecution of Christians worldwide, seeing in it a comeuppance for a church and a belief system for which they have long harbored hatred or self-loathing guilt. That Christians in Muslim lands are generally poor, disenfranchised, and worlds away from the oppressive force that is the Christianity of Leftist myth doesn't seem to enter their minds.

And so Islamic jihadists and Sharia supremacists, with ever increasing confidence and brutality, and virtually no protest from the West, continue to prey on the Christians in their midst. These embattled communities are now on the verge of extinction, with no one to speak up for them. Their continued existence and safety would require nothing short of a miracle.

Cognitive dissonance

In light of all this (and much more) evidence of an escalating global Islamic jihad against Christians, Peter Kreeft's assertion—that "an 'ecumenical jihad' is possible and is called for, for the simple and strong reason that Muslims and Christians preach and practice the same First Commandment: *islam*, total surrender, submission of the human will to the divine will"—seems ironic. At the very least, the impulse to wage a new war of all religions united against secularism is coming largely from Christians, without significant interest from the Muslim side. There is much more evidence of Muslim hatred and contempt for Christians, as evidenced by the global violence against them, than there is of Muslim interest in a common front with Catholics or any other Christians. To be sure, several years ago a large group of Islamic scholars did write to Pope Benedict and other Christian leaders, inviting them to dialogue (an initiative we'll examine in depth later on), but they have not managed to restrain their bloody-minded coreligionists.

The reasons for this may be many and elusive, but the reality of the escalating Muslim persecution of Christians and the comparatively small number of Muslims who have shown interest in anything like the common front that Kreeft advocates highlight the danger that, in their haste to gain an advantage in the culture wars, Western Catholics may be papering over vast and substantial differences between Catholicism and Islam solely in the hope of gaining an ally. And that way lies danger, for an ally gained by such means will hardly be dependable, and the ways in which that lack of dependability may manifest itself could have consequences nothing short of catastrophic.

Saladin: myth versus reality

Kreeft, and others like him, envision Muslims as devout, God-fearing, moral people who would naturally align themselves with others, such as Catholics, who share their concerns about galloping secularism and the erosion of moral values in society. In his book *The Enemy at Home,* conservative pundit Dinesh D'Souza advocates a common front between conservative Americans of all faiths and conservative Muslims, portraying these Muslims, whom he does not identify by name, as honorable, pious, humble, and appalled by contemporary Western popular culture. No doubt these qualities describe many Muslims. They certainly recall one particular Muslim: the semi-legendary sultan of the Crusader era, Saladin.

In the twelfth century, Saladin dealt decisive blows to the Crusader enterprise; but did it, according to prevailing historical myth, in a magnanimous and noble manner. Today Saladin is generally regarded as an exponent of the best aspects of Islam and proof that it need not be a religion of terrorism and intransigence. The Arab historian Amin Maalouf sums this up in his description of Saladin: "He was always affable with visitors, insisting that they stay to eat, treating them with full honours, even if they were infidels, and satisfying all their requests. He could not bear to let someone who had come to him depart disappointed, and there were those who did not hesitate to take advantage of this quality. One day, during a truce with the Franj [Franks], the 'Brins,' lord of Antioch, arrived unexpectedly at Saladin's tent and asked him to return a district that the sultan had taken four years earlier. And he agreed!"[44]

The real Saladin of history was not quite as magnificently noble of spirit and generous as he is usually portrayed. After his great victory over the Crusaders at Hattin on July 4, 1187, he ordered that his Christian captives "should be beheaded [in accordance with Qur'an 47:4: "When you meet the unbelievers, smite their necks"], choosing to have them dead rather than in prison. With him was a whole band of scholars and Sufis and a certain number of devout men and ascetics; each begged to be allowed to kill one of them, and drew his sword and rolled back his sleeve. Saladin, his face joyful, was sitting on his dais; the unbelievers showed black despair."[45]

Saladin was just as ruthless and bloodthirsty on other occasions.[46] Here again, his positive reputation in the modern West is more a matter of wishful thinking than of realism. And so it is with so much Catholic–Muslim interaction nowadays.

2

Three Great Abrahamic Faiths?

The idea that Judaism, Christianity, and Islam are sister faiths, differing but closely related elaborations of the same religious tradition, is so commonplace today that for many Catholics it is essentially everything they know about Islam. The Second Vatican Council and the *Catechism of the Catholic Church* say that the Muslims are "professing to hold the faith of Abraham." And to a Catholic opening the Qur'an for the first time, there certainly seems to be a great deal to confirm this idea.

Echoes of the Bible

Most Catholics would be surprised at how much biblical material the Qur'an contains, but Muslims are generally well aware of this; indeed, the similarities between the Bible and the Qur'an are a staple of the presentations of Muslim apologists. The Bible and the Qur'an appear, superficially, to breathe the same religious atmosphere. They appear to be distinct expressions of the same larger religious tradition. Christians and Muslims revere the same religious heroes, tell the same stories, and speak about God in the same way.

What Catholic could possibly object to one of the most beloved and oft-memorized verses of the Qur'an, the "Verse of the Throne"?

> "God there is no god but He, the Living, the Everlasting. Slumber seizes Him not, neither sleep; to Him belongs all that is in the heavens and the earth. Who is there that shall intercede with Him save by His leave? He knows what lies before them and what is after them, and they

comprehend not anything of His knowledge save such as He wills. His Throne comprises the heavens and earth; the preserving of them oppresses Him not; He is the All-high, the All-glorious." (2:255)

The biblical resonances in this passage are many; in fact, the first portion of the Verse of the Throne could practically be reconstructed from the Bible. "I am the LORD, and there is no other, besides me there is no God," relates the prophet Isaiah (45:5). "Behold, He who watches over Israel will neither slumber nor sleep," we're told in the Psalms (121:4). "Behold, to the LORD your God belong heaven and the heaven of heavens, the earth with all that is in it," says Deuteronomy (10:14).

The Qur'an teaches that there is one almighty God, the creator of heaven and earth. "There is no god but God, and assuredly God is the All-mighty, the All-wise" (3:62). He knows and sees all things: "The eyes attain Him not, but He attains the eyes; He is the All-subtle, the All-aware" (6:103). "To God belongs all that is in the heavens and earth. Whether you publish what is in your hearts or hide it, God shall make reckoning with you for it. He will forgive whom He will, and chastise whom He will; God is powerful over everything" (2:284).

Also found in the Qur'an are declarations that Jesus is the Messiah, the Word of God, who was born of the Virgin Mary, a birth that the Qur'an reverentially describes as a great work of God. One passage echoes the Annunciation, although in the Qur'an there is more than one angel doing the announcing: "The angels said, 'Mary, God gives thee good tidings of a Word from Him whose name is Messiah, Jesus, son of Mary; high honored shall he be in this world and the next, near stationed to God" (3:45).

In the Qur'an, as in the New Testament, Jesus is a miracle-worker: "And We gave to Moses the Book, and after him sent succeeding Messengers; and We gave Jesus son of Mary the clear signs [i.e., miracles]" (2:87).

One almighty God. Jesus, the Messiah and the Word of God, born of a Virgin and working miracles. The Qur'an's biblical resonances do not end there. Like the Bible and the Christian tradition, the Qur'an and Islamic tradition call men to faith in a message it says is divinely revealed. "And believe in that I have sent down, confirming that which is with you, and be not the first to disbelieve in it. And sell not My signs for a little price; and fear you Me" (2:41).

The Qur'an even says that that message is the same as that which was revealed to earlier prophets. Allah tells his prophet to tell the people about Moses: "And mention in the Book of Moses; he was devoted, and he was a Messenger, a Prophet. We called to him from the right side of the Mount, and We brought him near in communion. And We gave him his brother Aaron, of Our mercy, a Prophet" (19:51-53).

Then Allah sends Jesus with a message that confirms that of Moses: "And We sent, following in their footsteps, Jesus son of Mary, confirming the Torah before him and We gave to him the Gospel, wherein is guidance and light, and confirming the Torah before it, as a guidance and an admonition unto the godfearing" (5:46). Finally, Allah sends Muhammad with a new message that confirms the gospel, which in the Qur'anic view is a book that Allah delivered to the world through Jesus: "And We have sent down to thee the Book with the truth, confirming the Book that was before it, and assuring it" (5:48). "This is a Book We have sent down, blessed and confirming that which was before it" (6:92).

There are numerous other biblical figures in the Qur'an, including Noah: "Noah called to Us; and how excellent were the Answerers! And We delivered him and his people from the great distress, and We made his seed the survivors, and left for him among the later folk. 'Peace be upon Noah among all beings!'" (37:75-9). The Qur'an also says of Abraham: "And who is there that has a fairer religion than he who submits his will to God being a good-doer, and who follows the creed of Abraham, a man of pure faith? And God took Abraham for a friend" (4:125).

The Qur'an's echoes of the Bible don't end with the cast of characters. There even seems to be something of the Bible's natural theology in the Qur'an. Faintly echoing St. Paul's observation that "ever since the creation of the world his invisible nature, namely, his eternal power and deity, has been clearly perceived in the things that have been made" (Rom. 1:20), the Qur'an teaches that Allah has made his presence and power clearly known in this world: "And We have sent down unto thee signs, clear signs, and none disbelieves in them except the ungodly" (2:99).

The Qur'an also teaches that Allah has set out rules about how human beings should behave, and that at the end of this earthly existence, he will judge every individual on the basis of how well he has lived up to those rules: "When earth is shaken with a mighty shaking and earth brings forth her burdens, and Man says, 'What ails her?' upon that day she shall tell her tidings for that her Lord has inspired her. Upon that day men shall issue in scatterings to see their works, and whoso has done an atom's weight of good shall see it, and whoso has done an atom's weight of evil shall see it" (99:1-8). Everything that man does is recorded: "Everything that they have done is in the Scrolls, and everything, great and small, is inscribed" (54:52-3).

The Qur'anic Exodus

The story of the Exodus is told and retold in the Qur'an, and often sounds like a summary and recapitulation of the biblical account, with some notable differences. It gives the flavor of how the Qur'an treats biblical material, and the differences between the Qur'anic and biblical accounts are revelatory of larger differences between basic Catholic and Islamic beliefs.

The Qur'an tells the story of the Exodus many times, each time presenting different details of the story. The longest and most detailed of these accounts is found in *sura* 7, and starts without the preamble of Moses' birth and upbringing, although that is told elsewhere in the Qur'an (28:1-19). In this instance, preceding the story of Moses are accounts of some of the deeds of several other prophets. The Qur'anic order is not chronological; its logic is homiletic. Moses and the other prophets are mentioned in order to make and illustrate various theological points. The initial homiletic point here is that "workers of corruption" will be punished just as Pharaoh was for opposing Moses: "but they did them wrong; so behold thou, how was the end of the workers of corruption!"

But in this passage there is also a particularly detailed account of the Exodus, beginning with God sending Moses "with Our signs to Pharaoh and his Council." The story reads like a summary recapitulation of the biblical account:

> Moses said, "Pharaoh, I am a Messenger from the Lord of all Being, worthy to say nothing regarding God except the truth. I have brought a clear sign to you from your Lord; so send forth with me the Children of Israel." Said he, "If thou hast brought a sign, produce it, if thou speakest truly." So he cast his staff; and behold, it was a serpent manifest. And he drew forth his hand, and lo, it was white to the beholders. (7:103-108)

The way this story is told suggests that the hearers have heard it before: We see Moses telling Pharaoh to "send forth

with me the Children of Israel" (7:105), but the Qur'an as-
sumes that the reader will know that the Israelites were at
this time oppressed as slaves in Egypt; it is not mentioned
explicitly. Moses performs various miracles before Pharaoh,
as in the biblical account—although when Moses' hand becomes "white to the beholders" (7:108), one early commen-
tator on the Qur'an, Ibn Abbas, says this was "not because
of leprosy," which is contrary to Exodus 4:6.[47] The *Ruhul
Ma'ani*, another venerable commentary on the Qur'an, says
that Moses' hand shone brighter than the sun.[48] This may be
in keeping with the Qur'an's idea that prophets must not suffer defeat or loss; the foremost manifestation of this assumption is the Qur'an's denial that Jesus was crucified (4:157).

The "Council of the people" then suggests that Pharaoh
"put off" Moses and Aaron for a while, while sending "mus-
terers" into the cities of Egypt to summon "every cunning
sorcerer." The sorcerers duly arrive and demand payment
from Pharaoh if they best Moses, but it was not to be:

> They said, "Moses, wilt thou cast, or shall we be the cast-
> ers?" He said, "You cast." And when they cast they put a
> Spell upon the people's eyes, and called forth fear of them,
> and produced a mighty sorcery. And We revealed to Moses:
> "Cast thy staff!" And lo, it forthwith swallowed up their
> lying invention. So the truth came to pass, and false was
> proved what they were doing. So they were vanquished
> there, and they turned about, humbled. (7:115-119)

Although Pharaoh is as unimpressed in the Qur'an with
the wonders Moses performs as he is in the biblical story, his
magicians are so moved as to profess faith in "the Lord of all
Being, the Lord of Moses and Aaron" (7:121-122), whereupon Pharaoh threatens to "cut off alternately your hands and

feet, then I shall crucify you all together" (7:124). This bit of barbarity appears nowhere in Exodus, and is the same punishment Allah prescribes elsewhere in the Qur'an for those who wage war against Allah and Muhammad (5:33). The cunning sorcerers respond with a confession of faith in Allah:

> They said, "Surely unto our Lord we are turning. Thou takest vengeance upon us only because we have believed in the signs of our Lord when they came to us. Our Lord, pour out upon us patience, and gather us unto Thee surrendering." (7:125-126)

Significantly, the word translated here as *surrendering* is in Arabic "Muslims" (*muslimeen*). When the Qur'an depicts the sorcerers as converting to the religion of Moses, it shows them converting not to Judaism but to Islam. This seems anachronistic: How could Moses and the sorcerers have been Muslims so long before Muhammad?

The Qur'an does not mean that Moses was a believer in Muhammad as a prophet of Allah. But as Muhammad's message confirms that of Jesus, and Jesus' message confirms Moses', in the Qur'anic view the messages of all the prophets were identical in substance. Allah gave mankind a series of revelations, and all of these call on human beings to become "Muslims," or submitters to Allah. A genuine submitter to Allah will always recognize Allah's message and accept his new prophets.

This is not to say, however, that Islamic theology recognizes any significant distinction between pre-Islamic monotheistic submitters to Allah such as Moses and the sorcerers (and other significant personages, as we shall see) and Muslims who publicly proclaim the *shahadah*, the Islamic confession of faith: "There is no god but Allah and Muhammad

is his prophet." Islam presents itself to be pure monotheism, with nothing added or subtracted; hence, when Jews
and Christians protest that Moses and other biblical figures
were actually Israelites professing the faith of Israel, Muslims
will respond that that faith was Islam, and that Judaism and
Christianity, in all their varied forms today, are but corrup-
tions of that original monotheism and submission to Allah—that is, Islam.

In the Qur'anic account (found in Sura 7) of Moses and
Pharaoh, after the sorcerers become Muslims, the "Council
of the people" asks Pharaoh, "Wilt thou leave Moses and his
people to work corruption in the land, and leave thee and
thy gods?" The phrase "corruption in the land" is significant
in Islam. It is the offense for which crucifixion or amputation of the hands and feet on opposite sides is prescribed in
Qur'an 5:33. Pharaoh answers: "We shall slaughter their sons
and spare their women; surely we are triumphant over them!"

Moses then tells his people to pray and be patient, and
they respond with the same truculence they display in the
Exodus account, telling Moses: "We have been hurt before
thou camest to us, and after thou camest to us." But Allah
is on their side: "Then seized We Pharaoh's people with
years of dearth, and scarcity of fruits, that haply they might
remember." But the Egyptians miss the point: "So, when
good came to them, they said, 'This belongs to us'; but if any
evil smote them, they would augur ill by Moses and those
with him. Why, surely their ill augury was with God; but
the most of them knew not."

Thereafter follow "the flood and the locusts, the lice and
the frogs, the blood, distinct signs; but they waxed proud
and were a sinful people." When the sea is parted and the
Children of Israel arrive on the other side, they find an un-
named idolatrous nation and immediately demand that Mo-

ses fashion gods for them to worship. Moses responds: "You
are surely a people who are ignorant. Surely this they are
engaged upon shall be shattered, and void is what they have
been doing," and "What, shall I seek a god for you other
than God, who has preferred you above all beings?"

The charge that the people are ignorant, rather than simply sinful and rebellious, is noteworthy, for to this day Islamic spokesmen and apologists charge non-Muslims with
ignorance, including those who demonstrate that they understand the religion well. The mainstream media present
us with surveys alleging that people who dislike Islam or
distrust Muslims are simply suffering from a lack of knowledge.[49] This is in line with the Islamic scheme of things:
Allah did not send prophets and revelations so much to save
people from sin—although there is a moral framework in
Islam—but to save them from ignorance.

Thus, the Fatihah, the first *sura* of the Qur'an and the most
frequently repeated prayer in Islamic tradition and day-to-
day piety, has the believer saying to Allah, "Guide us in the
straight path, the path of those whom Thou hast blessed, not
of those against whom Thou art wrathful, nor of those who
are astray" (1:6-7). Although this may appear to be a statement enjoining good behavior and rejecting sinful behavior,
in fact, it is more of a confessional statement. At least that is
how Islamic scholars have generally understood it. The most
mainstream and widely accepted understanding of this passage among Muslims is that "the straight path" is Islam, while
"those against whom Thou art wrathful" are the Jews and
"those who are astray" are the Christians.[50] The problem with
the two groups is their erroneous beliefs, which they hold in
ignorance—although this ignorance is culpable.

In the Qu'ran, Allah recounts that he gave Moses the
Ten Commandments, with a stern warning to the unbe-

lievers but without specifying here (or anywhere else in the
Qur'an) what those commandments actually are:

> And We wrote for him on the Tablets of everything an
> admonition, and a distinguishing of everything: "So take
> it forcefully, and command thy people to take the fairest of
> it. I shall show you the habitation of the ungodly. I shall
> turn from My signs those who wax proud in the earth un-
> justly; though they see every sign, they will not believe in
> it, and though they see the way of rectitude they will not
> take it for a way, and though they see the way of error, they
> will take it for a way. That, because they have cried lies to
> Our signs and heeded them not." Those who cry lies to
> Our signs, and the encounter in the world to come—their
> works have failed; shall they be recompensed, except ac-
> cording to the things they have done? (7:145-147)

Shortly thereafter, as we hear about the Children of Israel's
dalliance with the golden calf, Allah says of the tablets he gave
to Moses that "in the inscription of them was guidance, and
mercy unto all those who hold their Lord in awe" (7:154) but
again, doesn't say exactly what that guidance was.

Those who worshipped the calf, meanwhile, will not
only be subject to the Lord's anger, but to "abasement in this
present life" (7:152)—a concept that recurs in many contexts
in Islamic teaching.

Moses, for his part, prays for forgiveness for the Children of Israel, noting: "My Lord, hadst Thou willed Thou
wouldst have destroyed them before, and me. Wilt Thou
destroy us for what the foolish ones of us have done? It is
only Thy trial, whereby Thou leadest astray whom Thou
wilt, and guidest whom Thou wilt"(7:155)." Allah responds
somewhat anachronistically:

My chastisement—I smite with it whom I will; and My mercy embraces all things, and I shall prescribe it for those who are godfearing and pay the alms, and those who indeed believe in Our signs, those who follow the Messenger, the Prophet of the common folk, whom they find written down with them in the Torah and the Gospel, bidding them to honor, and forbidding them dishonor, making lawful for them the good things and making unlawful for them the corrupt things, and relieving them of their loads, and the fetters that were upon them. Those who believe in him and succor him and help him, and follow the light that has been sent down with him—they are the prosperers. (7:156-157)

Since the messenger in question is apparently prophesied about in the Torah and the Gospels, in this passage Allah evidently refers to the prophet of Islam, Muhammad—even though he is supposed to be saying this to Moses many hundreds of years before Muhammad was born. The passage is not couched as a prophecy, but seems to presuppose that Muhammad has already appeared on the scene: a considerable lapse of attention for the Qur'anic narrator.

Ultimately, Allah curses the Sabbath-breaking Jews by transforming them into apes: "Be you apes, miserably slinking!"(7:166). This, too, is a theme to which the Qur'an returns, emblematic of an attitude toward Jews that would bring a blush to the cheeks of the most hardened anti-Semite.

In this retelling of the Exodus account, then, we discover numerous key differences between the biblical and Qur'anic accounts that are indicative of the differences between Christianity and Islam in general. Particularly significant are the lack of specification of the Ten Commandments and the failure of Moses actually to see God in the passage parallel to

that in which he sees God's "back" in Exodus. As we shall
examine in depth later, these differences manifest a moral
understanding and a vision of God sharply different from
the Christian view.

The Almost-Fall of Man

Other similarities between Catholicism and Islam, along with
some other striking and telling differences, can be found in
the Bible's foundational narrative, that of the fall of Adam
and Eve. Here again, this Qur'anic account reads practically
as if it were a summary interpretation of the biblical story,
with some intriguing and telling variations—although, like
the Qur'an's account of the Exodus, it also never appears in
any one place as a continuous narrative. At no point does the
Qur'an tell the story of our first parents whole and entire,
from beginning to end; instead, it is interspersed throughout
the Muslim holy book. And so, in the account that follows,
details are drawn from all over the book to present the details
of the story as the Qur'an has them, but in linear fashion.

In the Qur'an, as well as in the Bible, God creates Adam
and Eve and places them in a paradisal setting. In the Qur'an,
Allah teaches Adam the names of the animals (2:31), rather
than inviting him to name them himself. But the command
to avoid the forbidden fruit is the same in substance as it is in
the Bible: "And We said, 'Adam, dwell thou, and thy wife,
in the Garden, and eat thereof easefully where you desire;
but draw not nigh this tree, lest you be evildoers'" (2:35).
But "then Satan caused them to slip therefrom"—from the
Garden, that is—"and brought them out of that they were
in; and We said, 'Get you all down, each of you an enemy
of each; and in the earth a sojourn shall be yours, and enjoyment for a time'" (2:36).

Allah has created this first man "of a clay of mud molded" (15:26), or from dust, as we learn in a passage that affirms the thoroughly Christian doctrine of Jesus as the new Adam: "Truly, the likeness of Jesus, in God's sight, is as Adam's likeness; He created him of dust, then said He unto him, 'Be,' and he was" (3:59).

However, even though Jesus is likened to Adam, there is no indication in the Qur'an that Allah created mankind in the divine image (Genesis 1:26); although there are hints that the Qur'anic accounts were adapted from sources that took that image for granted. The Qur'an repeats no fewer than five times that Allah commands the angels to prostrate themselves before Adam (2:34; 7:11; 15:29; 18:50; 20:116). This command originated in Jewish tradition and depends upon the biblical notion of man's bearing the divine image. For if man did not bear God's image, the command that a greater being must prostrate before a lesser one would make no sense. Neither the Qur'an nor Islamic tradition, however, ever draws out these implications.

When Satan refuses to prostrate himself, the Qur'an tells us, he becomes "one of the unbelievers" (2:34)—an odd conflation of disobedience with disbelief. Allah asks him why he refused, and Satan answers pridefully, disparaging Adam: "I am better than he; Thou createdst me of fire, and him Thou createdst of clay" (7:12; cf. 38:76, 15:33, 17:61) Allah curses Satan for his disobedience (38:77-78) and banishes him from Paradise (7:13; 15:34)—but then Satan requests a reprieve until the Day of Judgment. Allah assents (15:37; 38:79-81), despite the fact that Satan boasts that he intends to use this reprieve to tempt Muslims away from Islam (7:16-17; 15:39). Recalling Satan's colloquy with God in the Book of Job, Satan challenges Allah over Adam: "What thinkest Thou? This whom Thou hast honored above me—if Thou deferrest me to the Day of Resurrection I shall assuredly master his seed, save a few" (17:62).

Satan vows to lead astray all of mankind "excepting those Thy servants among them that are sincere" (38:83; cf. 15:40), although Allah warns him that "over My servants thou shalt have no authority, except those that follow thee, being perverse" (15:42) and vows to fill hell with Satan's followers (38:85). "Depart!" he commands Satan. "Those of them that follow thee—surely Gehenna shall be your recompense, an ample recompense! And startle whomsoever of them thou canst with thy voice; and rally against them thy horsemen and thy foot, and share with them in their wealth and their children, and promise them!" (17:63-64). But this bounty is illusory; Satan "promises them naught, except delusion" (17:64).

Allah, meanwhile, warns Adam about him: "Adam, surely this is an enemy to thee and thy wife. So let him not expel you both from the Garden, so that thou art unprosperous. It is assuredly given to thee neither to hunger therein, nor to go naked, neither to thirst therein, nor to suffer the sun" (20:118-120). But Satan tempts him away from the delights of this place by inviting him to eat from what is known in the Bible as the Tree of Life—not, as the account in Genesis has it, the Tree of the Knowledge of Good and Evil: "Adam, shall I point thee to the Tree of Eternity, and a Kingdom that decays not?" (20:120).

And Adam and Eve succumb, in no particular order: "So the two of them ate of it, and their shameful parts revealed to them, and they took to stitching upon themselves leaves of the Garden. And Adam disobeyed his Lord, and so he erred" (20:121).

The differences between this account and the biblical one are not mere matters of detail: In the Qur'anic account, Adam and Eve are never mentioned as having been created in the image of God; that there is something singular about them is assumed— Allah bids the angels to bow down before human beings—but never explained. And when Adam and Eve rebel from Allah, they do so by eating of the fruit of the "Tree of Eternity," not the fruit of the Tree of the Knowledge of Good and Evil. This is significant because, as the Navarre Bible explains, "the fact that man had access to the 'tree of the knowledge of good and evil' means that God left the way open to the possibility of evil in order to ensure a greater good—the freedom that is man's endowment. By using his reason and following his conscience, man is able to discern what is good and what is evil; but he himself cannot *make* something good or evil."[51]

But reason, freedom, and discernment are all denied in Islam. In the Qur'an, human beings are not endowed with the dignity of bearing God's image, but are merely another group of his creatures. A hadith does say that "Adam is the image of Allah," but this does not carry over to mankind in general nor have the significance it does in Christianity.[52] Indeed, its only significance in Islamic tradition is a tendency toward literalistic anthropomorphism, as some Muslim divines picture Allah with a human body. But it has no significance for the nature of the human soul and spirit.

And the first couple are not tempted with the prospect of moral awareness, becoming "like God, knowing good and evil" (Gen. 3:5). Instead, the tempter offers them everlasting life. As Allah banishes them to earth (the Qur'anic Paradise in which Adam and Eve lived before the fall doesn't appear to have been an earthly one), he says: "Therein you shall live, and therein you shall die, and from there you shall be brought forth" (7:25). Yet, just as in the Christian conception of death and the afterlife, this earthly death is not the end of existence, for the blessed shall be resurrected to enjoy the delights of Paradise—although, as we shall see, the Qur'an envisions a Paradise that is markedly different from the Christian one.

In the meantime, the first parents' progeny do not bear the burden of separation from Allah. As he banishes Adam and Eve from Paradise, Allah tells them: "Get you down, both of you together, out of it, each of you an enemy to each; but if there comes to you from Me guidance, then whosoever follows My guidance shall not go astray, neither shall he be unprosperous" (20:123). That's all. Islam has no concept of original sin: Even though Islamic tradition echoes Catholic tradition by identifying only Jesus and Mary as sinless, in Islam man is no more alienated from God before the rebellion of Adam and Eve than he was before it, and all he need do is follow Allah's guidance so as not to go astray. The rebellion of Adam did not change the fundamental character of either man or creation; it was simply the rebellion of one man, instructive for others only insofar as they can see that disobedience to Allah will bring punishment.

Thus, the contemporary Canadian Muslim writer Abdul Rashid, a veteran of Christian-Muslim dialogue in Ottawa, explains that "the Holy Koran tells us that God created the human being on '*fitra*' (7:172; 20:30)"—that is, with knowledge of the Supreme Being and of the difference between right and wrong. "Thus," Rashid continues, "Islam rejects the notion that people are inherently sinful. Each child is born innocent and free of sin." Allah "revealed, through His chosen prophets, the right path but left it to human beings to follow it or to reject it."[53] And his ability to follow it is unhindered by any innate inclination toward sin, although Satan the tempter is always close at hand.

Slave of Allah

Because man is not made in Allah's image, he is in essence merely Allah's slave, and because he has, even as the result of his transgression, no knowledge of good and evil, he must obey Allah's commands purely as a matter of fiat—without reasoning from them or about them. Consequently, Islam never developed any kind of natural theology, and indeed never could have. And because there is no idea of original sin, there is, furthermore, no understanding that any community of human beings will of necessity be imperfect and incomplete. In other words, alien to Islam is the idea that it is impossible to establish the kingdom of God on earth.

"Of those We created," says Allah in the Qur'an, "are a nation who guide by the truth, and by it act with justice" (7:181). These are the Muslims, whom Allah addresses directly in a related passage: "You are the best nation ever brought forth to men, bidding to honor, and forbidding dishonor, and believing in God" (3:110). The Muslim community, because it is the "best nation" and guides by the truth, calling people to honor and forbidding dishonor, is able to establish a perfectly just society on this earth.

Yet even in this vision of a just society, we are already worlds away from the Christian understanding of the human person's having an innate dignity stemming from being made in the image of God and endowed with free will, albeit marred by original sin: a being, in the lapidary phrase of the Byzantine funeral service, "full of grandeur and weakness." For the Muslims are the best of people who "guide by the truth," even if they fall short now and again.

These examples from Christian and Muslim holy texts reveal only a few of the significant differences between the Muslim and Catholic understandings of how God deals with his creatures. Ultimately, these differences indicate significantly different conceptions of God himself.

What about Abraham?

Yet we are all still children of Abraham, aren't we? Jews, Christians, and Muslims all know and cherish the accounts of Abraham, who through his devotion to the true God

became "the father of a multitude of nations" (Gen. 17:4–
5)—don't we?

Certainly some people at the highest levels of the U.S.
government think so. In November 2011, President Barack
Obama sent greetings to Muslims worldwide on the occasion of Eid al-Adha, the Muslim feast day commemorating
Abraham's near-sacrifice of his son (who in Islamic tradition
was Ishmael, not Isaac) as a sign of his willingness to obey
God. "As Muslims celebrate this Eid," Obama wrote, "they
will also commemorate Abraham's willingness to sacrifice
his son by distributing food to those less fortunate around
the world. . . . The Eid and Hajj rituals are a reminder of the
shared roots of the world's Abrahamic faiths and the powerful role that faith plays in motivating communities to serve
and stand with those in need."[54]

Obama wasn't blazing any new trails. In December 2006,
his predecessor, George W. Bush, said this in his greetings
to Muslims on Eid al-Adha: "For Muslims in America and
around the world, Eid al-Adha is an important occasion to
give thanks for their blessings and to remember Abraham's
trust in a loving God. During the four days of this special
observance, Muslims honor Abraham's example of sacrifice
and devotion to God by celebrating with friends and family,
exchanging gifts and greetings, and engaging in worship
through sacrifice and charity."[55]

When President Bush spoke of "Abraham's example of
sacrifice and devotion to God," he probably had the Genesis accounts of Abraham in mind. In Genesis, the story of
Abraham is one of fidelity to God and how it is rewarded.
The Lord tells Abraham that his faith in God will redound
to the benefit of all mankind: "By your descendants shall all
the nations of the earth bless themselves, because you have
obeyed my voice" (Gen. 22:18).

And when President Obama spoke of "the shared roots of the world's Abrahamic faiths," he was apparently assuming that Islamic accounts of Abraham shared the same expansive and generous vision: one of God blessing all the nations of the earth because of, or even by means of, Abraham's immense faith.

However, Muslims do not accept Genesis as inspired Scripture. They believe that the Old and New Testaments contain the remains of what once were legitimate revelations from God, but which Jews and Christians have dared to tamper with to the extent that they cannot be trusted. What Muslims believe about Abraham comes primarily from the Qur'an, which does not present Abraham either as "the father of a multitude of nations" or as one through whom "all the nations of the earth" shall "bless themselves."

Although it lacks those elements, the Qur'an does hold up Abraham as a "good example" for the Muslims—*uswa hasana*, the same appellation given to Muhammad elsewhere (33:21). In Islamic theology, Muhammad's example is, with very few exceptions, the believer's supreme guide. When the Qur'an says that Abraham also is a "good example," however, it is in reference to a specific instance: when Abraham says to his pagan relatives, "We are quit of you and that you serve, apart from God. We disbelieve in you, and between us and you enmity has shown itself, and hatred for ever, until you believe in God alone" (60:4).

Abraham is held up to the Muslims as a model of emulation, then, only when he declares his everlasting enmity and hatred for those who do not follow what Muslims believe to be the true religion.

In that same verse, the Qur'an then adds a critical caveat: "Except that Abraham said unto his father, 'Certainly I shall ask pardon for thee; but I have no power to do aught for thee

against God.'" In other words, Abraham is a good example
for believers *except* when he says that he will pray that Allah
will pardon his pagan father. The *Tafsir al-Jalalayn*, a venerable and respected Qur'an commentary written by two
mainstream and revered Muslim scholars, emphasizes that
this is "an exception where the excellent example is concerned, meaning that you should not imitate him in that by
asking forgiveness for unbelievers."[56]

Abraham's hatred is exemplary; his prayer for forgiveness
is not.

"Shared roots of the world's Abrahamic faiths," indeed.
Although it is clear that Islam emerges from the Judeo-
Christian religious tradition, it so radically recasts that tradition as to render the value of any common-ground appeals
dubious at best.

3

The Same God?

In the Qur'an, Allah tells Muhammad not to argue with the "People of the Book"—that is, the Jews, Christians, and a few other groups who are considered to have received a genuine revelation from Allah, even though they later distorted that revelation: "Dispute not with the People of the Book save in the fairer manner, except for those of them that do wrong; and say, 'We believe in what has been sent down to us, and what has been sent down to you; our God and your God is One, and to Him we have surrendered'" (29:46).

Many Christians, including many Catholics, accept this assertion at face value, and not without reason. As we have seen, there are so many similarities between the Bible and the Qur'an—their main characters, their preoccupations, their perspectives on numerous issues—that it is easy at first glance to regard Muslims as close allies in theism against a common foe of unbelievers.

Supporting this is the linguistic identity between the two religions' names for God. Arabic-speaking Christians, including Eastern Catholics such as Maronites and Melkites, use the word "Allah" for the God of the Bible. Flowing from this is the common use among both Christians and Muslims of many Arabic interjections that feature the word "Allah": *Inshallah* ("God willing"), *Smallah* ("in the name of God"), *Wallah* ("by God"), *Allah ma'ak* ("God be with you"), and others.

Interestingly, Coptic Christians never use these expressions. Possibly due to centuries of Muslim harassment and persecution in Egypt, they replace the word *Allah* with *Rabb* ("Lord"). However, among Arabic-speaking Christians the

Copts are an exception in this. Most use the same expressions that Muslims use, although not in reference to the God of the Qur'an but to the God of the Bible.

In any case, Catholics accept that Muslims and Catholics worship the same God above all because the Second Vatican Council says so.

The mind of the Church

Any examination of Islam and its relationship to Catholicism should, of course, be guided by the mind of the Church. And so we turn to the Second Vatican Council's two statements on the Church's relationship with Muslims.

The more important of these is the briefer one, both because it is found in a dogmatic constitution while the other is in a declaration, and because in its two sentences it contains more statements of fact. *Lumen Gentium,* the Dogmatic Constitution on the Church, tells us that the "plan of salvation also includes those who acknowledge the Creator. In the first place amongst these there are the Mohammedans, who, professing to hold the faith of Abraham, along with us adore the one and merciful God, who on the last day will judge mankind" (16).

Here it is almost more important to clarify what this text does *not* say than what it does. For the first statement, that "the plan of salvation also includes" Muslims, has led some—mostly critics of the Church—to assert that the Council Fathers are saying that Muslims are saved and thus need not be preached the gospel, as they've already got just as much of a claim on heaven as do Christians.

This is obviously false. This statement on Muslims comes as part of a larger passage that begins by speaking of "those who have not yet received the gospel" and concludes by reaffirming "the command of the Lord, 'Preach the gospel to every creature.'" It speaks of the possibility of salvation for those who "through no fault of their own do not know the gospel of Christ or His Church, yet sincerely seek God and moved by grace strive by their deeds to do his will as it is known to them through the dictates of conscience."

Clearly, then, Muslims figure in the "plan of salvation" not in the sense that they are saved as Muslims, that is, by means of Islamic observance, but insofar as they strive to be attentive to and to obey the authentic voice of the creator whom they acknowledge and who speaks to them through the dictates of their conscience. The conciliar statement also wisely adds the qualification that Muslims *profess* to hold the faith of Abraham. The Church does not definitively affirm that Muslims do actually hold that faith, but only notes that they believe they do.

In affirming Allah's oneness, his omniscience and omnipotence, his mercy and judgment, Islam's concept of God coincides with Christianity's to an important degree. Thus, Peter Kreeft writes disapprovingly that "many Christians, both Protestant and Catholic, do not believe what the Church says about Islam . . . : that Allah is not another God, that we worship the same God."[57] Indeed, as far back as 1076 we find Pope St. Gregory VII writing to Anzir, the king of Mauritania, that "we believe and confess one God, although in different ways."[58]

But although the Church affirms that Catholics and Muslims worship the same God, obviously this does *not* mean that we believe in the same God in every particular. For the teachings of Islam describe a God who, although one and powerful and a judge, is in other important respects substantially different from the God of the Bible and the Catholic faith. Catholics do not believe that Muhammad was a prophet or that the Qur'an is God's word, and Muslims do not believe that Jesus is the son of God or the Savior of the world, or that God is triune, and so on. In declaring that both Muslims and Catholics together adore the one and merciful God, the council could not have meant that Muslims and Catholics regard God in exactly the same way, or that the differences are insignificant.

It would do no outrage to *Lumen Gentium,* then, to examine these differences carefully, and from them to speculate on the prospects for Catholic/Muslim cooperation.

The second Vatican II reference to Islam must be understood in light of that of the Dogmatic Constitution on the Church; it comes in the Declaration on Non-Christian Religions, *Nostra Aetate*:

> The Church regards with esteem also the Moslems. They adore the one God, living and subsisting in Himself; merciful and all-powerful, the Creator of heaven and earth, who has spoken to men; they take pains to submit wholeheartedly to even His inscrutable decrees, just as Abraham, with whom the faith of Islam takes pleasure in linking itself, submitted to God. Though they do not acknowledge Jesus as God, they revere Him as a prophet. They also honor Mary, His virgin Mother; at times they even call on her with devotion. In addition, they await the day of judgment when God will render their deserts to all those who have been raised up from the dead. Finally, they value the moral life and worship God especially through prayer, almsgiving and fasting.
>
> Since in the course of centuries not a few quarrels and hostilities have arisen between Christians and Moslems, this sacred synod urges all to forget the past and to work sincerely for mutual understanding and to preserve as well as to promote together for the benefit of all mankind

social justice and moral welfare, as well as peace and free-dom. (Nostra Aetate 3)

Although this is a bit more descriptive about Muslim be-lief than is *Lumen Gentium*, as it includes the Islamic clas-sification of Jesus as a non-divine prophet and Islam's re-spect for the Virgin Mary, it adds nothing of substance to the dogmatic constitution's statements about Muslims. Here again, we see the Church's careful use of language: Islam's identification with Abraham is presented not as fact, but as something Muslims claim, or "take pleasure" in claiming.

The rest of Catholic tradition on Islam

As Pope Benedict XVI has reminded us, Vatican II was not a super-council whose teachings superseded all previous Church teaching; rather, its teachings must be understood in light of tradition. "The council did not formulate anything new in matters of faith, nor did it wish to replace what was ancient," he said in October 2012. "Rather, it concerned itself with seeing that the same faith might continue to be lived in the present day, that it might remain a living faith in a world of change."[59] When it comes to Islam, the consis-tent focus in earlier statements about Islam is generally not on what Muslims believe but on the hostility of Muslims to Christians and Christianity. In that vein, Pope Benedict XIV, in 1754, reaffirmed an earlier prohibition on Albanian Catholics giving their children "Turkish or Mohammedan names" in baptism by pointing out that not even Protestants or Orthodox were stooping so low: "None of the schismat-ics and heretics has been rash enough to take a Moham-medan name, and unless your justice abounds more than theirs, you shall not enter the kingdom of God."[60]

Pope Callixtus III, in a somewhat similar spirit, in 1455 vowed to "exalt the true Faith, and to extirpate the diabolical sect of the reprobate and faithless Mahomet in the East."[61]

Some Catholics will argue that the statements of Benedict XIV and Callixtus III (and other statements like them from other popes) simply reflect a very different age from our own, and moreover that Vatican II's statements reflect a more mature spirit and a greater amount of the charity toward others that Christians ought to exhibit.

And that may well be so, although it must be noted that even though they are only fifty years old, the statements of Vatican II on Islam reflect the outlook of a vanished age no less than do those of the earlier popes. For in the 1960s, secularism and Westernization were very much the order of the day in many areas of the Islamic world. It was, for example, unusual in Cairo in the 1960s to see a woman wearing a *hijab*, an Islamic headscarf mandated by Muhammad's command that when appearing in public a woman should cover everything except her face and hands. Today, on the other hand, one would be surprised on the streets of the same city to see a woman who is *not* so attired.

The *hijabs* in Cairo are but one visible sign of a revolution—or, more properly, a revival—that has swept the Islamic world. Islamic values have been revived, including not only rigor in dress codes but also hostility toward Western ideas and principles. The "Arab Spring" uprisings that began late in 2010 have led to a reassertion of the political aspects of Islam, as opposed to Western political models, all across the Middle East. Western ideas of democracy and pluralism that were fashionable in elite circles all over the Islamic world in the first half of the twentieth century have fallen into disrepute.

In other words, the Islamic world that the Fathers of Vatican II had in mind is rapidly disappearing. What the Council affirms is true and demands our assent; however, the tone of these statements must be evaluated within the context of their times. For the documents of Vatican II are no less a product of their age than the statements of Benedict XIV and Callixtus III are a product of theirs. Just as the time of crusading knights has vanished, so has the time of a dominant secular West striding confidently into what it terms the "modern" age.

Although it will always be the Christian's responsibility to reach out with respect and esteem to Muslims, the hostility that the Islamic world had always displayed toward Christendom was never—at any time before or since—less in evidence than it was in the 1960s, and so a statement of friendship was never more appropriate. That situation does not prevail today, a fact that has a great many implications for the prospects for dialogue as well. Western-minded Muslims who have a favorable attitude toward the Catholic Church no longer have the influence among their co-religionists that they once had, at least in the Islamic world.

That is not to say, however, that we have returned to the world of Benedict XIV and Callixtus III, when Catholics understood that Mohammedanism, as it was then popularly styled (to the indignation of Muslims themselves), was steeped in falsehood—perhaps even diabolical—and dedicated to the destruction of the Church and to the conversion or subjugation of Christians. We are separated by centuries of cultural assumptions from the world in which it was even possible to think of one's faith as having enemies and needing to be defended. Catholics of the modern age have long assumed that such a world was gone forever, and there is some reason to believe that it is indeed.

But with Muslim persecution of Christians escalating worldwide, there is also considerable evidence that that rough old world is returning; that it may never have been as far away as it seemed.

And there are reasons for that embedded within the Qur'an and Islamic tradition.

Refrain from the Trinity

The most obvious difference between the Christian and Islamic conceptions of God is the Trinity. The Qur'an, several times, explicitly denies the Trinity, although it never actually states the Christian doctrine accurately. And so, in the Muslim holy book, Allah asks Jesus: "O Jesus son of Mary, didst thou say unto men, 'Take me and my mother as gods, apart from God'?" (5:116).

The Qur'an has Jesus disclaim any responsibility for Christians' worshipping him and his mother: "He said, 'To Thee be glory! It is not mine to say what I have no right to. If I indeed said it, Thou knowest it, knowing what is within my soul, and I know not what is within Thy soul; Thou knowest the things unseen" (5:116).

Here we have not only a merely human Jesus but also a misapprehension of the Trinity. The Qur'an envisions the Christian Trinity not as the Father, Son, and Holy Spirit—three Persons, one God—but as a trio of deities: Allah, Jesus, and Mary. Nonetheless, in another passage, the Qur'an warns Christians not to affirm a single Triune God either: "People of the Book, go not beyond the bounds in your religion, and say not as to God but the truth. The Messiah, Jesus son of Mary, was only the Messenger of God, and His Word that He committed to Mary, and a Spirit from Him. So believe in God and His Messengers, and say not, 'Three.' Refrain; better is it for you. God is only One God. Glory be to Him—That He should have a son! To Him belongs all that is in the heavens and in the earth; God suffices for a guardian" (4:171).

"Refrain; better is it for you." This may simply be a
warning that hellfire awaits those who take Jesus and Mary
as gods besides God, in line with another passage of the
Qur'an: "They are unbelievers who say, 'God is the Third
of Three.' No god is there but One God. If they refrain not
from what they say, there shall afflict those of them that disbelieve a painful chastisement" (5:73). However, given the
Qur'an's exhortation to Muslims to fight Christians "until
they pay the tribute out of hand and have been humbled"
(9:29), this warning also carries a hint of menace.

Allah is not a Father

The Allah of the Qur'an, in the first place, is not a father.
He is, above all, not the father of Jesus Christ. As we will
see in more detail in the next chapter, the Qur'an decisively
and repeatedly rejects, as an insult to Allah's transcendent
majesty, the idea that Jesus is his son; indeed, that he could
have any son at all.

The assumption behind verse 4:171 quoted above is that it
would somehow limit God if he had a son. In contradiction
of this unthinkable proposition, Allah says of himself: "To
Him belongs all that is in the heavens and in the earth; God
suffices for a guardian." The idea here is that Allah would
only have a son if he were too weak or insufficient to man-
age the universe himself, and so needed a partner to share
the work; but he is all-powerful, and doesn't need any help
to govern the heavens and the earth, and thus has no son.

The Qur'an dismisses the idea of divine fatherhood, which
Muslims assume must occur in physical terms. "It is not for
God to take a son unto Him. Glory be to Him! When He
decrees a thing, He but says to it 'Be,' and it is" (19:35). In
other words, Allah has no son because he can create by fiat

and so need not beget. What's more, Allah must not have
a son because he doesn't have a wife: "The Creator of the
heavens and the earth—how should He have a son, seeing
that He has no consort, and He created all things, and He
has knowledge of everything?" (6:101). "He—exalted be our
Lord's majesty! has not taken to Himself either consort or
a son" (72:3). In line with this, the warnings to Christians
to "say not, 'Three,'" and not to worship Jesus and Mary as
gods alongside Allah seem to stem from an assumption that
Christians believed that God had taken Mary as his wife and
begotten a son, Jesus, after the manner of the old pagan gods.

Catholics would reject this as a gross misunderstanding
of what the Trinity and the Fatherhood of God mean, but
it generally makes little headway to explain these misunderstandings to pious and knowledgeable Muslims. Hearing
that the Trinity is composed of the Father, Son, and Holy
Spirit—one God, rather than a divine trio of God, Jesus,
and Mary—Muslims generally point out that the Qur'anic
passage doesn't mention the Trinity anyway and so cannot
be assumed to be referring to it. They also usually go on to
point out that Christians nevertheless still worship Jesus as
God and maintain that this is still deification of a human
being and tantamount to polytheism. They also point, in a
manner reminiscent of Fundamentalist Protestants, to the
Church's veneration of Mary as evidence that she, too, is
worshipped as divine.

Jesus is not God's Son, and neither are you

Islam also rejects the idea of divine fatherhood in general.
In the Islamic view, in no sense can human beings be called
the children of Allah. The Qur'an dismisses such an idea
contemptuously, in an explicit rejection of the Jewish and

Christian view. Allah first recounts the claim of the Jews and Christians, and then instructs Muhammad (and the Muslims) how to respond to it: "Say the Jews and Christians, 'We are the sons of God, and His beloved ones.' Say: 'Why then does He chastise you for your sins? No; you are mortals, of His creating; He forgives whom He will, and He chastises whom He will.' For to God belongs the kingdom of the heavens and of the earth, and all that is between them; to Him is the homecoming" (5:18).

The Qur'an's assumption that a father would not punish his children for their wrongdoing is odd, but there it is. Whatever the reasoning, in Islam God is not a father to human beings. To a pious Muslim, a prayer like the Our Father is utterly alien. He would consider it presumptuous in the extreme to call Allah his Father. Instead, Allah is the master of the universe and human beings are his slaves. The hallmark of Islamic religious observance is external obedience, not likeness with the divine through an interior transformation.

This I once discovered to my considerable surprise when, early in my college career, I was showing off my knowledge of Arabic and recited the *shahadah*, the Islamic profession of faith, in Arabic to a Muslim: "There is no god but Allah, and Muhammad is his prophet."

The Muslim, hearing this, told me: "Now you are a Muslim!"

I was puzzled. "What do you mean?"

"You said the *shahadah*, you said it in Arabic, and you said it in the presence of a male Muslim witness. That means you are now a Muslim."

"But I didn't mean it!" I protested, growing more incredulous by the second.

"It doesn't matter," replied the Muslim with the utmost certainty. "You said it in the proper way. You had a witness. That is all that is needed. One's inner dispositions are irrelevant."

Allah's automatons

Not only are they irrelevant, they are apparently programmed from on high.

"God changes not what is in a people, until they change what is in themselves." So says the Qur'an (13:11), and all through the book there are so many exhortations to believe in its message that it is hard to imagine that Islam could reject the concept of free will. A medieval commentary on the Qur'an that is still widely read and respected among Muslims today, the *Tafsir al-Jalalayn,* says of the unbelievers that Allah does not remove "blessings from them" until they "exchange their good state for disobedience."[62] In other words, as long as they persist in sin, they have only themselves to blame.

Certainly there are contemporary Muslims who assert that Islam upholds the idea that man is free to choose or reject the path of Allah, although whether they do this intending to dissent from mainstream Islamic tradition and teaching on this matter, or simply to make Islam more palatable to non-Muslim Westerners, is unclear. The contemporary Canadian Muslim writer Abdul Rashid criticized the concept of original sin by invoking human freedom: "First, God Almighty revealed, through His chosen prophets, the right path but left it to human beings to follow it or to reject it. Secondly, it is a fundamental belief for Muslims that there is a life in the Hereafter where each human being will be accountable for his/her deeds in this world. Hereditary sin is contrary to both of these concepts—free will and accountability."[63]

Yet a very different message comes through in a curious Qur'anic passage in which Allah swears by various kinds of stars in the night sky ("slinkers,""runners," and "sinkers") that the message of his prophet is reliable:

No! I swear by the slinkers,
the runners, the sinkers,
by the night swarming,
by the dawn sighing,
truly this is the word of a noble Messenger
having power, with the Lord of the Throne secure,
obeyed, moreover trusty.
Your companion is not possessed;
he truly saw him on the clear horizon;
he is not niggardly of the Unseen.
And it is not the word of an accursed Satan;
where then are you going?
It is naught but a Reminder unto all beings,
for whosoever of you who would go straight;
but will you shall not, unless God wills, the Lord of all
Being. (81:15-29)

This message from a "noble Messenger" and not "the
word of an accursed Satan" will profit "whosoever of you
who would go straight" (81:28), but no one can "unless God
wills" (81:29).

There are numerous other passages of the Qur'an, as
well as indications from Islamic tradition, to the effect that
not only can no one believe in Allah except by his will, no
one can *disbelieve* in him except by his active will. "And to
whomsoever God assigns no light, no light has he" (24:40).

The issue of free will versus predestination has, of course,
vexed Catholics and Protestants for centuries, as different
biblical passages are given different weight in various traditions. Calvinism, of course, in its pure form is notorious
for its doctrine of double predestination, the idea that God
has destined people for hell as well as for salvation. But this
position is largely unique to them in the Christian tradition,

which generally holds that God desires all to be saved and gives everyone the means to attain this salvation. The idea that God would create men for hell contradicts the proposition that God "desires all men to be saved and come to the knowledge of the truth" (1 Tim. 2:4) and that he "takes no pleasure in the death of anyone" (Ezek. 18:32).

The situation in Islam is, on first glance, even worse, with the Qur'an's testimony on this, as on other matters, appearing to be hopelessly contradictory. The Qur'an, says the Qur'an, is "naught but a Reminder unto all beings, for whosoever of you who would go straight; but will you shall not, unless God wills, the Lord of all Being" (81:27-29). Those who would "go straight"—follow Allah's straight path—cannot do so "unless God wills."

This does not depart significantly from the Catholic understanding that no soul can approach God without having received the grace to do so. However, the Qur'an goes much further than that, into a more or less open determinism: "If God had willed, He would have made you one nation; but He leads astray whom He will, and guides whom He will; and you will surely be questioned about the things you wrought" (16:93). Even though everything is in Allah's hands, even the decision of the individual to obey him or not—for he leads astray those whom he wills, and guides to the truth whom he wills—human beings will still be held accountable for the things they have done.

The Qur'an repeats this idea many times: Those who have rejected Allah do so because he made it possible for them to do nothing else. And indeed, given the fact that in the Islamic scheme of creation and salvation, human beings are the slaves of Allah, not his children, the rejection of free will is not altogether surprising. Allah tells Muhammad that "some of them there are that listen to thee, and We lay veils upon their hearts lest they understand it, and in their ears heaviness; and if they see any sign whatever, they do not believe in it, so that when they come to thee they dispute with thee, the unbelievers saying, 'This is naught but the fairy-tales of the ancient ones'" (6:25-6).

Elsewhere in the Qur'an, Allah describes this veil as a seal and as a barrier, saying to his prophet: "As for the un-believers, alike it is to them whether thou hast warned them or hast not warned them, they do not believe. God has set a seal on their hearts and on their hearing, and on their eyes is a covering, and there awaits them a mighty chas-tisement" (2:6-7). The medieval Islamic scholar Ibn Kathir (1301-1372), whose commentary on the Qur'an is still enor-mously influential among Muslims, says in his commentary on this Qur'anic passage: "These Ayat [verses] indicate that whomever Allah has written to be miserable, they shall nev-er find anyone to guide them to happiness, and whomever Allah directs to misguidance, he shall never find anyone to guide him."[64] And elsewhere in the Qur'an: "And We have put before them a barrier and behind them a barrier; and We have covered them, so they do not see. Alike it is to them whether thou hast warned them or thou hast not warned them, they do not believe. Thou only warnest him who fol-lows the Remembrance and who fears the All-merciful in the Unseen; so give him the good tidings of forgiveness and a generous wage" (36:9-11).

If the prophet succeeds in warning only the one "who fol-lows the Remembrance and who fears the All-merciful in the Unseen," it would appear that the only people who will heed the call of Islam are those who have already been des-tined to do so: those who already in some way "fear the All-Merciful." There are even some to whom it doesn't matter whether or not the prophet preaches, for even if they hear his message they will not believe it. Allah has made them blind to its truth: He has "put before them a barrier and behind them a barrier; and We have covered them, so they do not see."

The obstinate unbelief of those who reject Islam thus appears to be entirely in accord with the will of Allah. The *Tafsir al-Jalalayn* explains that this passage offers a "metaphor for how the path of faith is closed" to the unbelievers.[65]

At first glance, this may seem to be not far from Jesus' words: "This is why I speak to them in parables, because seeing they do not see, and hearing they do not hear, nor do they understand. With them indeed is fulfilled the prophecy of Isaiah which says: 'You shall indeed hear but never understand, and you shall indeed see but never perceive. For this people's heart has grown dull, and their ears are heavy of hearing, and their eyes they have closed, lest they should perceive with their eyes, and hear with their ears, and understand with their heart, and turn for me to heal them'" (Matt. 13:13-15).

Indeed, Islamic tradition shares with Catholic tradition the idea that repeated defiance of God can render one's soul insensitive to grace. That appears to be the case in many passages of the Qur'an, such as one recounting the reaction of hypocrites to a new revelation that Muhammad has delivered: "And whenever a *sura* is sent down, they look one at another: 'Does anyone see you?' Then they turn away. God has turned away their hearts, for that they are a people who do not understand" (9:127).

But in Islam there is more. Another Qur'an commentary explains Qur'an 36:9 as meaning that Allah has "covered the insight of their hearts (so that they see not) the Truth and guidance."[66] Ibn Kathir, whose Qur'an commentary is one of the most widely respected among Muslims, records that one early Muslim also ascribed unbelief to Allah's will: "Allah placed this barrier between them and *Islam* and *Iman* [faith], so that they will never reach it."[67]

Other Qur'an passages state this explicitly. "We have created for Gehenna," Allah says in a Qur'anic passage that directly echoes Jesus' quoting of Isaiah, "many jinn and men: they have hearts, but understand not with them; they have eyes, but perceive not with them; they have ears, but they hear not with them. They are like cattle; nay, rather they are further astray. Those—they are the heedless" (7:179).

Despite the superficial similarity of the "eyes but see not and ears but hear not" motif, there is an immense gulf between this and the statement of Jesus, which most exegetes throughout the ages have taken to mean that some people harden themselves so in unbelief that when they hear the truth of God, they do not recognize it as such. In the Qur'anic passage, by contrast, Allah says that he actually created some people (as well as the mysterious spirit beings known as jinn) for hell—a doctrine that is hard to reconcile with the idea of a just and loving God.

Even as the Qur'an repeatedly affirms that no one can believe except by Allah's will, it also affirms that unbelievers bear responsibility for their actions. In this passage these two propositions are placed side by side with no hint that there is any difficulty: "And those who break the covenant of God after His compact, and who snap what God has commanded to be joined, and who work corruption in the earth—theirs shall be the curse, and theirs the Evil Abode" (13:26).

Thus far, we are in the realm of free will and personal responsibility. But then we read, "God outspreads and straitens His provision unto whomsoever He will. They rejoice in this present life; and this present life, beside the world to come, is naught but passing enjoyment" (13:27).

If Allah "outspreads and straitens His provision unto whomsoever He will," then the decision of whether someone will be a believer and be saved or an unbeliever and be

damned is up to him. When asked why he hasn't performed
a miracle that would be a definitive sign that his message really is divine, Allah tells his messenger to say essentially that:
"The unbelievers say, 'Why has a sign not been sent down
upon him from his Lord?' Say: 'God leads astray whomsoever
He will, and He guides to Him all who are penitent'" (13:28).

Allah shortly thereafter tells Muhammad: "Thus We have
sent thee among a nation before which other nations have
passed away, to recite to them that We have revealed to thee;
and yet they disbelieve in the All-merciful. Say: 'He is my
Lord—there is no god but He. In Him I have put my trust,
and to Him I turn'" (13:31). He dismisses the possibility that
those who have rejected the Islamic message would accept
it if they saw a great sign, and concludes by affirming that
the decision to believe or not believe is entirely up to Allah:

> If only a Koran whereby the mountains were set in mo-
> tion, or the earth were cleft, or the dead were spoken
> to—nay, but God's is the affair altogether. Did not the
> believers know that, if God had willed, He would have
> guided men all together? And still the unbelievers are
> smitten by a shattering for what they wrought, or it
> alights nigh their habitation, until God's promise comes;
> and God will not fail the tryst. (13:32)

And again:

> Nay; but decked out fair to the unbelievers is their devis-
> ing, and they are barred from the way; and whomsoever
> God leads astray, no guide has he. For them is chastise-
> ment in the present life; and the chastisement of the world
> to come is yet more grievous; they have none to defend
> them from God. (13:34-35)

"They have none to defend them from God."

In the New Testament, it is God who defends human beings from the condemnation of the accuser, Satan. In the
book of Revelation, Satan is referred to as "the accuser of our
brethren" who "accuses them day and night before our God"
(Rev. 12:10). But defending the brethren in the face of this
accuser is God himself, by virtue of the cross of Jesus Christ.
In the Qur'an, by contrast, the one whom Allah has decided
to condemn has no one to defend him from the Almighty.

The Qur'an even makes it clear that it did not have to be
this way. Had Allah wanted it that way, everyone on earth
would have believed in the true religion: "And if thy Lord
had willed, whoever is in the earth would have believed, all
of them, all together." He chides his prophet about trying too
hard to make these unbelievers believe, when Allah has already decreed that they would reject him: "Wouldst thou then
constrain the people, until they are believers? It is not for any
soul to believe save by the leave of God; and He lays abomination upon those who have no understanding" (10:99-100).

Mainstream Muslim exegetes have interpreted these verses to
mean exactly what they appear to mean. Says Ibn Kathir: "Allah
has decreed that they will be misguided, so warning them will
not help them and will not have any effect on them."[68]

In Islamic theological history, a party known as the
Qadariyya tried to advance the concept of individual free
will. The pioneering Islamic scholar Ignaz Goldziher explains that the Qadaryya were protesting against "an unworthy conception of God," and yet they "could not find a
large body of supporters" among Muslims. Their opponents
"battled them with the received interpretation of the sacred
scriptures."[69] And won. Ultimately, Muslim authorities declared the concept of human free will to be heretical.

A twelfth-century Muslim jurist, Ibn Abi Ya'la, fulminated that the Qadariyya wrongly "consider that they hold in their grasp the ability to do good and evil, avoid harm and obtain benefit, obey and disobey, and be guided or misguided. They claim that human beings retain full initiative, without any prior status within the will of Allah for their acts, nor even in His knowledge of them." Even worse, "their doctrine is similar to that of Zoroastrians and Christians. It is the very root of heresy."[70]

This "very root of heresy" does indeed involve "an unworthy conception of God." The idea that God created automatons that cannot but do as God wills—including reject him and suffer in hell for all eternity—is fundamentally incompatible with the Christian understanding of God. In Islam, not only is Allah not a father, he a slave master, and one so cruel that he creates beings for hell—in other words, he brings them into existence solely so that he may torture them. He does offer these wretched creatures a path to life, but bars them, solely on the basis of his arbitrary whim, from ever finding or embarking upon that path.

This is not the God who "so loved the world that he gave his only begotten son, so that whoever believes in him should not perish but have eternal life." Indeed, the God of the Qur'an has no son to give, since it would be an offense to his transcendent majesty even to have one.

A God of both light and darkness

As we have seen, the Catholic concept that mankind's alienation from God is manifested in an inclination toward sin is utterly alien to Islam. In Islam there is no concept of original sin. Although Adam and Eve begin in Paradise and are banished from it after their disobedience, and Satan vows to tempt the believers, ultimately even this is a manifestation of Allah's active will. In the Qur'an, it is only Allah who inspires in the soul both "lewdness and godfearing" (91:8). The world-renowned Pakistani Muslim political leader and theologian Syed Abul Ala Maududi (1902-1979), who wrote a popular and influential commentary on the Qur'an, explains that this verse means that "the Creator has imbedded in man's nature tendencies and inclinations towards both good and evil."[71]

That means that Allah is ultimately responsible not just for the soul's inclination toward good but for its inclination toward evil as well. In other words, in sharp contrast to the Christian understanding that evil is the rejection of God, in Islam God is the source of evil. This is worlds apart from the proposition that "God is light, and in Him there is no darkness at all" (1 John 1:5)—for to place evil in the soul, Allah must have it to give, which would be utterly impossible in the Christian conception, since evil is the absence of God.

The Islamic concept casts the very goodness of God into doubt, as well as the nature of what is good. The grand and powerful Christian conception of a God who is love, and who endowed his human creatures with freedom so that they could respond to him in love, and who sacrificed himself in order to overcome impediments to their ability to do so, is replaced by the idea of a remote God who for reasons unexplained put both good and evil within man's heart.

Allah is will

But for a believing Muslim, to suggest anything else would be blasphemous. No limits can be placed upon the sovereignty of Allah, the absolute monarch. That includes ones that would naturally arise from his being always good and true. Allah, the Qur'an says twice, is the best of "schemers": "And when the unbelievers were devising against thee, to confine thee, or slay thee, or to expel thee, and were devising, and God was devising; and God is the best of devisers" (8:30; cf. 3:54). In this "devising," Allah has no limitations whatsoever.

Indeed, at one point the Qur'an excoriates the Jews for suggesting limits to God's power. The passage is ambiguous, but its principal import is plain enough: They dared to say that there was something Allah could not do: "The Jews have said, 'God's hand is fettered.' Fettered are their hands, and they are cursed for what they have said. Nay, but His hands are outspread; He expends how He will" (5:64). Neither does he have any obligation to disclose any consistency or anything else in what he does: "He shall not be questioned as to what He does" (21:23).

What could the Jews have possibly meant, if any Jews ever said it at all? It is possible that they meant that God, being good, would be consistent, and would operate the universe according to consistent and observable laws. This would not have been so much a limitation on what God *could* do, but upon what he *would* do. As St. Thomas Aquinas explained: "Since the principles of certain sciences—of logic, geometry, and arithmetic, for instance—are derived exclusively from the formal principals of things, upon which their essence depends, it follows that God *cannot* make the contraries of these principles; He *cannot* make the genus not to be predicable of the species, nor lines drawn from a circle's center to its circumference not to be equal, nor the three angles of a rectilinear triangle not to be equal to two right angles" (emphasis added).[72]

This proposition of divine consistency was all-important for the development of scientific inquiry. "The rise of science," observes social scientist Rodney Stark, "was not an extension of classical learning. It was the natural outgrowth of Christian doctrine: nature exists because it was created by God. In order to love and honor God, it is necessary to fully appreciate the wonders of his handiwork. Because God is perfect, that handiwork functions in accord with *immutable principles*. By the full use of our God-given powers of reason and observation, it ought to be possible to discover those principles." That process of discovery became the foundation of modern science. "These were the crucial ideas," says Stark, "that explain why science arose in Christian Europe and nowhere else."[73]

Indeed, for an Islamic culture to affirm that God's creation operates according to immutable principles would be nothing short of blasphemy. Allah's hand is not fettered by consistency or by anything else. Allah is free to do anything he wills to do, without any expectations or limitations deriving from logic, love, or anything else. This idea made sure that scientific exploration in the Islamic world would be stillborn.

According to the physicist priest Fr. Stanley L. Jaki, the great Muslim philosopher al-Ghazali "denounced natural laws, the very objective of science, as a blasphemous constraint upon the free will of Allah."[74] Al-Ghazali (1058-1111), although himself a philosopher, delivered what turned out to be the coup de grace to Islamic philosophical investigation, at least as a vibrant mainstream force, in his monumental attack on the very idea of Islamic philosophy, *Incoherence of the Philosophers*.

Muslim philosophers such as Avicenna and Averroes, according to al-Ghazali, were not intellectual trailblazers worthy of respect and careful consideration. In positing that there could be truth that was outside of or even contradicted what Allah had revealed in the Qur'an, they had shown themselves to be nothing more than heretics who should be put to death and their books burned. Al-Ghazali accused them of "denial of revealed laws and religious confessions" and "rejection of the details of religious and sectarian [teach-ing], believing them to be man-made laws and embellished tricks."[75] He declared that the doctrines of Muslim philoso-phers such as al-Farabi and Avicenna "challenge the [very] principles of religion."[76]

Al-Ghazali, said scholar Tilman Nagel, "was inspired by a notion that we frequently see in Islam's intellectual history: the notion that everything human beings can possibly know is already contained in the Koran and the *hadith* [the volu-minous traditions of Muhammad's words and deeds]; only naïve people can be made to believe that there is knowledge beyond them."[77]

At the end of *The Incoherence of the Philosophers,* Al-Ghaza-li reveals how high the stakes are: "If someone says: 'You have explained the doctrines of these [philosophers]; do you then say conclusively that they are infidels and *that the killing of those who uphold their beliefs is obligatory?*"[78] He then con-cludes that they should indeed be pronounced infidels, and therefore, presumably, be executed.

Although Islamic philosophy lived on, it was never the same; it had effectively been put to death. After al-Ghazali and the defeat of the relatively rationalistic Mu'tazilite party, there was no large-scale attempt to apply the laws of rea-son or consistency to Allah, or, therefore, to the world he had created. Fr. Jaki explains: "Muslim mystics decried the notion of scientific law (as formulated by Aristotle) as blas-phemous and irrational, depriving as it does the Creator of his freedom."[79] The social scientist Rodney Stark notes the existence of "a major theological bloc within Islam that con-demns all efforts to formulate natural laws as blasphemy in that they deny Allah's freedom to act."[80]

By contrast, Fr. Jaki explains, in the Old Testament, "the faithfulness of the God of history is supported not only with a reference to another saving intervention of God into human affairs, but very often also by a pointed and detailed reference to the faithfulness of the regular working and permanence of a nature created by God."[81] In contrast, the Qur'an affirms Allah's changeability, even in what he reveals to mankind: "And for whatever verse We abrogate or cast into oblivion, We bring a better or the like of it; knowest thou not that God is powerful over everything?" (2:106).

The God whose message the Catholic Church preaches to the world has power over everything, but he does not exercise it with anything like this despotic inconsistency. In his absolute and unfettered sovereignty, Allah has doomed the Islamic world to over a millennium of intellectual stagnation and anti-intellectualism: A recurring idea in the Islamic world is that the Qur'an and Sunnah contain all that is needed for the proper functioning of human society, and everything else is either superfluous or heretical.

At this point we are worlds away from the God who blessed creation and human endeavor even to the point of becoming incarnate to save his creatures, and who in his goodness is consistent, such that observation of his creation and all intellectual endeavors are praiseworthy and worthy of the divine blessing. The Catholic notion of God, derived from biblical revelation, the Judeo-Christian tradition, and a venerable philosophical tradition, offers a notion of God that is almost diametrically opposed to the lone, capricious Allah of Islam. The God of Islam is not love. The God of Islam is *will*: absolute, untrammeled, unlimited will.

And so we do indeed worship the same God, as the Second Vatican Council tells us, but the operative aspects of that affirmation are, as we have seen in this chapter, extremely limited. Catholics and Muslims both consider themselves to be within the Abrahamic tradition, although they understand it in different ways, and believe in one God who created the heavens and the earth *ex nihilo*, although they understand him in vastly different ways as well. Catholics would be wise to avoid false irenicism, or worse, the indifferentism that arises from misreading what the Council is trying to say. Catholics have a responsibility to preach the gospel to Muslims just as much as to everyone else.

4

The Same Jesus?

"I feel a divine jealousy for you," St. Paul tells the Corinthians, "for I betrothed you to Christ to present you as a pure bride to her one husband. But I am afraid that as the serpent deceived Eve by his cunning, your thoughts will be led astray from a sincere and pure devotion to Christ. For if someone comes and preaches another Jesus than the one we preached, or if you receive a different spirit from the one you received, or if you accept a different gospel from the one you accepted, you submit to it readily enough. (2 Cor. 11:2-4)

More in common than we think?

Interestingly, while Muslims and Arabic-speaking Christians call God by the same name, they differ on the name of Jesus: Muslims call him *Isa*, whereas to Arabic-speaking Christians he is *Yasua*. The latter is similar to the Hebrew *Yeshua* or Joshua, while the Muslim usage more closely resembles the name Esau. Clearly, there are also differences in how Christians and Muslims view Jesus—or else Muslims would be Christians. But since Muslims use the presence of Jesus in Islam as a basis for outreach to Christians, the identity and role of Jesus in Islam bears close examination.

Several years ago, Ibrahim Hooper, an American convert to Islam and spokesman for the Council on American-Islamic Relations (CAIR), the highest-profile Muslim organization in the United States, wrote an essay entitled, "Muslim and Christians: More in common than you think," which has been and continues to be reprinted in all sorts of publications, usually around Christmastime.

Hooper begins with an evocative quotation: "Behold! The angels said: 'O Mary! God giveth thee glad tidings of a Word from Him. His name will be Jesus Christ, the son of Mary, held in honor in this world and the Hereafter and in (the company of) those nearest to God.'"

Then he comes right to the point: "Before searching for this quote in the New Testament, you might first ask your Muslim co-worker, friend or neighbor for a copy of the Quran, Islam's revealed text. The quote is from verse 45 of chapter 3 in the Quran." Hooper then explains: "It is well known, particularly in this holiday season, that Christians follow the teachings of Jesus. What is less well understood is that Muslims also love and revere Jesus as one of God's greatest messengers to mankind."

He then goes on to adduce other Qur'anic passages about Jesus, saying that if Christians and Muslims understood all that they had in common, this mutual understanding would defuse a great many conflicts in the world: "As forces of hate in this country and worldwide try to pull Muslims and Christians apart, we are in desperate need of a unifying force that can bridge the widening gap of interfaith misunderstanding and mistrust. That force could be the message of love, peace and forgiveness taught by Jesus and accepted by followers of both faiths."

Hooper adds: "When Muslims mention the Prophet Muhammad, they always add the phrase 'peace be upon him.' Christians may be surprised to learn that the same phrase always follows a Muslim's mention of Jesus or that we believe Jesus will return to earth in the last days before the final judgment. Disrespect toward Jesus, as we have seen all too often in our society, is very offensive to Muslims." He acknowledges that "Muslims and Christians do have some differing perspectives on Jesus' life and teachings," but doesn't explore those, leaving the impression that they are largely insignificant.

In keeping with his irenic thrust, he says that Jesus' "spiritual legacy offers an alternative opportunity for people of faith to recognize their shared religious heritage" and claims that "America's Muslim community stands ready to honor that legacy by building bridges of interfaith understanding and challenging those who would divide our nation along religious or ethnic lines."

"We have," Hooper concludes, "more in common than we think."[82]

Another CAIR presentation asserts that "like Christians, Muslims respect and revere Jesus. Islam teaches that Jesus is one of the greatest of God's prophets and messengers to humankind. Like Christians, every day, over 1.3 billion Muslims strive to live by his teachings of love, peace, and forgiveness. Those teachings, which have become universal values, remind us that all of us, Christians, Muslims, Jews, and all others have more in common than we think."[83]

Hooper's article and the CAIR piece are both canny and compelling. They are reasonable, they are conciliatory, and they resonate with the spirit of the age—the spirit that would prefer to focus upon what we have in common rather than upon what divides us, and to see in every present or historical enemy a potential friend.

And there is apparently a great deal to recommend this point of view.

Less than meets the eye

Jesus in the Qur'an, as we have seen, is the Word of God, "a Spirit from him," born of a Virgin, a miracle worker who numbered among his followers apostles who were exemplary in righteousness. Allah says that he "gave Jesus son of Mary the clear signs, and confirmed him with the Holy Spirit." But then dissension arose among his followers—a fact with which no Christian could possibly disagree, although in the Qur'an it is attributed to Allah's agency: "And had God willed, those who came after him would not have fought one against the other after the clear signs had come to them; but they fell into variance, and some of them believed, and some disbelieved; and had God willed they would not have fought one against the other; but God does whatsoever He desires" (2:253).

It is noteworthy, however, that although Hooper quotes Qur'an 3:45, which calls Jesus "a Word from Him," that is, from Allah, he does not explain that the Qur'an's understanding of what it means for Jesus to be the "Word of God" is significantly different from the biblical one. In the Qur'an there is nothing of the exalted theology of the *Logos* through whom the world was created. The idea that "the Word was with God, and the Word was God" (John 1:1) is anathema to Islam. Rather, the Qur'an explains the term in language strongly reminiscent of the Christian theology of Jesus as the New Adam: "Truly, the likeness of Jesus, in God's sight, is as Adam's likeness; He created him of dust, then said He unto him, 'Be,' and he was" (3:59).

However, this is not an assertion of Christ the New Adam, as in St. Paul's lapidary formulation that "as in Adam all die, so in Christ all are made alive" (1 Cor. 15:22). It is merely an affirmation of the Virgin Birth: Both Jesus and Adam have no earthly father, but were created by divine fiat, the divine word. While it is momentous enough that the Qur'an affirms the Virgin Birth, this miracle is given no greater significance in Islamic tradition than any of the other signs of the divine power. In fact, at one point the Qur'an even uses this same language in the context of another denial that Jesus is the Son of God: "It is not for God to take a son unto Him. Glory be to Him! When He decrees a thing, He but says to it 'Be,' and it is" (19:35).

Jesus says of himself (miraculously, as an infant in the cradle): "Lo, I am God's servant; God has given me the Book, and made me a Prophet" (19:30). He is not divine; he is a servant of Allah (*Abdullah*, or slave of Allah: 4:172; 19:30; 43:59). The gospel is not a message about him but a book that he has received from Allah, who by this delivery made him a prophet.

Not the Son

The centerpiece of the Qur'an's teaching about Jesus, in line with all this, is another sharp departure from orthodox Christianity: The Qur'an repeatedly and strenuously denies that Jesus is the son of God (to say nothing of God the Son). "The Jews say, 'Ezra is the Son of God,'" the book asserts, although no Jews have ever been found who actually did say any such thing; "the Christians say, 'The Messiah is the Son of God.' That is the utterance of their mouths, conforming with the unbelievers before them. God assail them! How they are perverted!" (9:30). The Qur'an emphasizes that Allah has no son no fewer than twelve times (2:116; 10:68; 17:111; 18:4; 19:35; 19:88; 19:91; 19:92; 21:26; 23:91; 39:04; 43:81).

Not only does Allah "assail" those who affirm that Christ is the Son of God; as we have seen, he also warns them not to deify Jesus: "The Messiah, Jesus son of Mary, was only the Messenger of God, and His Word that He committed to Mary, and a Spirit from Him. . . . God is only One God. Glory be to Him—That He should have a son!" (4:171).

The Qur'an declares that to say that Allah has a Son would be to impugn his total power and sovereignty. In-

deed, to affirm that he has a son is "something hideous"
that upsets the entire equilibrium of creation: "And they say,
'The All-merciful has taken unto Himself a son. You have
indeed advanced something hideous! The heavens are well
nigh rent of it and the earth split asunder, and the mountains
well nigh fall down crashing for that they have attributed to
the All-merciful a son; and it behoves not the All-merciful
to take a son" (19:88-92). The idea of divine sonship is conceived of in physical terms more appropriate to the Greek
myths than to Christian theology, as the Qur'an dismisses
the possibility that Allah could have a son on the grounds
that he has no wife: "The Creator of the heavens and the
earth—how should He have a son, seeing that He has no
consort, and He created all things, and He has knowledge
of everything?" (6:101).

Here again, we see the assumption that to affirm that Allah has a son would somehow impugn the ideas that he created everything and is omniscient. The first is reasonably easy
to understand, as apparently the Qur'an was envisioning a
God with a son after the fashion of ancient pagan schemata in
which one god was responsible for the creation of one part of
the universe, while another god created a different part. Why
having a son would challenge Allah's omniscience is less clear.
The assumption is apparently that Allah would regard a son
the way a farmer might: as someone who could help him with
his tasks and make up for his deficiencies. Since in Allah there
are no deficiencies, hence he has no son.

The Qur'an says that Jesus is "a sign unto men and a mercy
from Us" (19:21)—that is, from Allah. Mary, too, is called a
sign (21:90; 23:50). But a sign of what? In what way are Jesus
and Mary signs of Allah in a way that the other prophets,
and their mothers, weren't? No explanation is given.

In Islam, not only is Jesus not the son of God, but to assert that he is renders one an infidel: "They are unbelievers who say, 'God is the Messiah, Mary's son.' Say: 'Who then shall overrule God in any way if He desires to destroy the Messiah, Mary's son, and his mother, and all those who are on earth?' For to God belongs the kingdom of the heavens and of the earth, and all that is between them, creating what He will. God is powerful over everything" (5:17). The beginning of that passage appears again in the Qur'an, as if it were a kind of refrain: "They are unbelievers who say, 'God is the Messiah, Mary's son.' For the Messiah said, 'Children of Israel, serve God, my Lord and your Lord. Verily whoso associates with God anything, God shall prohibit him entrance to Paradise, and his refuge shall be the Fire; and wrongdoers shall have no helpers'" (5:72).

The Qur'an envisions the Incarnation not as God becoming man but as a heavenly being visiting the earth without fully taking on human form. Thus it warns the Christians: "The Messiah, son of Mary, was only a Messenger; Messengers before him passed away; his mother was a just woman; they both ate food. Behold, how We make clear the signs to them; then behold, how they perverted are!" (5:75). Offering the fact that Jesus ate food as evidence that Jesus is not the Son of God manifests a deep misunderstanding of the nature of the Incarnation. The Qur'an apparently envisions it solely as God's taking the form of a man but not becoming a man in any real sense; the idea that God would have "become like us in all things except sin" (Heb. 2:17) is a concept completely alien to the Qur'an and Islam in general. Where the Qur'an envisions the Incarnation at all, it does so only in the sense of God taking flesh as a garment, rather like a boss going incognito among his employees to see what they really think of him, but not becoming a fellow employee in any genuine sense.

A miracle worker, by Allah's permission

In the Qur'an, this messenger of Allah, although emphatically just a human, does have the ability to perform miracles and even to raise the dead. But this is not to indicate (as in the Gospels) that he is divine, with his own authority and power over life and death; instead, he performs all his miracles only with Allah's permission. Jesus tells the children of Israel: "I have come to you with a sign from your Lord. I will create for you out of clay as the likeness of a bird; then I will breathe into it, and it will be a bird, by the leave of God. I will also heal the blind and the leper, and bring to life the dead, by the leave of God. I will inform you too of what things you eat, and what you treasure up in your houses. Surely in that is a sign for you, if you are believers" (3:49).

This is a sharp contrast to Muhammad, who works no miracles. When the unbelievers demand a miracle from the new prophet — "And they that know not say: Why does God not speak to us? Why does a sign not come to us?" (2:118; cf. 6:37; 10:20; 13:7; 13:27) —Allah tells him how to respond: by saying that even if he did come to the unbelievers with a miracle, they would reject him anyway: "Indeed, We have struck for the people in this Koran every manner of similitude; and if thou bringest them a sign, those who are unbelievers will certainly say, 'You do nothing but follow falsehood'" (30:58). It is significant that even though the Qur'an exalts Muhammad as the "Seal of the Prophets" (33:40) and Islamic tradition even further exalts him as the supreme example of human behavior (an idea based on the Qur'an's designation of him as a "good example" (33:21)—indeed, *the* good example), it is Jesus who in the Qur'an is the miracle worker, not Muhammad. Jesus is designated the Word of God, not Muhammad. Jesus is born of a Virgin, not Muhammad. These and other undigested bits of orthodox Christianity in the Qur'an, and the Muslim holy book's general exaltation of Jesus over Muhammad, are left unexplained in Islamic tradition, since it lacks a rational theology and a tradition of reasoning from Scripture: The divine fiat is all. But they remain as hints of a greater truth that over the centuries have led many a Muslim to discover a far greater truth than Islam encompasses.

They preach Christ not crucified

The Qur'an frequently criticizes the Jews, whom it terms "the most hostile of men to the believers" (5:82) and the slayers of the prophets (4:155). Yet they also draw the divine ire "for their saying, 'We slew the Messiah, Jesus son of Mary, the Messenger of God'—yet they did not slay him, neither crucified him, only a likeness of that was shown to them" (4:157).

This recalls Christian Gnostic texts that denied the Crucifixion on the grounds that, the material world being evil, Jesus appeared on earth as a mere phantasm, taking on only the *appearance* of human form, not its substance. Hence the crucifixion had to be an illusion. A Gnostic document called *The Second Treatise of the Great Seth* has Jesus recounting what actually happened:

> For my death, which they think happened, (happened) to them in their error and blindness, since they nailed their man unto their death. For their Ennoias did not see me, for they were deaf and blind. But in doing these things, they condemn themselves. Yes, they saw me; they punished me. It was another, their father, who drank the gall and the vinegar; it was not I. They struck me with the reed; it was another, Simon, who bore the cross on his shoulder. It was another upon Whom they placed the crown of thorns. But

I was rejoicing in the height over all the wealth of the archons and the offspring of their error, of their empty glory. And I was laughing at their ignorance.[84]

Gnostics who left the Roman Empire to escape persecution in the fifth, sixth, and seventh centuries may have made their way into Arabia, for this idea of an illusory and deceptive Crucifixion certainly infiltrated the Qur'an and Islamic tradition. The idea that another was crucified in Jesus' place often led the Gnostics to identify the crucified one as the apostle Thomas, since he was "called the twin" (John 11:16). In Gnostic literature, Thomas is frequently called "Judas Thomas," a name he never bears in the canonical Gospels, but one which easily led to the idea that the one who was crucified was actually Judas Iscariot—a notion that is found in Muslim tradition.[85]

Other Muslim sources offer other candidates for the one who was crucified and elaborate on the theme that someone was made to resemble Jesus. Ibn Kathir claims that the Jews compelled "the king of Damascus at that time, a Greek polytheist who worshipped the stars," to have Jesus arrested. Jesus, in response, asked his companions: "Who volunteers to be made to look like me, for which he will be my companion in Paradise?"

When one young man agreed to take on this task, "Allah made the young man look exactly like 'Isa, while a hole opened in the roof of the house, and 'Isa was made to sleep and ascended to heaven while asleep." Then, "those surrounding the house saw the man who looked like 'Isa, they thought that he was 'Isa. So they took him at night, crucified him and placed a crown of thorns on his head. The Jews then boasted that they killed 'Isa, and some Christians accepted their false claim, due to their ignorance and lack of reason."[86]

However the deception was accomplished, Muslim scholars generally explain that Jesus could not have been crucified because it would have been impossible for Allah's prophet to be so defeated and destroyed. Considering, however, how often the Qur'an excoriates the Jews for killing the prophets,[87] this explanation is curious, and raises more questions than it answers.

One of the most important questions that it raises concerns the Resurrection of Christ. Right after saying that it only *appeared* to the Jews that they had crucified Jesus, the Qur'an says that Allah "raised him up to Him" (4:157). Does this mean that he ascended into heaven? There is no such belief in Islamic tradition, although another Qur'anic passage also has Jesus saying: "Peace be upon me, the day I was born, and the day I die, and the day I am raised up alive!" (19:33). These cryptic statements seem to assume that Jesus rose from the dead and ascended into heaven, but this is nowhere stated in Islam; all that is stated positively is that he was not crucified. When Islamic authorities deal with the segments of these verses about Allah raising up Jesus to himself, they cast them in the future.[88]

Jesus, nephew of Moses

The third chapter of the Qur'an is entitled "The Family of Imran." Imran is Amram, who was the father of Moses and Aaron (Ex. 6:20). Moses and Aaron had a sister, Miriam, who was a prophetess (Exod. 15:20). In Arabic, the names "Miriam" and "Mary" are identical: *Maryam*. Apparently confusing the two, the Qur'an records Mary the mother of Jesus as being born to Imran's wife: "When the wife of Imran said, 'Lord, I have vowed to Thee, in dedication, what is within my womb. Receive Thou this from me; Thou hear-est, and knowest.' And when she gave birth to her she said, 'Lord, I have given birth to her, a female.' (And God knew very well what she had given birth to; the male is not as the female.) 'And I have named her Mary, and commend her to Thee with her seed, to protect them from the accursed Satan'" (3:35-36).

This is the same Mary to whom angels appear in the Qur'an's version of the Annunciation: "When the angels said, 'Mary, God gives thee good tidings of a Word from Him whose name is Messiah, Jesus, son of Mary; high honoured shall he be in this world and the next, near stationed to God" (3:45). Indeed, the Qur'an states that when Mary came to her relatives with the baby Jesus, they assumed that she had been unchaste, and in passing called her by a most striking title: "Then she brought the child to her folk carrying him; and they said, 'Mary, thou hast surely committed a monstrous thing! Sister of Aaron, thy father was not a wicked man, nor was thy mother a woman unchaste'" (19:27-28).

Early on in their interactions with Muslims, Christians picked up on this confusion, and charged Muhammad with mistaking Mary the mother of Jesus with Miriam the sister of Moses, thereby making Jesus into Moses' nephew. And so in a *hadith*, Muhammad is reported as being asked about this, and responding that "sister of Aaron" was merely a title of honor, and that the Qur'an never actually meant to say that Mary was Aaron's literal sister at all: "The (people of the old age) used to give names (to their persons) after the names of Apostles and pious persons who had gone before them."[89]

This is a deft explanation, but it leaves unanswered why Mary's mother is "the wife of Imran," unless this, too, was an example of someone being nicknamed with the name of an apostle and pious person.

What is much more likely, obviously, is that here as elsewhere the Qur'an appropriates half-digested and sometimes
dimly understood biblical traditions, generally recasting
them in fundamental ways, while often leaving traces of
Jewish and Christian theology that remain unexplained in
their new Islamic setting.

Traces of the truth

For example, "I will inform you too of what things you eat,
and what you treasure up in your houses" (3:49) sounds like
a summary restatement of half-remembered New Testament
passages about the Mosaic dietary laws (such as when Jesus
"declared all foods clean" in Mark 7:19) or the Eucharist,
as well as perhaps the parable of the rich man who busies
himself with building larger storehouses for his crops and is
suddenly taken unawares, his soul required of him that very
night (Luke 12:13-21), or the parable of the sower, in which
Jesus exhorts his hearers to "look at the birds of the air: they
neither sow nor reap nor gather into barns, and yet your
heavenly Father feeds them" (Matt. 6:26).

From the enigmatic Qur'anic text, however, none of this
can be discerned, and so Muslim scholars have to guess at the
meaning. The *Tafsir al-Jalalayn* sees this as yet another of Jesus'
miracles: that he knew what people were eating inside their
homes, even though he wasn't present. "I will inform you too
of what things you eat, and what you treasure up, store, in
your houses, and what I have never seen, and he would inform
people what they had eaten and what they would eat. Surely in
that, mentioned, is a sign for you, if you are believers."[90]

Nor is this strange phrase the only vestige of authentic
New Testament teaching in the Qur'an. In Qur'an 5:114-
115, Jesus prays: "'O God, our Lord, send down upon us a

Table out of heaven, that shall be for us a festival, the first and last of us, and a sign from Thee. And provide for us; Thou art the best of providers.' God said: 'Verily I do send it down on you; whoso of you hereafter disbelieves, verily I shall chastise him with a chastisement wherewith I chastise no other being.'"

Many scholars of all creeds and perspectives have pointed out that the prospect of Jesus' asking Allah for a table from heaven that "shall be for us a festival" bears more than a hint of Eucharistic theology. The philologist Christoph Luxenberg points out that Jesus prays that this Table from heaven be "a feast ('id) for us and a sign (ayah) from thee" (5:114)."The Arabic word 'id," says Luxenberg, "borrowed from the Syriac, has been, in conformity with its Arabic meaning, correctly translated by 'celebration' [or 'feast,' in the liturgical sense]."[91] The Jesuit priest Samir Khalil Samir, a noted scholar of Islam, points out that "according to unanimous scholarly opinion [the Arabic word 'id] is a borrowing from the Syriac 'ida, which signifies 'Feast' or 'liturgical festival.'"

Fr. Samir uses this to explain the nature of this strange "Table from heaven": "This ma'ida [table] is thus defined by two terms: 'id and aya, a 'Feast' or 'liturgical festival' and a 'sign.' Is this not the most appropriate definition of the Eucharist of Christians, which is a festive celebration and a sacramental sign? Even more, it seems evident that in this passage we are dealing with a rather faithful description of Christian faith, otherwise not shared by Muslims."[92]

Luxenberg further notes that the Qur'anic passage ends with a stern warning from Allah: "God said, 'Verily I do send it down on you; whoso of you hereafter disbelieves, verily I shall chastise him with a chastisement wherewith I chastise no other being'" (5:115). He concludes: "Islam was not impressed by this divine injunction with its threats of the most severe punishments, not having grasped its significance. If the Muslim exegetes had understood these passages as the Koran intended them, there would have been a liturgy of the Last Supper in Islam."

A Jesus smorgasbord

And so, although the Qur'an presents itself as the correction of the biblical record, in reality its teachings on Jesus are a curious amalgam of material from the New Testament and the writings of heretical and schismatic sects. In a certain sense, there is something for everyone: a bit of orthodox Christianity (the Virgin Birth, the idea of Jesus as the Word of God, even if improperly understood), a bit of Gnosticism (the illusory crucifixion), a bit of hyper-Arianism (the denial of Christ's divinity) and Ebionism (the Qur'an calls Jesus "messiah" but rejects his divinity, as did the Judaizing Ebionite sect).

Islamic theology draws out none of the implications or the orthodox Christian understandings of these various privileges, titles, and singularities. All are suborned to the overarching principle that Jesus is not the son of God; the Virgin Birth is not a manifestation of the singularity of Jesus but only of Allah's power. Compare, for example, the words of the angel Gabriel to Mary in Luke's Gospel and in the Qur'an:

> Do not be afraid, Mary, for you have found favor with God. And behold, you will conceive in your womb and bear a son, and you shall call his name Jesus. He will be great, and will be called the Son of the Most High; and the Lord God will give to him the throne of his father David, and he will reign over the house of Jacob forever; and of his kingdom there will be no end. (Luke 1:30-33)

Mary, God gives thee good tidings of a Word from Him whose name is Messiah, Jesus, son of Mary; high honoured shall he be in this world and the next, near stationed to God. He shall speak to men in the cradle, and of age, and righteous he shall be. (Qur'an 3:45-46)

Although Jesus is to be "high honored" both "in this world and the next," and even be "near stationed to God," there is no hint in this that he is to be the son of the Most High, and even his title as Messiah doesn't involve his attaining to the throne of his father David. Instead, "Messiah" in the Qur'an is essentially just a name, as it is indeed identified in this passage. Although the Qur'an frequently refers to Jesus as the Messiah (3:45, 4:157, 4:171-2, 5:17, 5:72, 5:75, 9:30-1), these references don't carry the significance that they do in Christianity. There is no hint in the Qur'an or Islamic tradition that the Jews were expecting a savior, still less that Jesus was he.

There are traces, however, of the idea that the name "Messiah" has something to do with the way in which Jesus is "high honored." One early Qur'an commentary containing exegesis from Ibn Abbas, one of Muhammad's early followers, explains, "[T]he Messiah means the king (Jesus, son of Mary, illustrious in the world), he has standing and position amidst people in the life of this world (and the Hereafter) he has standing and position with Allah (and one of those brought near), unto Allah in the Garden of Eden."[93]

Ibn Kathir records traces of the literal meaning of messiah, "anointed one." As one touches in order to anoint, he sees the name as a reference to Jesus' touching people in order to heal them: "Isa was called 'Al-Masih' (the Messiah) because when he touched (*Mash*) those afflicted with an illness, they would be healed by Allah's leave."[94] Yet still there is no larger salvific expectation involved in this; no idea that the entire people are afflicted with a spiritual illness that Jesus would heal by his touch.

In another place in the Qur'an, Allah sends "Our Spirit that presented himself to [Mary] a man without fault." This spirit then tells her, "I am but a messenger come from thy Lord, to give thee a boy most pure" (19:17, 19). That's all Jesus is in the Qur'an: "most pure," but most emphatically and insistently not the "son of the Most High."

The Muslim Jesus is, however, a miracle worker. The miracle that he says he will perform when he speaks from the cradle, that of bringing clay birds to life, appears to be a reminiscence of a tradition that is recorded in the Infancy Gospel of Thomas, which dates from the second century:

> And a certain Jew when he saw what Jesus did, playing upon the Sabbath day, departed straightway and told his father Joseph: Lo, thy child is at the brook, and he hath taken clay and fashioned twelve little birds, and hath polluted the Sabbath day. And Joseph came to the place and saw: and cried out to him, saying: Wherefore doest thou these things on the Sabbath, which it is not lawful to do? But Jesus clapped his hands together and cried out to the sparrows and said to them: Go! and the sparrows took their flight and went away chirping. And when the Jews saw it they were amazed, and departed and told their chief men that which they had seen Jesus do.[95]

As we have seen, since Islam has no concept of rational theology, the elements of the Islamic picture of Jesus that seem to make him greater than Muhammad—being the Word of God, being born of a virgin, sinlessness, the ability to work miracles, returning at the end of the world—are never considered as to their implications for Jesus' identity or for his status vis-à-vis Muhammad. Islamic theology never attaches any significance to the fact that Jesus was born of a virgin, but Muhammad was not; the latter is still the last and greatest prophet, the "seal of the prophets" (33:40).

Jesus is not the last of these prophets or their seal; nor is he the greatest among them. (The Qur'an actually counsels against ranking the prophets according to greatness.) For all his striking particularities, for all the singular privileges Allah inexplicably gave his penultimate prophet rather than to the "seal of the prophets," Jesus is merely one in a chain from Adam to Muhammad.

Prepare ye the way for Muhammad

Nonetheless, in the Qur'an, one of Jesus' primary missions is to prepare the way for Muhammad and to announce his coming: "And when Jesus son of Mary said, 'Children of Israel, I am indeed the Messenger of God to you, confirming the Torah that is before me, and giving good tidings of a Messenger who shall come after me, whose name shall be Ahmad.' Then, when he brought them the clear signs, they said, 'This is a manifest sorcery'" (61:6).

"Ahmad" is etymologically related to Muhammad; both mean "Praised One." And so, Muslims understand Jesus to have proclaimed the coming of Muhammad, correcting the biblical account of Jesus' words about the coming of the Holy Spirit (John 14:16-17). The word "Paraclete" is from the Greed *parakletos,* meaning counselor—very similar in sound to *periklytos,* which means "famous" or "renowned." Hence, some Muslim scholars claim that the original text read *periklytos* and was then changed to *parakletos* by Christians who hated Muhammad or had some personal gain in view by effacing Jesus' reference to him. In this vein, the twentieth-century Islamic scholar Abdullah Yusuf Ali, author of one of the most popular translations of the Qur'an into English, explains that "'Ahmad,' or 'Muhammad,' the Praised One, is almost a translation of the Greek word *Periclytos*." Almost! He explains that "our doctors contend that *Paracletos* is a corrupt reading for *Periclytos*, and that it would apply to the Holy Prophet."[96]

In reality, there is not one New Testament manuscript containing the word *periklytos* in that passage. However, documentary evidence, or lack thereof, generally leaves Islamic apologists unmoved. The view that Islam is a correction of the false teachings of Christianity about Jesus is mainstream in Islam. Muslims even see the multiplicity of divisions among Christians as evidence that Allah is displeased with them over their distortion of his prophet's message.

Enmity and hatred

Indeed, Muslims to this day point to the huge number of Christian sects as confirmation that Allah has stirred up "enmity and hatred" among Christians for "forgetting a portion of that they were reminded of." There is a related idea among many Muslims that Christians (and, indeed, all non-Muslims) actually know better: They know Islam is true but refuse to accept it out of a desire for personal gain or from sheer perversity.

Muhammad's first biographer, Ibn Ishaq, whose biography is more fanciful hagiography than sober historiography, but nonetheless records a great deal that is illuminating about (among many other things) Islamic beliefs and assumptions, reports that at one time a group of Christians, including a bishop from southern Arabia, journeyed to see Muhammad.

Along the way, the Christians argued among themselves, in keeping with the Qur'anic assertion that Allah had "stirred up among them enmity and hatred." However, Ibn Ishaq is none too clear about the nature of the disagreements. He says that they "differed among themselves in some points, saying [Jesus] is God; and He is the son of God; and He is the third person of the Trinity, which is the doctrine of Christianity." When they go in to meet Muhammad, he challenges them to draw down the curse of Allah upon those who are speaking falsehood. They ask for time to talk amongst themselves privately. During this private meeting, one of the Christian leaders says:

> O Christians, you know right well that Muhammad is a prophet sent (by God) and he has brought a decisive declaration about the nature of your master. You know too that a people has never invoked a curse on a prophet and seen its elders live and its youth grow up. If you do this you will be exterminated. But if you decide to adhere to your religion and to maintain your doctrine about your master, then take your leave of the man and go home.[97]

Resuming their meeting with Muhammad, they present Christian doctrine to him and proclaim themselves to be true worshippers of God. Muhammad responds bluntly: "You lie. Your assertion that God has a son, your worship of the cross, and your eating pork hold you back from submission."[98] These are, in other words, manifestations of perversity, not conviction. The Christians decline Muhammad's challenge, thus confirming his assertion of their insincerity. The Qur'an makes a similar charge: "And when God took compact with those who had been given the Book: 'You shall make it clear unto the people, and not conceal it.' But they rejected it behind their backs and sold it for a small price—how evil was that their selling!" (3:187).

There are all too many Muslim clerics who agree with the Saudi Sheikh Abd Al-Muhsin Al-Qadhi, who several years ago harshly criticized Christianity in line with mainstream Islamic beliefs about Christ and Christianity:

> Today we will talk about one of the distorted religions, about a faith that deviates from the path of righteousness . . . about Christianity, this false faith, and about the people whom Allah described in his book as deviating from the path of righteousness. We will examine their faith, and we will review their history, full of hate, abomination, and wars against Islam and the Muslims. In this distorted and deformed religion, to which many of the inhabitants of the earth belong, we can see how the Christians deviate greatly from the path of righteousness by talking about the concept of the Trinity. As far as they are concerned, God is the Father, the Son, and the Holy Ghost: three who are one. . . .
>
> They see Jesus, peace be upon him, as the son of Allah. . . . It is the Christians who believe Jesus was crucified. According to them, he was hanged on the cross with nails pounded through his hands, and he cried, "My God, why have you forsaken me?" According to them, this was so that he would atone for the sins of mankind. . . . Regardless of all these deviations from the path of righteousness, it is possible to see many Muslims . . . who know about Christianity only what the Christians claim about love, tolerance, devoting life to serving the needy, and other distorted slogans. . . . After all this, we still find people who promote the idea of bringing our religion and theirs closer, as if the differences were miniscule and could be eliminated by arranging all those [interreligious] conferences, whose goal is political.[99]

"Love, tolerance, devoting life to serving the needy, and other distorted slogans." Those who have wondered why there has arisen no Muslim Mother Teresa, no Muslim St. Francis of Assisi, no Muslim who has ever won renown for his charity or humility, need look no further.

Jesus saves us—from Christianity

In Islamic theology, the person who will correct the Christians' "distorted and deformed religion" is Jesus himself. Muhammad prophesies a vision of the end times that has the Muslim prophet Jesus actually making war against Christians and Christianity: "The Hour will not be established until the son of Mary [Jesus] descends amongst you as a just ruler, he will break the cross, kill the pigs, and abolish the Jizya tax. Money will be in abundance so that nobody will accept it [as charitable gifts]."[100]

He will break the cross because it is an insult to Allah's transcendent power to suggest that one of his prophets could have been victimized, that Jesus was God in the flesh who died and rose from the dead for our salvation. He will kill the pigs because they represent the failure of the Christians to accept Muhammad's new revelations and their attendant dietary restrictions; at this point, the world is to be conquered and Islamized entirely, and so no one will have any use for pigs at all.

He will abolish the *jizya* tax, which is the hallmark of the subjugated status of the People of the Book as mandated in the Qur'an (9:29). There will be no need to collect it anymore, because the People of the Book who remain alive at this time will all have converted to Islam. "Money will be in abundance," as a true era of peace and happiness dawns upon the world, presumably amid the corpses of millions of pigs and Christians who refused to convert and were duly killed by Jesus himself.

"During his time," says Ibn Kathir, "Allah will destroy all religions except Islam and Allah will destroy Al-Masih Ad-Dajjal (the False Messiah)."[101]

And thus the true age of peace will dawn: when Jesus has saved the world by destroying Christianity.

5

Are We All Muslims Now?

The Qur'anic "correction" of biblical stories, as we have seen, makes over Moses and Jesus into prophets whose teachings were congruent with those of Muhammad. But the Islamic critique of Judaism and Christianity doesn't stop there.

One of the least-noted aspects of Islam is its thorough-going historical revisionism, aimed at the complete and utter delegitimizing of Christianity. Muslim spokesmen in the West routinely point to Jesus' status as a prophet in the Qur'an as an indication of Islam's ecumenical broad-mindedness. In reality, however, Islam treats Christianity as a perversion of the original teaching of Jesus (which is identical to the message of the Qur'an and Islam). This robs Christianity of any legitimate manifestation; to Islam, all Christians are essentially apostate Muslims.

In the Qur'an, not just Moses and Jesus but all the biblical figures who appear are presented as Muslims. Abraham, for example, of whom the Qur'an says: "No; Abraham in truth was not a Jew, neither a Christian; but he was a Muslim and one pure of faith; certainly he was never of the idolaters" (3:67).

It may seem preposterous to non-Muslims that the Qur'an makes this claim, since Abraham lived millennia before Muhammad. But actually, the claim presents no problem of anachronism for Muslims, because they consider Islam to be the original and true religion of all true prophets. Thus, any deviations from the substance of Islam in the message of a true prophet (such as are found in Christian and Jewish scriptures) are simply evidence that the followers of that prophet altered his message.

Note the clear contrast with the way Christians view Judaism. Christianity originated as a sect of Judaism. The

Jews at its foundation, Sts. Peter and Paul, and all the other New Testament authors except for St. Luke, read the Old Testament as Scripture. They understood it differently, particularly in regard to the messianic prophecies, than did the leaders of the Jewish people, but they wouldn't have dreamed of claiming that its text had been tampered with, or that it was not reliably the word of God. Rather than re-writing Judaism to accommodate itself, Christianity has sought to harmonize its teachings with its Jewish roots.

In contrast to this accommodating and inclusive view, Islam views Judaism and Christianity as distorted and renegade versions of the true messages of Moses and Jesus. The people who originated them and the people who follow them today are perverse, rejecting the true faith even though they know it to be true. Islamic doctrine holds that the true teachings of Moses and Jesus corresponded to those of Muhammad, and that they delivered to the world written revelation—the original, unadulterated Torah and Gospels—that reflected this correspondence. These original texts have been lost, but fortunately, Muslims contend, the Qur'an contains the substance of their true messages.

The corruption of Scripture

In the Qur'an, the Christians have not so much fabricated as forgotten what Allah told them through Jesus. Despite the Qur'an's dependence upon biblical material as one of its most obvious sources (and the only source that makes coherent much of what it says about Jesus), the Qur'an criticizes the Christians for not faithfully preserving the revelations they received: "And with those who say 'We are Christians' We took compact; and they have forgotten a portion of that they were reminded of. So We have stirred up among them enmity and hatred, till the Day of Resurrection; and God will assuredly tell them of the things they wrought" (5:14).

These charges are much milder than those the Qur'an levels against the Jews, who have not only "forgotten a part of what they were reminded of," but also are busy "perverting words from their meanings," which apparently amounts to a charge that they were willfully misinterpreting the Scripture: "So for their breaking their compact We cursed them and made their hearts hard, they perverting words from their meanings; and they have forgotten a portion of that they were reminded of; and thou wilt never cease to light upon some act of treachery on their part, except a few of them. Yet pardon them, and forgive; surely God loves the good-doers" (5:13).

Yet the Christians' corruption of their own scriptures, according to the Qur'an, goes beyond simple forgetfulness. The Qur'an also asks of the Jews and Christians, "And who does greater evil than he who conceals a testimony received from God? And God is not heedless of the things you do" (2:140). Apparently, then, the Christians have not just forgotten a part of divine revelation, but are deliberately concealing some of what Allah told them. This implies a moral guilt that all Christians carry—or, if it is restricted only to the perpetrators of this corruption, at the very least the Christians of today are misled and ignorant of the true teachings of Jesus.

This moral guilt comes through clearly in the Qur'an when it says that there are among the People of the Book (the Qur'an's term for groups that have received written revelations from Allah—principally Jews and Christians) some "evildoers" who claim that what they recite is divine revelation, when actually it is of their own devising: "Then the evildoers substituted a saying other than that which had been said to them; so We sent down upon the evildoers wrath out of heaven for their ungodliness" (2:59). These "sayings" that are substituted one for another apparently involve Jews and Christians' passing off human writings as inspired Scripture: "And there is a sect of them twist their tongues with the Book, that you may suppose it part of the Book, yet it is not part of the Book; and they say, 'It is from God,' yet it is not from God, and they speak falsehood against God, and that wittingly" (3:79).

This warning appears to be in connection with the Christian proclamation of Christ's divinity, since immediately following it comes an oblique reference to Christians' worshipping Christ as God: "It belongs not to any mortal that God should give him the Book, the Judgment, the Prophethood, then he should say to men, 'Be you servants to me apart from God.' Rather, 'Be you masters in that you know the Book, and in that you study.' He would never order you to take the angels and the Prophets as Lords; what, would He order you to disbelieve, after you have surrendered?" (3:80-81).

This passage clearly identifies the orthodox Christian understanding of the divinity of Christ as a sinful deification of a human being and a twisting of Jesus' message. In the Qur'an, the true Christians are those who hold Jesus to be a merely human prophet who taught the absolute oneness and singularity of God. This Christianity, however, has long since vanished from the earth. Mainstream Muslim belief is that orthodox Christianity is nothing more than a subterfuge, a massive hoax designed to fool the believers and lead them astray.

Some of those who engage in this subterfuge not only recite false revelations but write them down and even sell them to the ignorant and unwary: "And some there are of them that are common folk not knowing the Book, but only fancies and mere conjectures. So woe to those who write the Book with their hands, then say, 'This is from God,' that

they may sell it for a little price; so woe to them for what
their hands have written, and woe to them for their earn-
ings" (2:79).

Oddly enough, however, even while charging that the
Christians "have forgotten a portion of that they were reminded of," the Qur'an directs Christians to determine the
question of whether or not Islam is true by consulting the
Gospel, "wherein is guidance and light":

> And We sent, following in their footsteps, Jesus son of
> Mary, confirming the Torah before him and We gave to
> him the Gospel, wherein is guidance and light, and con-
> firming the Torah before it, as a guidance and an admo-
> nition unto the godfearing. So let the People of the Gos-
> pel judge according to what God has sent down therein.
> Whosoever judges not according to what God has sent
> down—they are the ungodly. (5:46-47)

The Qur'an refers to the "Gospel" in this and other passages as if it were a book delivered to Jesus, in much the
same way as the Qur'an was said to have been delivered
to Muhammad. Jews and Christians will find prophecies
of Muhammad's coming in their own scripture—that is, in
the unadulterated Torah and Gospel that Muslims say taught
Islam but have vanished from the earth. Allah says: "My
chastisement—I smite with it whom I will; and My mercy
embraces all things, and I shall prescribe it for those who are
godfearing and pay the alms, and those who indeed believe
in Our signs, those who follow the Messenger, the Prophet
of the common folk, whom they find written down with
them in the Torah and the Gospel" (7:156-157).

Not only are Christians thus directed to consult their
own scripture in order to determine the veracity of Mu-

hammad's prophetic claim, but Allah even tells Muhammad to do the same thing:

> So, if thou art in doubt regarding what We have sent down to thee, ask those who recite the Book before thee. The truth has come to thee from thy Lord; so be not of the doubters, nor be of those who cry lies to God's signs so as to be of the losers. (10:94-95)

These passages put Muslims in an awkward position. The Qur'an itself says that the gospel contains "guidance and light" and tells Christians and even Muhammad to consult it; and yet the New Testament does not confirm Muhammad's message; indeed, it teaches numerous doctrines that Islam denies (notably the divinity of Christ). Muslim theologians have found a solution to this conundrum in claiming that the true Gospel that was delivered to Jesus Christ (as the Qur'an puts it) is not the New Testament of Christianity. The Muslim charge that Christians have corrupted their scripture is pointed: Those who changed the text are supposed to have done so in order to remove references to Muhammad and correspondences to Islamic doctrine. So the Gospel that was delivered to Jesus the Muslim prophet contained "guidance and light," but the New Testament does not.

Twentieth-century translator of the Qur'an, Abdullah Yusuf Ali, explains: "The *Injil* [Gospel] mentioned in the Qur'an is certainly not the New Testament, and it is not the four Gospels, as now received by the Christian Church, but an original Gospel which was promulgated by Jesus as the *Tawrah* [Torah] was promulgated by Moses and the Qur'an by Muhammad al Mustafa."[102]

The existence of this "original Gospel which was promulgated by Jesus" is a staple of Muslim belief. Extrapolating from the Qur'an's claim that Christians "have forgotten a portion of that they were reminded of" and have altered the scripture they received from Jesus, Islam generally teaches that the New Testament, as it stands today, is a corrupted version of the true gospel, altered at the hands of venal churchmen.

Gospel of Barnabas: the real deal?

There is, however, no documentary evidence whatsoever of this original Gospel. Not only has it never been found, nothing corresponding to it is even referred to in early Christian literature. No documents, whole or fragmentary, have been found to support the idea that there ever existed an account of Jesus' life that conformed to Islamic doctrine about him.

Some Muslims point to the Gospel According to Barnabas, a relatively wordy text that exists only in a couple of manuscripts that date from the sixteenth century. Iran's Basij Press claimed in May 2012 that a copy of the Gospel of Barnabas in the possession of the Turkish government actually dated from the fifth century, and claimed far-reaching implications for this: "The discovery of the original Barnabas Bible will now undermine the Christian Church and its authority and will revolutionize the religion in the world. The most significant fact, though, is that this Bible has predicted the coming of Prophet Mohammad and in itself has verified the religion of Islam, and this alone will unbalance the powers of the world and create instability in the Christian world."[103]

Some Muslim websites contain claims that early Christians accepted it as part of the canon of Scripture. However, says one such site, the first ecumenical council—Nicaea in 325—"ordered that all original Gospels in Hebrew script should be destroyed. An Edict was issued that any one in possession of these Gospels will be put to death."[104]

This is utterly fanciful—the Council of Nicaea didn't even deal with issues pertaining to the canon, much less violently suppress possessors of some Muslim proto-Gospel. (Claims of this sort have become popular in recent years, though, thanks in part to Dan Brown's anti-Catholic historical fiction *The Da-Vinci Code*.) Still, Islamic apologists in the U.S. frequently refer to the suppression of the Scripture at the Council of Nicaea as if it were established historical fact. Somewhat ironically, Islamic tradition contends that the caliph Uthman collected all the manuscripts of the Qur'an in the year 653, standardized the text, and burned all the variants (although this incident is highly questionable from a historical standpoint).

In any case, we find not even a mention of a Gospel of Barnabas until the sixth century, and no extant copy older than the sixteenth. It is no more likely to be the original Gospel, or even an accurate account of Jesus' life, than the libretto of *Jesus Christ Superstar*. Numerous small errors destroy its credibility: For example, it records that "Pilate was governor in the priesthood of Annas and Caiaphas" when Jesus was born; Pontius Pilate did not actually become procurator of Judea until the year A.D. 26. It refers to "casks of wood" that are "filled with wine," even though the storage of wine in wooden casks did not begin until several hundred years after the time of Jesus, and even then only in Europe.

No, the Gospel of Barnabas shows all the signs of being produced to fill a need: a need for a Muslim Jesus. It contains all the teachings about Jesus found in the Qur'an and *hadith*, along with material from the canonical Gospels that is recast in order to fit into this Islamic framework. Accordingly, in it Jesus excoriates as "impious" the idea that he is divine:

> As God lives, in whose presence my soul stands, I am not the Messiah whom all the tribes of the earth expect, even

as God promised to our father Abraham, saying: 'In your seed will I bless all the tribes of the earth.' But when God shall take me away from the world, Satan will raise again this accursed sedition, by making the impious believe that I am God and son of God, whence my words and my doctrine shall be contaminated, insomuch that scarcely shall there remain thirty faithful ones: whereupon God will have mercy upon the world, and will send his Messenger for whom he has made all things who shall come from the south with power, and shall destroy the idols with the idolaters who shall take away the dominion from Satan which he has over men. He shall bring with him the mercy of God for salvation of them that shall believe in him, and blessed is he who shall believe his words.[105]

In describing this coming messenger, who is, of course, Muhammad, Jesus sounds more like John the Baptist than himself, saying: "Unworthy though I am to untie his hosen, I have received grace and mercy from God to see him." He says that the messenger "shall destroy every false opinion of me, and his faith shall spread and shall take hold of the whole world, for so has God promised to Abraham our father. And that which gives me consolation is that his faith shall have no end, but shall be kept inviolate by God."[106]

When Jesus reveals that Muhammad is the "blessed name" of this messenger, the crowd cries out, "O God send us your Messenger: O Muhammad, come quickly for the salvation of the world!"[107]

The Gospel of Barnabas is so clearly inauthentic that, although it remains popular in some Muslim apologetic quarters, most Muslim scholars today follow Abdullah Yusuf Ali's lead, contenting themselves with charging that the New Testament has so clearly been tampered with that it

no longer had any value as a record of Jesus' teachings. (Of
course, they do not offer an unaltered version of what they
say is Jesus' original message; indeed, they cannot do so.)

In any case, believing that the original religion of all the
prophets is Islam, and that Christianity is a corrupt version
of the true message of Jesus, Muslims accordingly enter into
dialogue with Christians regarding them as at best ignorant,
at worst deliberately rebellious. It should therefore come as
no surprise that virtually all Muslim attempts at outreach to
Christians are actually thinly veiled invitations to accept Islam, not genuine efforts at dialogue and mutual understanding. Islam simply does not consider Christianity, a deliberately twisted version of the original message of their prophet
Jesus, or Christians, the "vilest of creatures" (Qur'an 98:6),
as worthy of respect. Some individual Muslims may accord
Christians that respect, of course, but if they do, it is respect
that springs from their common humanity, not from the
teachings of Islam.

Most Catholics who engage in interfaith dialogue regard
their dialogue partners as equals, and assume that they're
returning the favor. But mainstream Islam does not mandate
regarding orthodox Christians as equals, but instead as reb-
els from the true faith and the true God. Catholics who enter into this dialogue should be aware of this. The extreme
religious chauvinism of Muslims makes genuine dialogue as
equals essentially impossible.

It bears noting in conclusion that this chauvinism goes far
beyond any Catholic view of Protestantism (in any of its forms)
as a corrupted and incomplete version of the true teaching of
Christ. Whereas Catholics can recognize in separated Christians a shared divine revelation and a common confession of
the salvific work of the Son of God, Islam sees in Christianity
only apostasy and idolatry. Furthermore, Islam holds apos-

tates and hypocrites in furious contempt, prescribing death for both. However dimly a Catholic may regard the errors of Protestantism, he recognizes that he is bound to regard all Protestants in charity—a virtue that is notably absent in Islam's commands about how to treat unbelievers.

6

A Common Desire for Justice?

Catholics may be tempted to dismiss the revisionism of Islam's replacement theology. After all, we have serious theological disagreements with adherents of all other faiths, too, but we can make common cause with them—for example, on moral issues, as we have done with Muslims in the past. When it comes to contemporary debates in the moral sphere, Catholics might wish to look past theological disagreements to the many moral beliefs they presume Christianity and Islam hold in common.

Some Catholics go even further than that. Appraising the moral compromises of comfortable American middle-class Catholicism, they see in Islam not only a potential moral partner on life issues but also a positive moral exemplar.

In this vein, Peter Kreeft has compiled a list of "what Christians should *obviously* [emphasis in original] learn from Muslims," including "the absoluteness of the moral laws and of the demand to be just and charitable."[108] Dinesh D'Souza argued in his 2007 book *The Enemy at Home* that it is the West's "social and moral corruption" that have largely motivated Islamic jihadists, asserting that "the Muslims who hate us the most are the ones who have encountered Western decadence, either in the West or in their own countries."[109]

It's true that Western immorality is a frequent feature of the Islamic critique of the post-Christian West, as well as a target for the morality police of Sharia states.[110] In the summer of 2009, Iranian authorities even published a list of hairstyles that were acceptably moral and Islamic, as opposed to "decadent" Western imports, among which were the ponytail and the mullet.[111]

That same Western decadence is indeed also a frequent preoccupation of Islamic jihadists. In December 2010, a Muslim named Taimour Abdulwahab al-Abdaly set off explosives on a street in Stockholm that was crowded with Christmas shoppers, killing himself and injuring two others. His wife, who was later arrested for helping plan the attack, explained that Abdulwahab "disliked the decadent side of society here."[112]

Christian writers such as Kreeft and D'Souza seem to think the Islamic world has something to teach today's decadent West. Yet although it is obvious that Christians should learn "the absoluteness of the moral laws and of the demand to be just and charitable," it is far less clear that Muslims have these laws to teach, or believe them themselves.

It is all-important to examine whether Muslims do or not, for it is on the basis of their vision of Muslims as upright, moral, God-fearing, and pious that many Catholics see them as potential allies and are apt to regard criticism of Islam's violent and supremacist doctrines, or of the Muslim persecution of Christians in Muslim lands, as self-defeating.

In reality, Islamic morality is quite different from what these Catholics want to believe. Not only does it have much less common ground with Catholic morality than most Catholics assume, but in fostering genuine virtues it compares unfavorably even with the decadent West.

Moral absolutes and the raid at Nakhla

First and foremost, in Islamic morality there are no absolutes. After Muhammad and the earliest Muslims moved from Mecca to Medina in 622, the event known as the *hijra* (flight) that is generally understood to mark the beginning of Islam, he began ordering his followers to raid the caravans of the Quraysh, the pagan Arabs of Mecca who had rejected Muhammad's claim to be a prophet. (Muslims would say this was an instance of a prophet's not being without honor except in his own country, as Muhammad was a member of the Quraysh tribe and had grown up among them.)

On one occasion, Muhammad ordered nine of his men to raid a Quraysh caravan that was making its way back to Mecca. He gave the leader of the Muslim raiders, Abdullah bin Jahsh, sealed instructions with orders not to open and read them until his group had already journeyed for two days away from Medina.

Once two days had passed, Abdullah read Muhammad's instructions, which said, "When you have read this letter of mine proceed until you reach Nakhla between Mecca and Al-Ta'if. Lie in wait there for Quraysh and find out for us what they are doing."

Thereupon, Abdullah told his men, "The apostle has commanded me to go to Nakhla to lie in wait there for Quraysh so as to bring us news of them. He has forbidden me to put pressure on any of you, so if anyone wishes for martyrdom let him go forward, and he who does not, let him go back; as for me I am going on as the Prophet has ordered." None went back. Abdullah was referring to martyrdom not in the Christian sense but in the Islamic sense: A martyr is one who "fight[s] in the way of God; they kill, and are killed" (Qur'an 9:111).

Abdullah and his men spotted the Quraysh caravan earlier than they had expected: It was the last day of the month of Rajab, one of the four "sacred months" of the pagan Arab calendar. During these months, by mutual agreement of the various Arab tribes, it was forbidden to take up arms. However, this presented Abdullah's band with a dilemma: "If you leave them alone tonight they will get into the sacred area and will be safe from you; and if you kill them, you will kill them in the sacred month." Nonetheless, they eventually decided, in the words of Muhammad's first biographer, Ibn Ishaq, to "kill as many as they could of them and take what they had."

When they returned to Medina, they found Muhammad wrathful: "I did not order you to fight in the sacred
month."[113] He refused to accept the fifth of the spoils that
they had set aside for him. The moral absolute that fighting was prohibited during the sacred month was paramount,
and Abdullah and his men had violated it.

However, then Allah revealed this passage of the Qur'an
to Muhammad: "They will question thee concerning the
holy month, and fighting in it. Say: 'Fighting in it is a heinous thing, but to bar from God's way, and disbelief in Him,
and the Holy Mosque, and to expel its people from it—that
is more heinous in God's sight; and persecution is more heinous than slaying'" (2:217).

Ibn Ishaq explained what this meant: The Quraysh "have
kept you back from the way of God with their unbelief in
Him, and from the sacred mosque, and have driven you
from it when you were with its people. This is a more serious matter with God than the killing of those whom you
have slain."[114] Thus, the Muslim raiders' fighting during the
sacred month was justified, and Muhammad thereupon took
his share of the spoils of the raid.

This incident taught a profound lesson that future Muslims would take to heart: In Islam, any moral law can be
set aside for the good of the Muslims. That is Islam's only
functional moral absolute.

Honor thy father and mother . . . unless they're infidels

In the Qur'an's many retellings of the exodus of the children
of Israel from Egypt, the one notable omission is any spe-
cifics about the contents of the "tablets" that Moses brings
down from the mountain, beyond that "in the inscription of
them was guidance" (Qur'an 7:154). There is, however, one

key passage of the Qur'an that does contain what appears to
be a set of moral principles on the order of (and reminiscent
of) the Ten Commandments:

> Set not up with God another god, or thou wilt sit con-
> demned and forsaken.
>   Thy Lord has decreed you shall not serve any but Him,
> and to be good to parents, whether one or both of them
> attains old age with thee; say not to them 'Fie,' neither
> chide them, but speak unto them words respectful, and
> lower to them the wing of humbleness out of mercy and
> say; 'My Lord, have mercy upon them, as they raised me
> up when I was little.' Your Lord knows very well what is
> in your hearts if you are righteous, for He is All-forgiving
> to those who are penitent. (17:22-23)

Yet even in the believer's relationship with his parents,
the overarching principle is that Muslims must be "hard
against the unbelievers, merciful one to another" (48:29).
The Qur'an says: "O believers, fight the unbelievers who are
near to you; and let them find in you a harshness; and know
that God is with the godfearing" (9:123). This includes unbelievers of one's immediate family: The Muslim holy book
specifically forbids believers from being friendly with their
non-believing relatives:

> O believers, take not your fathers and brothers to be your
> friends, if they prefer unbelief to belief; whosoever of you
> takes them for friends, those—they are the evildoers. Say:
> "If your fathers, your sons, your brothers, your wives, your
> clan, your possessions that you have gained, commerce you
> fear may slacken, dwellings you love—if these are dearer to
> you than God and His Messenger, and to struggle in His

way, then wait till God brings His command; God guides not the people of the ungodly." (9:23-24)

Explains Ibn Kathir: "Allah commands shunning the disbelievers, even if they are one's parents or children, and prohibits taking them as supporters if they choose disbelief instead of faith." Unlike superficially similar recommendations in the New Testament,[115] such statements in an Islamic context are not balanced by exhortations to universal charity and prayer for the unbelievers. Recall that the Qur'an holds up Abraham as an example for Muslims in his hatred for his unbelieving family, but specifically rules him out as an example when he says he will pray for his unbelieving father.

The Qur'an emphasizes not only that a Muslim must have nothing to do with his parents if they are unbelievers but that he should not even pray for them: "It is not for the Prophet and the believers to ask pardon for the idolaters, even though they be near kinsmen, after that it has become clear to them that they will be the inhabitants of Hell" (9:113).

In a Qur'anic account of Noah and the great flood, when the flood kills Noah's son, Noah appeals to Allah on the basis of his promise to save Noah's family: "And Noah called unto his Lord, and said, 'O my Lord, my son is of my family, and Thy promise is surely the truth. Thou art the justest of those that judge'" (11:45). But Allah responds: "Noah, he is not of thy family; it is a deed not righteous," referring to Noah's son saying that he would flee to the top of a mountain to save himself from the flood (11:43, 46).

Lying is a sin . . . except when it is a positive good

The prophet of Islam was unequivocal about the Muslim's responsibility to be truthful: "It is obligatory for you to tell the truth, for truth leads to virtue and virtue leads to Paradise, and the man who continues to speak the truth and endeavors to tell the truth is eventually recorded as truthful with Allah, and beware of telling of a lie, for telling of a lie leads to obscenity and obscenity leads to Hell-Fire, and the person who keeps telling lies and endeavors to tell a lie is recorded as a liar with Allah."[116]

However, Muhammad also said, "War is deceit" and that lying is permissible in wartime. He said that lying was permissible when a husband needed to keep the peace in the household by deceiving his wife.[117] Shi'ite Islam has elaborated doctrines of deception (*taqiyya* and *kitman*) to which the believer may resort when in danger for his life, but since the Qur'an also teaches that this deception is allowed, this is not solely a Shi'ite concept: "Let not the believers take the unbelievers for friends, rather than the believers—for whoso does that belongs not to God in anything—unless you have a fear of them. God warns you that you beware of Him, and unto God is the homecoming" (Qur'an 3:28). A Muslim is thus not to take non-Muslims as friends unless he has "a fear of them" and is only feigning friendship to protect himself.

Ibn Kathir explains this verse: "Allah prohibited His believing servants from becoming supporters of the disbelievers, or to take them as comrades with whom they develop friendships, rather than the believers." However, exempt from this are "those believers who in some areas or times fear for their safety from the disbelievers. In this case, such believers are allowed to show friendship to the disbelievers outwardly, but never inwardly."[118] He explains, "the scholars agreed that if a person is forced into disbelief, it is permissible for him to either go along with them in the interests of self-preservation, or to refuse."[119]

Syed Abul Ala Maududi, an internationally influential twentieth-century Islamic scholar and Pakistani political leader, explained that this verse "means that it is lawful for a believer, helpless in the grip of the enemies of Islam and in imminent danger of severe wrong and persecution, to keep his faith concealed and to behave in such manner as to create the impression that he is on the same side as his enemies." In severe circumstances, "he may even state that he is not a believer."[120]

This outright and explicit deception goes far beyond the Christian idea of mental reservation that St. Raymond of Penyafort (1175-1275) first enunciated:

> I believe, as at present advised, that when one is asked by murderers bent on taking the life of someone hiding in the house whether he is in, no answer should be given; and if this betrays him, his death will be imputable to the murderers, not to the other's silence. Or he may use an equivocal expression, and say "He is not at home," or something like that. And this can be defended by a great number of instances found in the Old Testament. Or he may say simply that he is not there, and if his conscience tells him that he ought to say that, then he will not speak against his conscience, nor will he sin. Nor is St. Augustine really opposed to any of these methods.[121]

This amounts to allowing for misleading but strictly true statements to be employed in extreme circumstances, in order to stave off an even greater evil than the deception itself. Muslims would argue, of course, that their doctrine is the same: One may resort to deception only in extreme circumstances, and even then only in the service of justice.

In the case of Islam, however, justice is equated with positive Islamic law, underscoring a vision of the good that is markedly different from that of the Church. These differences can be found at the very heart of Islam's moral framework, particularly in Islam's directives regarding how Muslims should treat non-Muslims.

Stealing from unbelievers? Fine

The Qur'an's punishment for theft is draconian: "And the thief, male and female: cut off the hands of both, as a recompense for what they have earned, and a punishment exemplary from God; God is All-mighty, All-wise" (5:38).

But the Qur'an also contains instructions for the distribution of the spoils of war: "Know that, whatever booty you take, the fifth of it is God's, and the Messenger's, and the near kinsman's, and the orphans', and for the needy, and the traveler, if you believe in God and that We sent down upon Our servant on the day of salvation, the day the two hosts encountered; and God is powerful over everything" (8:41). This "booty" comes from warfare against unbelievers.

At one point, Muhammad signs a treaty with the Quraysh, the Treaty of Hudaybiyyah, which many of his followers saw as a defeat for the Muslims. To mollify them, Muhammad presented them with a Qur'anic revelation promising future victories and much booty: "When God was well pleased with the believers when they were swearing fealty to thee under the tree, and He knew what was in their hearts, so He sent down the Shechina upon them, and rewarded them with a nigh victory and many spoils to take; and God is ever All-mighty, All-wise. God has promised you many spoils to take; these He has hastened to you, and has restrained the hands of men from you, and that it may be a sign to the believers, and to guide you on a straight path" (48:18-20).

In Islam, the spoils are an essential component of warfare. Islamic tradition records that Muhammad once wrote to a conquered Jewish tribe, the Banu Janbah, in great detail about the spoils that he and the victorious Muslims were owed: "Verily, for the Apostle of Allah will be the booty which you receive on making peace (with some party) and every slave you get, as well as animals and other objects, except that which the Apostle of Allah or his envoy remits. Verily, it is binding on you to pay one-fourth of the yield of your date-palms, and one-fourth of your game from the rivers, and one-fourth of what your women spin."[122]

In addition to the spoils of war, Islamic law mandates the plunder of the conquered and subjugated infidels (*dhimmis*) as well, in the form of a poll tax or tribute (*jizya*) that non-Muslims must pay: "Fight those who believe not in God and the Last Day and do not forbid what God and His Messenger have forbidden—such men as practice not the religion of truth, being of those who have been given the Book—until they pay the tribute out of hand and have been humbled" (9:29).

In that spirit, Muhammad is recorded as once having written to a Christian ruler:

> I will not fight against you unless I write to you in advance. So, join the fold of Islam or pay the *jizyah*. Obey Allah and His Apostle and the messengers of His Apostle, honor them and dress them in nice clothes. . . . Provide Zayd with good clothes. If my messengers will be pleased with you, I shall also be pleased with you. . . . Pay three *wasaq* of barley to Harmalah.[123]

The *jizya* was so important to the early Muslims that the caliph Umar (d. 644) once told his people, "I advise you to fulfill Allah's *dhimma* (financial obligation made with the *dhimmi*) as it is the *dhimma* of your Prophet and the source of the livelihood of your dependents (i.e., the taxes from the *dhimmi*.)"[124]

Many Muslims still regard it in the same way today. The last Islamic empire, the Ottoman Empire, abolished the *dhimma* and the *jizya* in 1856, when as "the sick man of Europe" it could no longer withstand Western pressure to do so. However, the subjugation of the People of the Book and their payment of this tax to the believers remain part of Islamic law as all eight of the schools of Islamic jurisprudence teach it.

Consequently, calls to re-impose the *jizya*, or attempts to do so, periodically reappear among Muslims. In March 2007, Muslim gangs knocked on doors in Christian neighborhoods in Baghdad, demanding payment of the *jizya*.[125] In December 2011, Yassir Al-Burhami, a leader of the Salafists, an Egyptian movement of rigorist Muslims, reiterated some of the classic Islamic laws regarding the *dhimmis*: "Appointing infidels to positions of authority over Muslims is prohibited. Allah said: 'Never will Allah grant the infidels a way [to triumph] over the Believers'" (Qur'an 4:141). He also declared that the Muslims of Egypt should begin again to collect the jizya from the Christians:

> Can the Christians of Egypt be compared to the Jews of Al-Medina? The case of the Jews of Al-Medina is one example of the relations between the Muslims and the infidels. The Muslims can implement any form of conduct used by the Prophet Muhammad. When the Prophet Muhammad was still in Mecca, he dealt with the infidels in a certain way, and when the Muslims are weak, they should deal with the infidels this way. "Refrain from action, pray, and pay the zakkat."
>
> In many infidel countries, such as occupied Palestine, we instruct Muslims to do just that. We are not telling the Muslims in Gaza to launch rockets every day, which would lead to the destruction of the entire country. We tell them to adhere to the truce.

When the Prophet Muhammad first arrived in Al-
Medina, he signed a treaty with the Jews without forcing
them to pay the *jizya* poll tax. This was necessary at the
time, but when they breached the treaty, he fought them,
and eventually, he imposed the *jizya* upon the People of
the Book.

The Christians [of Egypt] can be dealt with like the
Jews of Al-Medina. This is possible.[126]

The Coptic Orthodox priest Yohanna Qulta responded to this suggestion with firm resolve: "We will oppose
this fiercely, to the point of martyrdom. Returning to the
Middle Ages is out of the question. We will not turn to
the U.N. or to the Western countries but to Al-Azhar, to
Islamic moral values, and to the vast majority of Muslims,
who are moderate. Gone are the days of paying the *jizya*, the
days of slavery."[127]

Despite Fr. Qulta's confidence in the moderate majority of Muslims, Islamic hardliners have always exploited the
texts and teachings of Islam in order to call moderate believers back to a more rigorous observance of their faith.
For support they can appeal to the words of the Qur'an and
to the example of Muhammad—Muslims who believe in a
peaceful pluralistic society cannot.

Meanwhile, there are other forms of collecting the *jizya*,
even before an Islamic state is established in any given land.
Muslim immigrants in Europe exist on the dole in large
numbers, with the active encouragement of Muslim leaders,
who tell them that taking money from the infidels is their
right, in lieu of the payment of the *jizya*.[128]

Thus, Islamic morality excuses lying, stealing, and dis-
loyalty to one's parents (and more), provided such acts are
committed against non-Muslims.

Devaluing of non-Muslims

Islamic law forbids a Muslim woman from marrying a non-Muslim man, although a Muslim man may marry a non-Muslim woman (since it is assumed that the woman will enter her husband's household). Meanwhile, conversion from Islam by either spouse immediately annuls the marriage. This is in accord with the general dichotomy in Islam between Muslims and non-Muslims: The convert from Islam has left the community of "the best nation ever brought forth to men" (Qur'an 3:110) and joined that of "the unbelievers of the People of the Book and the idolaters," who are "the worst of creatures" (Qur'an 98:6).

This contrast is consistent throughout the entirety of Islamic teaching, in which there is nothing comparable to the Christian call for universal charity. Indeed, with regard to charitable works in particular, Islamic law expressly forbids the *zakat*, the alms that all Muslims are required to give, to be given to non-Muslims.[129]

The devaluation of the lives of unbelievers doesn't end there. In fact, Islamic law states that the lives of non-Muslims are literally less valuable than those of Muslims. This comes in the context of blood money, an indemnity that Islamic law allows a person who has killed someone to pay to the family members of his victim, if they are willing to accept it. The amount to be paid depends upon the religion of the victim, with the indemnity for non-Muslims heavily discounted.[130]

A leading Muslim authority in Iran, Sheikh Sultanhussein Tabandeh, actually defended the idea that a non-Muslim's life was worth less than that of a Muslim in his critique of the United Nations' Universal Declaration of Human Rights:

> Thus if [a] Muslim commits adultery his punishment is 100 lashes, the shaving of his head, and one year of banishment.

But if the man is not a Muslim and commits adultery with
a Muslim woman his penalty is execution. . . . Similarly if a
Muslim deliberately murders another Muslim he falls under
the law of retaliation and must by law be put to death by the
next of kin. But if a non-Muslim who dies at the hand of a
Muslim has by lifelong habit been a non-Muslim, the penalty
of death is not valid. Instead the Muslim murderer must pay
a fine and be punished with the lash. . . . Since Islam regards
non-Muslims as on a lower level of belief and conviction, if
a Muslim kills a non-Muslim . . . then his punishment must
not be the retaliatory death, since the faith and conviction he
possesses is loftier than that of the man slain. . . . Again, the
penalties of a non-Muslim guilty of fornication with a Muslim woman are augmented because, in addition to the crime
against morality, social duty and religion, he has committed
sacrilege, in that he has disgraced a Muslim and thereby cast
scorn upon the Muslims in general, and so must be executed.
. . . Islam and its peoples must be above the infidels, and never
permit non-Muslims to acquire lordship over them.[131]

Thou shalt not kill . . . except . . .

Once the unbeliever's life is devalued, it is not a large jump
to considering it lawful to murder them under certain circumstances.

And slay not the soul God has forbidden, except by right.
Whosoever is slain unjustly, We have appointed to his
next-of-kin authority; but let him not exceed in slaying;
he shall be helped (17:33).

Note all the caveats. This is not quite equivalent to
"Thou shalt not kill." Anyone with even the most glancing

awareness of Catholic tradition and the Christian tradition in general knows that absolute pacifism has been a minority view. Christians, at least since the time of Constantine, have acknowledged a right to self-defense for individuals and nations, and have distinguished between murder and killing that could, for various reasons, be justified.

Thus, the problem with Qur'an 17:33 is not that it allows for killing under certain circumstances, and that it speaks of those who are "slain unjustly," which opens up the possibility that others might be slain justly. The problem is the way in which the Qur'an and Islamic law determine the justice of a particular slaying.

One of the most famous verses in the entire Qur'an is known in Islamic tradition as the "Verse of the Sword": "Then, when the sacred months are drawn away, slay the idolaters wherever you find them, and take them, and confine them, and lie in wait for them at every place of ambush. But if they repent, and perform the prayer, and pay the alms, then let them go their way; God is All-forgiving, All-compassionate" (9:5).

The "sacred months" were four months of the pre-Islamic Arab calendar when, by mutual agreement of the otherwise warring Arab tribes, fighting was forbidden. The Muslims are here commanded to fight against the idolaters, which would include Christians, until they "repent, and perform the prayer, and pay the alms." These are three of the well-known Five Pillars of Islam: the confession of faith (shahada), signifying repentance from one's previous life of ignorance and alienation from the true faith of Islam; the regular performance of five daily prayers; and almsgiving, required annually from Muslims as a percentage of their income. Thus, this passage is saying that Muslims must fight against those whom Islam considers to be idolaters until they convert to Islam (or, if they are "People of the Book," submit to dhimmitude).

The most notorious part of this verse, "slay the idolaters wherever you find them," recurs two other times in the
Qur'an. In one passage, Allah gives the Muslims the same
instructions, to slay those who have expelled them from
their homes and persecuted them:

> And fight in the way of God with those who fight with
> you, but aggress not: God loves not the aggressors. And
> slay them wherever you come upon them, and expel them
> from where they expelled you; persecution is more griev-
> ous than slaying. But fight them not by the Holy Mosque
> until they should fight you there; then, if they fight you,
> slay them—such is the recompense of unbelievers—but if
> they give over, surely God is All-forgiving, All-compas-
> sionate. Fight them, till there is no persecution and the
> religion is God's; then if they give over, there shall be no
> enmity save for evildoers. (2:190-193)

This passage is one of the foundations for the frequent
Muslim apologetic claim that the Qur'an allows for fighting only in self-defense, since Allah does not love aggressors. Some schools of Islamic jurisprudence, however, teach
that non-belief in Islam is itself an act of aggression, since
Islam is the original religion of all mankind, and no one can
reject it in good faith. Maulana Bulandshahri, an Islamic
scholar who has written a contemporary commentary on
the Qur'an, explains: "The worst of sins are Infidelity (*Kufr*)
and Polytheism (*shirk*) which constitute rebellion against Allah, The Creator. To eradicate these, Muslims are required
to wage war until there exists none of it in the world, and
the only religion is that of Allah."[132] This would be a *defensive* war, for unbelief in Islam is inherently aggressive.

In any case, Muslims must fight against those who have

expelled and persecuted them until "there is no persecution and the religion is God's." This is an open-ended call to make war against non-Muslims solely on the basis of their not being Muslims. For "the religion" will not be entirely "God's" until all people accept the truly divine religion, which is Islam. Furthermore, Islam does not envision a world that is entirely Muslim until the end times, when Jesus returns and "breaks the crosses"; consequently, this directive to fight until "the religion is God's" (repeated in Qur'an 8:39) is an open-ended command to remain in a state of warfare with non-Muslims, and to work toward their subjugation under the Islamic law, until the consummation of all things.

The third occurrence of the "slay them wherever you find them" phrase in the Qur'an refers to the "hypocrites," who initially accepted Islam but then rejected it:

> How is it with you, that you are two parties touching the hypocrites, and God has overthrown them for what they earned? What, do you desire to guide him whom God has led astray? Whom God leads astray, thou wilt not find for him a way. They wish that you should disbelieve as they disbelieve, and then you would be equal; therefore take not to yourselves friends of them, until they emigrate in the way of God; then, if they turn their backs, take them, and slay them wherever you find them; take not to yourselves any one of them as friend or helper. (4:88-9)

This verse offers Qur'anic support for Muhammad's pronouncement of a death sentence on those who apostatize from Islam: "If anyone changes his religion, kill him." These hypocrites who are trying to lure other Muslims to discard their faith as well are not to be befriended until they "emigrate in the way of God," in other words, until they leave their homes in Mecca and join the Muslim community in Medina. The death penalty for apostates is still part of Islamic law, taught by all eight schools of Islamic jurisprudence: the four principal Sunni schools, the Shafi'i, Maliki, Hanafi, and Hanbali; the smaller Ibadi school that is found principally in Oman; the even smaller Zahiri school; and the Shi'ite Jafari and Zaidi schools.

This strikes at the heart of the Catholic idea of the dignity of every human person and the right of that person, endowed by God with free will, to exercise his conscience without coercion. Islam claims that "there is no compulsion in religion" (Qur'an 2:256) but hedges around this apparent concession to religious liberty and the freedom of conscience with so many caveats, not least among them being onerous restrictions on the freedom and livelihood of non-Muslims in the Islamic state, that it becomes effectively meaningless.

Pope Benedict XVI has written, "Muslims share with Christians the conviction that no constraint in religious matters, much less the use of force, is permitted."[133] This is certainly true, although all too often honored in the breach. However, Islamic doctrine does not consider the depriving of non-Muslim *dhimmis* of basic rights, or the death penalty for apostates from Islam, to be "constraint in religious matters." The convert from Islam is free to continue in his apostasy and be killed, and the *dhimmi* is free to continue as a non-Muslim in the Islamic state, suffering institutionalized discrimination. The death penalty for apostasy and the second-class status mandated for *dhimmis* are not considered constraint but simple justice.

Since the foundation of Catholic morality is equal dignity of all human beings before God, this also strikes at the heart of the compatibility on life issues that many Catholics assume exists between Catholicism and Islam.

What's more, at its very core Islamic morality owes more to coercion and conformity than to the cultivation of genuine virtue and as such stands yet again at the polar opposite of Christian morality.

The empire of fear

The Mufti of Australia, Sheikh Taj al-Din al-Hilali, once complained that "Australian law guarantees freedoms up to a crazy level."[134] (A "mufti" is a Sunni Muslim scholar who interprets Islamic law in a way that his followers regard as authoritative.) Yet freedom is an indispensable prerequisite for any cultivation of real virtue. Thus, in guaranteeing freedom even a post-Christian West makes it more possible to be virtuous than the seemingly more upright Islamic world. With its stonings, amputations, and death penalties for an array of offenses including apostasy, Islam has created not a framework in which people can become genuinely good but an empire of fear.

Muslims don't dare step out of line; not because of love for God or a real desire to please him, but because they are afraid of what would happen to them if they departed from Islam's vision of morality. Catholics concur with Muslims on many of the sins for which Islam prescribes these draconian punishments; there is no disagreement between the two on whether theft or adultery or blasphemy is sinful. But when the punishments for them are as harsh as Islam commands, the obedience that follows is not the free decision of the human being to choose the good but a simple conformism of terror.

That kind of conformism is the foundation of Islamic morality. For theft, the divinely ordained penalty is amputation: "And the thief, male and female: cut off the hands of both, as a recompense for what they have earned, and a punishment exemplary from God; God is All-mighty, All-wise" (Qur'an 5:38). This is also the penalty, along with crucifixion, for the ill-defined sin of doing corruption on Earth: "This is the recompense of those who fight against God and His Messenger, and hasten about the earth, to do corruption there: they shall be slaughtered, or crucified, or their hands and feet shall alternately be struck off; or they shall be banished from the land. That is a degradation for them in this world; and in the world to come awaits them a mighty chastisement" (5:33).

The Qur'an does not contain a command to stone adulterers, but this penalty is prescribed in Islamic law as based on Muhammad's example. One *hadith* explains:

> The Jews brought to the Prophet a man and a woman from among them who had committed illegal sexual intercourse. The Prophet said to them, "How do you usually punish the one amongst you who has committed illegal sexual intercourse?" They replied, "We blacken their faces with coal and beat them." He said, "Don't you find the order of *Ar-Rajm* (i.e., stoning to death) in the Taurat (Torah)?" They replied, "We do not find anything in it." 'Abdullah bin Salam (after hearing this conversation) said to them, "You have told a lie! Bring here the Taurat and recite it if you are truthful." (So the Jews brought the Taurat.) And the religious teacher who was teaching it to them put his hand over the Verse of *Ar-Rajm* and started reading what was written above and below the place hidden with his hand, but he did not read the Verse of *Ar-Rajm*. 'Abdullah bin Salam removed his (i.e., the teacher's) hand from the Verse of *Ar-Rajm* and said, "What is this?" So when the Jews saw that Verse, they said, "This is the Verse of *Ar-Rajm*." So the Prophet or-

dered both the adulterer and the adulteress to be stoned
to death, and they were stoned to death near the place
where biers used to be placed near the mosque. I saw her
companion (i.e., the adulterer) bowing over her so as to
protect her from the stones.[135]

Another *hadith* places the command to stone adulterers in
the original Qur'an: Ubayy ibn Ka'b, whom Islamic tradition identifies as an early compiler of the Qur'an, explained
that the Muslim holy book's thirty-third chapter once contained 213 additional verses, including this one: "The for-
nicators among the married men (*ash-shaikh*) and married
women (*ash-shaikhah*), stone them as an exemplary punishment from Allah, and Allah is Mighty and Wise."[136]

The second caliph, Umar, was worried:

I am afraid that after a long time has passed, people may
say, "We do not find the Verses of the Rajam (stoning to
death) in the Holy Book." And consequently they may
go astray by leaving an obligation that Allah has revealed.
Lo! I confirm that the penalty of Rajam be inflicted on
him who commits illegal sexual intercourse, if he is already married and the crime is proved by witnesses or
pregnancy or confession. . . . Surely Allah's Apostle carried out the penalty of Rajam, and so did we after him.[137]

The Christian, in rejecting these harsh punishments,
must not allow himself to be maneuvered into the opposite
extreme position that society has no right or responsibility
to proscribe immoral activity. Certainly in the past there
were Western societies more Christian than our own that
set forth strict moral codes. Still, in the Christian scheme,

for moral choices to be a manifestation of virtue they must be made in freedom, out of a desire to do good—not merely to avoid punishment, or under the power of coercion.

Islam does not see virtue this way. Iran's Ayatollah Khomeini once thundered, "Whatever good there is exists thanks to the sword and in the shadow of the sword! People cannot be made obedient except with the sword! The sword is the key to Paradise, which can be opened only for the Holy Warriors!"[138] Thus, it is no surprise that hardline Muslim groups like the Taliban in Pakistan and Afghanistan, al-Shabaab in Somalia and Kenya, and others like them enforce Islamic morality by means of terror. The headlines give us no shortage of recent examples: Al-Shabaab in May 2012 bombed a Mombasa nightclub that served alcohol, just as Muslims in Lebanon the previous month bombed a Christian-owned restaurant that served alcohol.[139] In January 2012, a Muslim named Sami Osmakac was arrested in Florida with a plan to bomb Tampa-area nightclubs.[140] Also in May 2012, a group of devout Muslims in Morocco stoned and assaulted a woman whom they thought was dressed in too revealing a manner, stripping her naked in public.[141]

Such instances are distressingly common in the Islamic world. Needless to say, the idea of enforcing moral codes by violence and terror is utterly alien to the spirit of Catholicism.

Even Dinesh D'Souza, perhaps before he came to agree with the Islamic critique of Western immorality, wrote in 2004, "Consider the woman in Afghanistan or Iran who is required to wear the veil. There is no real modesty in this, because the woman is being compelled. Compulsion cannot produce virtue; it can only produce the outward semblance of virtue."[142] Yet three years later D'Souza warned, "When you make America synonymous with permissiveness, when you dismiss serious moral offenses with a no-big-deal attitude . . . you are driving the traditional Muslims into the arms of the radicals."[143]

D'Souza appeared to be unaware that something quite similar to Western "permissiveness" was already written into Islamic law, albeit with a fig leaf of morality over it.

A similar Muslim fig leaf lies over the objective evils found in that area where many Christians most strongly presume to have an ally in Islam: marriage and sexual morality.

7

A Shared Sexual Ethic?

Indeed, in the area of sexual morality, the correspondence of Islamic statutes with Catholic teaching seems exact. The Qur'an instructs:

And approach not fornication; surely it is an indecency, and evil as a way. (17:32)

Fornication, adultery, the sanctity of marriage, the importance of bearing children—in all such areas, many Catholics believe that Catholic and Muslim moral teaching are essentially identical. Yet, there are serious differences that have up to now received far less attention than the similarities, although they are no less important. For although fornication and adultery are indeed forbidden in Islam as in Christianity, and there are other apparent moral similarities between the two religions, the Muslim understanding of marriage and sexual morality differs so greatly from the Christian understanding that it renders those similarities void of meaning.

What's more, Islamic morality allows for practices that Catholicism abhors, including contraception, child marriage, polygamy, female genital mutilation, and even sexual slavery of non-believing women.

Contraception

Some modern Muslim scholars hold that Islam forbids contraception, framing the argument in terms that will be familiar to orthodox Catholics, and giving hope to those who dream of allying with Islam to fight the spirit of the age:

> In general, most forms of contraception and birth control
> are forbidden. But since Islam is a complete religion, we
> have the benefit of the Quran, the *hadith* and traditions
> of Prophet Muhammad (peace be upon him), the com-
> panions, and many learned scholars to help us come to an
> informed decision.
>
> First, any sort of permanent birth control that is not for
> medical reasons is forbidden. So any medical procedure that
> leads to complete sterilization and is not medically required,
> is not allowed. This goes against the teachings of our Proph-
> et Muhammad and if not done for medical reasons, is usu-
> ally done for vain, selfish or impractical purpose.
>
> For instance, some people have the foolish notion that
> the world is becoming overpopulated and the earth's re-
> sources are running out. But Allah has made His earth
> bountiful, and if we trust in Him, there is certainly
> enough food and water and air to go around.
>
> Wherever there is starvation in the world, there is
> needless gluttony and waste elsewhere. So the problem is
> not a lack of resource but a lack of compassion for those
> who are less fortunate than us.[144]

But in reality, Islamic teaching regarding birth control and
artificial contraception is ambiguous. The *hadith*, the volumi-
nous collections of Muhammad's words and deeds, are full of
contradictory material in which Muhammad appears to speak
in favor of both sides of a disputed issue. This is because much
of the *hadith* material was composed well over a century after
Muhammad is supposed to have lived, at a time when com-
peting factions attempted to gain support for the positions
they espoused by inventing sayings of Muhammad.

Since the ninth century, Islamic scholars have attempted to isolate authentic sayings of Muhammad and accounts of his actions on the basis of the chain of *isnad*: the list of people who have passed on the tradition in question from the time of Muhammad and the eyewitnesses who saw the event to the time that it was written down. A chain that is unbroken and contains names of people known for their reliability is considered evidence of an authentic tradition. No consideration is given to the possibility that the chain itself could be forged, as well as the tradition; but nonetheless, on the basis of study of the chain of transmitters, early medieval Islamic scholars have delineated a body of traditions that they generally regarded as authentic, and those have become normative for Muslim faith and practice.

Islamic law regarding artificial contraception is derived from several sayings of Muhammad regarding *coitus interruptus* (in Islamic law, *azl*); however, in these he seems to come down on both sides of the question. On one occasion one of the believers asks Muhammad: "O Allah's Apostle! We get female captives as our share of booty, and we are interested in their prices, what is your opinion about *coitus interruptus*?" Muhammad answers: "Do you really do that? It is better for you not to do it. No soul that which Allah has destined to exist, but will surely come into existence."[145] Some of the early Muslims believed that Muhammad's saying it was "better for you not to do it" amounted to a prohibition: "Yahya related to me from Malik from Nafi that Abdullah ibn Umar did not practice *coitus interruptus* and thought that it was disapproved."[146] Another concluded from Muhammad's words: "By Allah, (it seems) as if there is upbraiding in it (for *azl*)."[147]

However, another Muslim asked Muhammad about this practice, mentioning that the Jews likened it to infanticide. Muhammad's response was predictable in its venom against those whom the Qur'an terms the worst enemies of the

Muslims (5:82): "The Jews told a lie. If Allah intends to create it, you cannot turn it away."[148]

This was still ambiguous, but seemed to be more in favor of the practice. Completely unambiguous was the recollection of Jabir, one of Muhammad's early companions, who in later life recalled, "We used to practice *azl* during the lifetime of Allah's Messenger (may peace be upon him). This (the news of this practice) reached Allah's Apostle (may peace be upon him), and he did not forbid us."[149]

The early Muslim jurist Imam Malik declared the practice permissible with free women and wholly acceptable with slave girls, "Malik said, "A man does not practice *coitus interruptus* with a free woman unless she gives her permission. There is no harm in practicing *coitus interruptus* with a slave-girl without her permission. Someone who has someone else's slave-girl as a wife, does not practice *coitus interruptus* with her unless her people give him permission."[150] The distinction here between the women from whom one must seek permission and those from whom one need not do so is based solely on the dignity of the free woman versus the slave, not on anything analogous to the Catholic understanding of the unitive and procreative ends of sexual intercourse.

The contemporary Muslim scholar Sa'diyya Shaikh, a professor of Islamic Studies and Feminist Theory at the University of Cape Town in South Africa, wrote in 2003 about the permissibility of contraception in Islam in terms that contrasted starkly with Catholic teaching:

Contraception has a long history in Islam that needs to be situated in relation to the broader Islamic ethos of marriage and sexuality. In Islam if one chooses to marry, this is not automatically linked to procreation. Within the Islamic view of marriage, an individual has the right to sexual pleasure within marriage, which is independent of one's choice to have children. This type of approach to sexuality is compatible with a more tolerant approach to contraception and family planning.

Historically the various Islamic legal schools with an overwhelming majority have permitted *coitus interruptus*, called *azl*, as a method of contraception. This was a contraceptive technique practiced by pre-Islamic Arabs and continued to be used during the time of the Prophet with his knowledge and without his prohibition.[151]

Likewise, the Shi'ite scholar S. M. Rizvi writes:

According to the Shi'ah *fiqh* [jurisprudence], family planning as a private measure to space or regulate the family size for health or economic reasons is permissible. Neither is there any Qur'anic verse or *hadith* against birth control, nor is it *wajib* [absolutely required] to have children in marriage. So basically, birth control would come under the category of *ja'iz*, lawful acts. Moreover, we have some *ahadith* (especially on the issue of *azl, coitus interruptus*) which categorically prove that birth control is permissible.[152]

Thus, the average Muslim who goes to his local imam and asks about the permissibility of artificial contraception will likely be told that it is just fine, since, after all, Muhammad—who is the supreme example of conduct for believers—allowed for *coitus interruptus*. Foreign to Islam is the Catholic idea of the inseparability of the unitive and procreative aspects of the marital act.

This is not really surprising, since in general Islam lacks a marital/sexual teleology. As we have seen, there is no extensive tradition of rational theology in Islam. Allah rules by fiat, and one does not question, or reason from, his commands.

Abortion

Unfortunately, the same situation prevails with abortion, even though many Catholics believe that Muslims are pro-life and thus reliable comrades-in-arms on life issues—and indeed, the Qur'an repeatedly warns of the heinousness of killing one's own children. One poetic early passage about the last day and the divine judgment condemns the pagan Arab practice of burying alive girl infants:

> When the sun shall be darkened,
> when the stars shall be thrown down,
> when the mountains shall be set moving,
> when the pregnant camels shall be neglected,
> when the savage beasts shall be mustered,
> when the seas shall be set boiling,
> when the souls shall be coupled,
> when the buried infant shall be asked
> for what sin she was slain,
> when the scrolls shall be unrolled,
> when heaven shall be stripped off;
> when Hell shall be set blazing,
> when Paradise shall be brought nigh,
> then shall a soul know what it has produced. (81:1-14)

Another passage condemns child-killing in a straightforward manner:

> And slay not your children for fear of poverty; We will provide for you and them; surely the slaying of them is a grievous sin. (17:31)

Yet this does not carry over to abortion. The Muslim scholar Sayyid Sabiq summarizes Islam's classic view of abortion as being something to avoid, but not impermissible in the first trimester, since Islamic belief is that Allah blows the spirit into a soul only after that point:

> Abortion is not allowed after four months have passed since conception because at that time it is akin to taking a life, an act that entails penalty in this world and in the Hereafter. As regards the matter of abortion before this period elapses, it is considered allowed if necessary. However, in the absence of a reasonable excuse it is detestable.

The best he can offer pro-lifers is a difference of opinion among traditional jurists over whether early abortion is allowable:

> The author of "Subul-ul-Maram" writes: "A woman's treatment for aborting a pregnancy before the spirit has been blown into it is a matter upon which scholars differed on account of difference of opinion on the matter of 'azal (i.e., measures to hinder conception). Those who allow 'azal consider abortion as allowable and vice versa." The same ruling should be applicable for women deciding on sterilization. Imam Ghazzali opines: "Induced abortion is a sin after conception." He further says: "The sin incurred thus can be of degrees. When the sperm enters the ovaries [sic], mixes with the ovum and acquires potential of life, its removal would be a sin. Aborting it after it grows into a germ or a leech would be a graver sin and the graveness of the sin increases very much if one does so after the stage when the spirit is blown into the fetus and it acquires human form and faculties."[153]

The contemporary Islamic scholar Azizah al-Hibri sums up the prevailing view: "The majority of Muslim scholars permit abortion, although they differ on the stage of fetal development beyond which it becomes prohibited." Furthermore, says al-Hibri, all the schools of Islamic jurisprudence "permit abortion for exigencies such as saving the mother's life."[154] Another Islamic scholar, the American convert Sherman Jackson, explains that only a "minority of jurists" believe that Islam forbids abortion "even during the first trimester," and counsels Muslims against engaging in any kind of pro-life activism:

> [W]hile abortion, even during the first trimester, is forbidden according to a minority of jurists, it is not held to be an offense for which there are criminal or even civil sanctions. On this understanding, Muslim-Americans who oppose abortion should assiduously limit their activism to the moral sphere and avoid supporting positions that favor the imposition of criminal or civil sanctions in an area into which Islamic law itself never contemplated injecting these.[155]

In light of all this, it is hard to understand why the idea is so widespread among conservative Catholics that Muslims would make good partners for action on life issues. In reality, the Islamic moral schema differs so sharply from the Catholic one that they have hardly any common ground at all. That is why, as we have seen, at the Beijing conference "many conference delegates said the Vatican seriously miscalculated its potential clout in the debate, especially among . . . Islamic governments to which it had appealed for support."[156] The Muslims opposed Vatican efforts to call for an end to abortion in all circumstances.

Polygamy

Even though Islam sanctions polygamy, Muslims in the West do not practice it openly, thereby leading some Catholics to want to enlist their help in the fight to defend traditional marriage. However, even if not every individual Muslim practices polygamy, Islam's approval of it results in an idea of marriage that differs sharply from the Christian view. Polygamy dehumanizes women, reducing them to the status of commodities, and allows only accidentally for the mutual self-giving in love of Christian marriage. The Qur'an directs, "If you fear that you will not act justly towards the orphans, marry such women as seem good to you, two, three, four; but if you fear you will not be equitable, then only one, or what your right hands own; so it is likelier you will not be partial" (4:3).

It should be noted that Islamic polygamy is not just a matter of the letter of the law that is no longer practiced among modern Muslims. In fact, it is more widespread among Muslims, even in the West, than most people realize. A New York City house fire in March 2007, in which a Muslim named Moussa Magassa was killed but his two wives survived, shed some light on Islamic polygamy in the U.S. The *New York Times* reported: "Immigration to New York and other American cities has soared from places where polygamy is lawful and widespread, especially from West African countries like Mali, where demographic surveys show that 43 percent of women are in polygamous marriages."[157]

Mufti Barkatullah, a senior imam in London, stated in 2004 that there were as many as 4,000 polygamous families in Great Britain. Ghayasuddin Siddiqui of the Muslim Parliament of Great Britain (which describes itself as "a forum whose purpose is to debate, campaign and lobby on issues concerning the Muslim community in Britain") estimated that there were fewer than that, but still a great many: "I've come across one man who has five wives and I would estimate that there are 2,000 men in polygamous marriages in Britain.

Of those, 1,000 have multiple wives based here and the other 1,000 have one here and others in different countries."[158]

Polygamy is permitted by law in most Islamic countries, and is spreading quickly outside their borders—particularly in Europe, which has been host to waves of Islamic immigration. The *Jerusalem Post* noted that "Europe, while welcoming the reform of the Family Law in Morocco that made polygamy almost impossible, and pressuring Turkey to put an end to the practice (the country's ban on polygamy is commonly overridden), is at the same time turning a blind eye to the existence of the practice within its own borders.... Immigrants from Mali, Egypt, Mauritania, Pakistan and other countries who come to live in Europe often bring along their extended families, which may contain two, three and even four wives, and all of their offspring."[159]

Ibrahim Hooper of the Council on American-Islamic Relations (CAIR), an Islamic advocacy group, said in 2007 that a "minority" of Muslims in America practiced polygamy, and noted "Islamic scholars would differ on whether one could do so while living in the United States."[160] Significantly, he didn't say anything about the fact that polygamy is against American law; perhaps he realized even then that the legalization of same-sex marriage, a battle that was just beginning, would unlock the floodgates to all manner of hitherto unconventional familial arrangements being given the sanction of law. As numerous Catholic theologians and controversialists have pointed out, once marriage is separated from the natural birth and rearing of children, and a man can "marry" another man, all other restrictive definitions of marriage become arbitrary. Why then can't a man enter into any kind of marital arrangement he wishes, including marrying four women at once? Multiculturalism, combined with the acceptance and legalization of same-sex marriage, has left the field clear for the legalization of polygamy in the U.S., and thereby also the further legal devaluation of the Catholic concept of marriage.

This also explains why the supposed pro-life, pro-family Muslims have generally not stood with Catholics and Evangelicals on the front lines of the battle for marriage.[161]

Divorce

Neither will Catholics find in Islam an ally against the harm that easy divorce has done to the institution of marriage. In contrast to Catholic teaching on marriage's indissolubility, a Muslim husband can divorce his wife at any time for any reason. All he has to do is say to his wife, "You are divorced."[162] The Qur'an mandates only a waiting period to determine whether or not the woman is pregnant (65:1), a period of approximately three months (2:228).

It may seem that the simplicity of this procedure makes it all too easy for men to divorce their wives in a fit of anger. But this, too, is taken into account. A man may take his wife back twice after divorcing her. However, if he divorces her three times and then wants to take her back, it is not so easy. The Qur'an stipulates that she first must marry someone else and be divorced by him; only then can she lawfully return to her first husband (2:229-230).

Women, too, can seek divorce in Islam, but it is not so easy for them. The Qur'an says, "If a woman fear rebelliousness or aversion in her husband, there is no fault in them if the couple set things right between them; right settlement is better; and souls are very prone to avarice. If you do good and are god-fearing, surely God is aware of the things you do" (4:128).

Muhammad's favorite wife, his child bride Aisha, explains the manner in which a couple may "set things right between them."

This verse, she says, "concerns the woman whose husband does not want to keep her with him any longer, but wants to divorce her and marry some other lady, so she says to him: 'Keep me and do not divorce me, and then marry another woman, and you may neither spend on me, nor sleep with me.'"[163]

In other words, the Muslim couple sets things right between them when the woman adopts a position of begging supplicant.

Child marriage

Islam sets out a deficient and dangerous standard for the age at which a girl can marry—following Muhammad's own example. Aisha recalls that she was six when Muhammad wedded her. He did not, however, take her into his household as his wife for another three years. Then he came for her. Aisha recounts:

> My mother, Umm Ruman, came to me while I was playing in a swing with some of my girl friends. She called me, and I went to her, not knowing what she wanted to do to me. She caught me by the hand and made me stand at the door of the house. I was breathless then, and when my breathing became normal, she took some water and rubbed my face and head with it. Then she took me into the house. There in the house I saw some Ansari [recent Muslim converts] women who said, "Best wishes and Allah's Blessing and a good luck." Then she entrusted me to them and they prepared me (for the marriage). Unexpectedly Allah's Messenger came to me in the forenoon and my mother handed me over to him, and at that time I was a girl of nine years of age.[164]

According to Islamic tradition, too, Muhammad "married Aisha when she was a girl of six years of age, and he consummated that marriage when she was nine years old."[165] He was, at this time, fifty-four years old.

Marriage to relatively young girls was not all that unusual for its time, but because in Islam Muhammad is the supreme example of conduct (cf. Qur'an 33:21), he is considered exemplary in this unto today. And so in April 2011, the Bangladesh Mufti Fazlul Haque Amini declared that those trying to pass a law banning child marriage in that country were putting Muhammad in a bad light: "Banning child marriage will cause challenging the marriage of the holy prophet of Islam . . . [putting] the moral character of the prophet into controversy and challenge." He added a threat: "Islam permits child marriage and it will not be tolerated if any ruler will ever try to touch this issue in the name of giving more rights to women."[166] The Mufti said that 200,000 jihadists were ready to sacrifice their lives for any law restricting child marriage.

Likewise, the influential website Islamonline.com in December 2010 justified child marriage by invoking not only Muhammad's example but the Qur'an as well:

The Noble Qur'an has also mentioned the waiting period [i.e., for a divorced wife to remarry] for the wife who has not yet menstruated, saying: "And those who no longer expect menstruation among your women—if you doubt, then their period is three months, and [also for] those who have not menstruated" [Qur'an 65:4]. Since this is not negated later, we can take from this verse that it is permissible to have sexual intercourse with a prepubescent girl. The Qur'an is not like the books of jurisprudence which mention what the implications of things are, even if they are prohibited. It is true that the prophet entered into a marriage contract with A'isha when she was six years old,

however he did not have sex with her until she was nine
years old, according to al-Bukhari.[167]

Other countries make Muhammad's example the basis
of their laws regarding the legal marriageable age for girls.
Article 1041 of the Civil Code of the Islamic Republic of
Iran states that girls can be engaged before the age of nine,
and married at nine: "Marriage before puberty (nine full lu-
nar years for girls) is prohibited. Marriage contracted before
reaching puberty with the permission of the guardian is valid provided that the interests of the ward are duly observed."
     Iran's Ayatollah Khomeini himself married a ten-year-
old girl when he was twenty-eight. Khomeini called marriage to a prepubescent girl "a divine blessing," and advised
the faithful to give their own daughters away accordingly:
"Do your best to ensure that your daughters do not see their
first blood in your house."[168] When he took power in Iran,
he lowered the legal marriageable age of girls to nine, in accord with Muhammad's example.
     Unsurprisingly, such laws are a boon to pedophiles, who, as
Time magazine reported in 2001, can "marry poor young girls
from the provinces, use and then abandon them," all within the
bounds of Islamic law.[169] The United Nations Children's Fund
(UNICEF) reports that more than half of the girls in Afghanistan and Bangladesh are married before they reach the age of
eighteen. In early 2002, researchers in refugee camps in Afghanistan and Pakistan found half the girls married by age thirteen. In an Afghan refugee camp, more than two out of three
second-grade girls were either married or engaged, and virtually all the girls who were beyond second grade were already
married. One ten-year-old was engaged to a man of sixty.
     Because of the Prophet's example, such unsavory arrange-
ments are resistant to reform. In an attempt to quash legis-

lation that would raise the minimum marriage age to seventeen, in 2009 Muslim clerics in Yemen issued a religious decree, or *fatwa*, declaring that opposition to child marriage makes one an apostate from Islam.[170] That law was passed but then quickly repealed after some Yemeni legislators dubbed it un-Islamic.[171] The Moroccan imam Mohamed al-Maghraoui issued a *fatwa* in 2008 declaring that marriage with a nine-year-old girl was acceptable according to Islamic law; more Western-minded Moroccan Islamic authorities nullified al-Maghraoui's ruling, but al-Maghraoui defiantly repeated it in 2011.[172]

In Malaysia in December 2010, a government minister, Nazri Aziz, said at a press conference that the Malaysian government had no plans to legislate against child marriage, because of Islam: "If the religion allows it, then we can't legislate against it."[173] Aziz did stipulate that the girl had to have reached puberty and begun to menstruate, but since the Qur'an contains regulations for divorcing a wife who has not yet begun to menstruate (65:4), even that was a Westernization.

And in July 2011, the Saudi cleric Salih bin Fawzan, a member of Saudi Arabia's highest religious council, issued a *fatwa* of his own, declaring that Islamic law set no minimum age for marriage at all, and that therefore girls could be lawfully married off "even if they are in the cradle."

As with other aspects of Islamic law and practice, immigration has extended child marriage into Western countries. The Iranian and Kurdish Women's Rights Organisation (IKWRO) declared that in England in 2010, at least thirty girls in Islington, a neighborhood of greater London, were forced into marriage, and that some were as young as nine years old.[174] In Sweden, there are several hundred reported incidences of child marriage every year.[175]

Islamic apologists in the West frequently deny that Aisha
was only nine when Muhammad consummated his marriage
with her, but they cannot explain why so many Muslim clerics and Islamic nations base their stance on the legal age for
marriage on Muhammad's example. Many also invoke traditions that say that the Blessed Mother was in her early teens
at the time that she gave birth to Jesus; here again, however,
the Catholic Church does not legislate on the basis of this.
Certainly the marriage of pubescent girls as young as fourteen
or fifteen has been common at various times in Europe and
America. However, the marriage of prepubescent girls has
been unheard of in the West, and is known to cause them
great physical and psychological harm. Today, child marriage
causes this harm to girls all over the Islamic world, makes a
mockery of the institution of marriage, and belies the common assumption among Catholics that Islamic morality is essentially identical to Catholic morality.

And that is not all, by any means.

Concubinage and sexual slavery

The Qur'an forbids Muslim men to have sexual relations
with "wedded women, save what your right hands own"
(4:4; see also 23:1–6). Those whom their "right hands own"
are slaves; since the Qur'an takes slavery for granted, it is
still part of Islamic law. There has never been an abolitionist
movement within Islam, for the fundamental principle of
the Christian abolitionist movement, the equal dignity of all
people before God, does not exist in Islam.

Slavery is rooted in the Qur'an, which matter-of-factly
allows a man four wives, plus an unspecified number of sex
slaves, women captured in the course of battle with non-Muslims: "O Prophet, We have made lawful for thee thy wives

whom thou hast given their wages and what thy right hand
owns, spoils of war that God has given thee" (33:50). Muhammad, the supreme example for Muslims, was a slave owner.

Of course the Bible, too, takes slavery for granted. But
biblical justifications for slavery—the application of the
curse of Ham to the Negro race was especially popular in
the antebellum American South—were never understood
among Christians to be as universal or strong as Muslim
scholars have understood those in the Qur'an to be. Despite
the Bible's seeming acceptance of slavery, the early Church
and medieval Church actively opposed it, and in modern
times abolitionist movements arose among Christians in
England and America because of the Christian idea of the
universal dignity of the human person.

In Islam, by contrast, no abolitionist movement has ever
arisen. Muhammad's exemplary status precludes it, as does
the sharp and all-pervasive dichotomy between believers
and unbelievers. The enslaving of unbelievers is not considered to be a violation of their human dignity; after all, the
Qur'an mandates that they offer "willing submission" to the
Muslims, and "feel themselves subdued" (9:29).

And even when the slaves are Muslims, the practice continues. Slavery is still practiced more or less openly today in
Sudan and Mauritania, and there is evidence that it continues beneath the surface in some majority-Muslim countries
as well—notably Saudi Arabia, which only abolished slavery
in 1962; Yemen and Oman, both of which ended legal slavery in 1970; and Niger, which didn't abolish slavery until
2004. In Niger, the ban is widely ignored, and according to
a Nigerian study, as many as one million people remain in
bondage there.[176] These bans have been imposed by Western
pressure; they have not arisen from an abolitionist movement within Islam.

Inextricable from the concept of Islamic slavery as a whole is sex slavery, which is rooted in Islam's devaluation of the lives of non-Muslims. The Qur'an's stipulation that a man may take four wives as well as hold slave girls as sex slaves has been taken in Islamic law to refer to women captured in wartime, who are considered the spoils of war. Here again, Islam avoids the appearance of impropriety, declaring that the taking of married women as sex slaves does not constitute adultery, for their marriages are ended at the moment of their capture. A manual of Islamic law directs: "When a child or a woman is taken captive, they become slaves by the fact of capture, and the woman's previous marriage is immediately annulled."[177]

This is by no means an eccentric or outdated view in Islam. The Salafist Egyptian Sheikh Abu-Ishaq al-Huwayni declared in May 2011 that "we are in the era of jihad" and that "if we could conduct one, two, or three jihadist operations every year, many people throughout the earth would become Muslims." And those who rejected the invitation to convert to Islam (da'wa) would be enslaved:

And whoever rejected this da'wa, or stood in our way, we would fight against him and take him prisoner, and confiscate his wealth, his children, and his women—all of this means money. Every mujahid who returned from jihad, his pockets would be full. He would return with three or four slaves, three or four women, and three or four children. Multiply each head by 300 dirhams, or 300 dinar, and you have a good amount of profit. If he were to go to the West and work on a commercial deal, he would not make that much money. Whenever things became difficult (financially), he could take the head (i.e., the prisoner) and sell it, and ease his (financial) crisis. He would sell it like groceries.[178]

After his words touched off a furor, he clarified what he meant in a subsequent interview:

> Jihad is only between Muslims and infidels. . . . Do you understand what I'm saying? Spoils, slaves, and prisoners are only to be taken in war between Muslims and infidels. Muslims in the past conquered, invaded, and took over countries. This is agreed to by all scholars—there is no disagreement on this from any of them, from the smallest to the largest, on the issue of taking spoils and prisoners. The prisoners and spoils are distributed among the fighters, which includes men, women, children, wealth, and so on.
>
> When a slave market is erected, which is a market in which are sold slaves and sex-slaves, which are called in the Qur'an by the name *milk al-yamin*, "that which your right hands possess" [Qur'an 4:24]. This is a verse from the Qur'an which is still in force, and has not been abrogated. The *milk al-yamin* are the sex-slaves. You go to the market, look at the sex-slave, and buy her. She becomes like your wife, (but) she doesn't need a (marriage) contract or a divorce like a free woman, nor does she need a *wali*. All scholars agree on this point—there is no disagreement from any of them. [. . .] When I want a sex slave, I just go to the market and choose the woman I like and purchase her.[179]

Around the same time, on May 25, 2011, a female Kuwaiti activist and politician, Salwa al-Mutairi, also spoke out in favor of the Islamic practice of sexual slavery of non-Muslim women, emphasizing that the practice accorded with Islamic law and the parameters of Islamic morality.

Peace, mercy, and blessings of Allah be upon you. My

name is Salwa al-Mutairi. I received a message that was
a little strange. A merchant told me that he would like to
have a sex slave. He said he would not be negligent with
her, and that Islam permitted this sort of thing. He was
speaking the truth. The topic that he brought up is an old
topic. I have been working on it for two years now.

I was working with this man, a young man, who
(liked) women a lot. I was sympathetic to his situation,
and also dedicated to my work. I was given the opportunity to visit Mecca, and when I did so, I brought up (this
man's) situation to the muftis in Mecca. I told them that
I had a question, since they were men who specialized
in what was *halal*, and what was good, and who loved
women. I said, "What is the law of sex slaves?"

The mufti said, "With the law of sex slaves, there must
be a Muslim nation at war with a Christian nation, or a
nation which is not of the religion, not of the religion of
Islam. And there must be prisoners of war."

"Is this forbidden by Islam?" I asked.

"Absolutely not. Sex slaves are not forbidden by Islam.
On the contrary, sex slaves are under a different law than
the free woman. The free woman must be completely
covered except for her face and hands. But the sex slave
can be naked from the waist up. She differs a lot from the
free woman. While the free woman requires a marriage
contract, the sex slave does not—she only needs to be
purchased by her husband, and that's it. Therefore the sex
slave is different than the free woman."

Of course, I also asked religious experts in Kuwait
(about this issue), and they told me about the problem
with the passionate man, or even the man who is committed to his religion. For every good man in our religion, the only solution for him—when forbidden women

come around, if he's tempted to sin, then the solution to this issue is for him to purchase sex slaves. I hope that Kuwait will enact the law for this category, this category of people—the sex slaves. . . .

I hope that a law will be enacted for this category, and they will open the door for this, just as they have opened the door for servants (to come into the country). They should open the door for sex slaves, by enacting a sound law, so that our children don't waste away in the abyss of adultery and moral depravity. Allah-willing, this will work out. I believe, look, the (sex slaves could come from) a country like Chechnya, where there is a war between an (Islamic) state and another state. Certainly there are prisoners. These prisoners could be purchased. They could be purchased and sold to the merchants in Kuwait. This is better than (the merchants) committing that which is forbidden. There is nothing wrong with this.

Harun al-Rashid [caliph, or successor of Muhammad as leader of the Muslims, from 786 to 809] had many more sex slaves than this. When he died he had 2,000 sex slaves. But he only had one wife. This was not forbidden. Our *shari'a* permits such a thing as this. Praise be to Allah, here in Kuwait there are many merchants who are committed (to Islam). I hope the best for Kuwait, Allah-willing.[180]

"He had only one wife. This was not forbidden. Our *shari'a* permits such a thing as this." Lest anyone think that Mutairi was joking, she reiterated her views on another occasion:

A Muslim state must [first] attack a Christian state—sorry, I mean any non-Muslim state—and they [the women, the future sex-slaves] must be captives of the raid. Is this forbidden? Not at all; according to Islam, sex slaves are not at all forbidden. Quite the contrary, the rules regulating sex-slaves differ from those for free women [i.e., Muslim women]: the latter's body must be covered entirely, except for her face and hands, whereas the sex-slave is kept naked from the belly button on up—she is different from the free woman; the free woman has to be married properly to her husband, but the sex-slave—he just buys her and that's that.[181]

All this is in accord, then, with Islam's prohibition of fornication and restriction of sex to marriage. The "free woman has to be married properly to her husband," but the sex slave does not. Yet, in the Islamic view, there is no sin involved if a man obtains such a slave.

This doesn't appear to be the view solely of a couple of reactionary Muslim thinkers. Britain, in recent years, has seen a recurring phenomenon of "Asian" (a common euphemism for "Muslim" in the British media) "sex gangs": groups of Muslim men who cajole or kidnap British non-Muslim girls, often in their early teens, and force them into prostitution.[182] Muslims from the Twin Cities area in Minnesota ran an interstate sex trafficking ring until they were caught and indicted in late 2010.[183] It's true that the savage exploitation of girls and young women is an unfortunately cross-cultural phenomenon, but only in Islamic law does it carry anything approaching divine sanction.

Temporary marriage

When easy divorce, multiple wives, and sex slaves do not give adequate satisfaction, Shi'ites also practice temporary marriage, which is simply a marriage contract with a deadline; in effect, a fig-leaf of morality placed over what is plainly and simply prostitution. "Temporary wives" are commonly found in seminary towns where young men are on their own for the first time and vulnerable to offers of companionship. A diary entry written by the Shi'ite student Aqa Najafi Quchani early in the twentieth century epitomizes the moral sham of temporary marriage:

> Fortunately, the woman was at home and I married her for a while. When I had quietened [sic] my desire and enjoyed the pleasure of the flesh from my lawful income, I gave the woman the *qeran* [an old Iranian monetary unit]. . . . It is reported that the Imams have said that whoever makes love legitimately has in effect killed an infidel. That means killing the lascivious spirit. It is obvious that when a *talabeh* [student] has no problem with the lower half of his body he is happier than a king.[184]

In a kind of parody of Christian sexual self-mastery, Aqa Najafi Quchani believed that he had engaged in "killing the lascivious spirit," not by resisting it so that it flees but by giving in to it and engaging the services of a prostitute. Then, searching for a comparison for how beneficial it is for him to have "made love legitimately" rather than indulged in fornication, he refers to the highest authorities in Shi'ite Islam, the Imams, saying "whoever makes love legitimately has in effect killed an infidel."

Today in the West, some accuse the so-called Christian Right of carrying out a "war on women," and modern feminists read Christian history as an endless string of oppression. But in reality, Christian anthropology has elevated, protected, and liberated women, while Islam, a religion toward which contemporary feminists are much less vocal in criticism, blatantly objectifies and subjugates them. No good Catholic who loves and respects women—and that should be all of us—can get too friendly with Muslims as allies in the culture wars, given this great chasm between us.

Still, the key point to remember here is not that Catholics are unable to pursue or sustain meaningful moral alliances with Muslims simply because Islam allows awful things that Catholicism does not. Rather, Islam's acceptance of these things reveals fundamentally misplaced principles about sex, marriage, and women such that any alliance based on puta- tively shared values will founder on the ineluctable fact that these values are not actually shared at all.

8

An Honest Desire for Dialogue?

In the name of interreligious dialogue, it's not uncommon for Muslim spokesmen to visit Christian churches, including Catholic parishes, with the stated goal of clearing up "misconceptions" about Islam. Such sessions often include the Muslim speaker's downplaying the reality of jihad activity and Muslim persecution of Christians, and offering his Christian audience bland assurances that such things have nothing to do with authentic Islam.

On a larger scale, Muslims have engaged in several high-profile attempts at dialogue with Catholics in recent years, to which Catholics have generally responded with enthusiasm. Yet, there is less to these attempts at outreach than meets the eye. The two most visible and well-publicized attempts by Muslims to reach out to Catholics turn out, on close examination, to be thinly veiled exercises in proselytizing. All of these attempts at "dialogue" share several common characteristics, including most notably a downplaying and glossing-over of the differences between Christianity and Islam, an over-emphasis on the similarities between the two religions, and a call to Christians to abandon or modify certain of their core beliefs, while never budging an inch on Islamic doctrines.

These invitations to dialogue were both published in the wake of one of the most unfortunate episodes of modern Catholic-Muslim relations: the violent aftermath of Pope Benedict XVI's Regensburg address.

"Things only evil and inhuman"

On September 12, 2006, in Regensburg, Germany, Pope Benedict XVI dared to enunciate some truths about Islam that proved to be unpopular and unwelcome among Muslims worldwide. Most notoriously, the Pope quoted the fourteenth-century Byzantine emperor, Manuel II Paleologus: "Show me just what Muhammad brought that was new, and there you will find things only evil and inhuman, such as his command to spread by the sword the faith he preached."

Less frequently noted is that the pope followed this by recounting that Manuel II then

> goes on to explain in detail the reasons why spreading the faith through violence is something unreasonable. Violence is incompatible with the nature of God and the nature of the soul. "God," he says, "is not pleased by blood—and not acting reasonably is contrary to God's nature. Faith is born of the soul, not the body. Whoever would lead someone to faith needs the ability to speak well and to reason properly, without violence and threats. . . . To convince a reasonable soul, one does not need a strong arm, or weapons of any kind, or any other means of threatening a person with death."

Pope Benedict then demonstrated his awareness that talk about the nature of God would not impress those who commit the most religious violence—Muslims—because "for Muslim teaching, God is absolutely transcendent. His will is not bound up with any of our categories, even that of rationality." He recalled the medieval Muslim philosopher Ibn Hazm (994-1064), who "went so far as to state that God is not bound even by his own word, and that nothing would oblige him to reveal the truth to us. Were it God's will, we would even have to practice idolatry."[185]

Later, after these words touched off an international furor, Pope Benedict emphasized repeatedly that he was not endorsing Paleologus's characterization of Muhammad's teachings, and reiterated his hope for the beginning of a "genuine dialogue of cultures and religions so urgently needed today."

The initial response was not promising. Muslims rioted and in several countries murdered Christians who had, of course, nothing whatsoever to do with what the pope had said. And several days after the Regensburg address, a group of Muslim clerics in Gaza issued an invitation to the pope to convert to Islam, or else: "We want to use the words of the Prophet Muhammad and tell the pope: *'Aslim Taslam'*"— that is, embrace Islam and you will be safe.[186] The implication, of course, was that the one to whom this "invitation" is addressed would *not* be safe if he declined to convert.

Then, a month later, came what seemed to be a ray of hope. On October 13, 2006, thirty-eight Muslim leaders and scholars, including some of the most prominent in the world, wrote an "Open Letter to the Pope" responding to what he had said at Regensburg. They established at the outset a respectful tone distinguishing them from the rioters and their clerical counterparts in Gaza, addressing the pope "in the spirit of open exchange" and heading up the letter with a verse from the Qur'an as an epigraph: "*In the Name of God, the Compassionate, the Merciful, Do not contend with people of the Book except in the fairest way.* . . . (The Holy Qur'an, *al-Ankabut,* 29:46)."[187]

"While we applaud your efforts to oppose the dominance of positivism and materialism in human life," the scholars told the pope, "we must point out some errors in the way you mentioned Islam as a counterpoint to the proper use of reason, as well as some mistakes in the assertions you put forward in support of your argument." Among the errors they enumerated was the pope's claim that the Qur'anic statement "there is no compulsion in religion" (2:256) came

from early in Muhammad's career and was later superseded
by more bellicose material. The scholars note, in accord
with mainstream Islamic theology, that this passage actually
came from late in Muhammad's prophetic career, and "was
a reminder to Muslims themselves, once they had attained
power, that they could not force another's heart to believe."

They were right on both counts. The passage did not
come from the time when, as the pope had said at Regensburg, "Mohammed was still powerless and under threat."
And Islamic law does forbid forced conversion, although
this is a law that throughout Islamic history and today has
often been honored in the breach. While quoting several
other Qur'anic verses that appear to support the freedom
of conscience, however, the scholars did not mention the
imperative in Islamic law, founded upon another passage of
the Qur'an, to wage war against non-Muslims and subjugate
"the People of the Book" under the rule of Islamic law:
"Fight those who believe not in God and the Last Day and
do not forbid what God and His Messenger have forbidden—such men as practice not the religion of truth, being
of those who have been given the Book—until they pay the
tribute out of hand and have been humbled" (9:29).

Although the Christians who have been fought against
and "humbled" under the rule of the Muslims are free,
within certain restrictions, to practice their religion, their
state of being "humbled" is manifested not just in the payment of "tribute" (*jizya*) but in a complex of humiliating
and discriminatory regulations designed to remind them
that because of their rejection of Muhammad and the
Qur'an, Allah has condemned them to suffer in this world
and the next. Islamic law traditionally forbids the *dhimmis*,
or protected people (the Islamic legal term for the "People
of the Book" subjugated under Muslim rule), from building

new churches or repairing old ones, holding authority over Muslims, making a public display of their worship (processions and even crosses on the outside of church buildings are forbidden), and more.

These laws are no longer fully enforced anywhere in the Islamic world, but they remain part of Islamic law, and Islamic supremacists today have, on several occasions, signaled their intention to revive them when they have the power to do so. In December 2011, Jordanian Sheikh Ahmad Abu Quddum explained Islam's doctrine of jihad on Jordanian television: "This fighting is in order to remove obstacles. It is waged against countries, not against individuals. When we declare Jihad against Germany, for instance, it is declared against the German state, for refusing to allow Islam to spread to the people of Germany. We give them a choice: Either to convert to Islam, or to pay the *jizya* and submit to the laws of Islam."[188] That same month, Sheikh Nader Tamimi, the mufti of the Palestinian Authority, declared, "To the rulers of the West, this is the religion of Allah. Either you pay the *jizya* poll tax, or else you will bring the sword to your necks."[189] Hamas has stated that it will re-impose the *dhimmi* laws once it gains full control of the Palestinian Authority.[190] And some Muslim Brotherhood leaders in Egypt, poised to take power after the "Arab Spring" uprisings, have indicated their intention to re-impose these laws, which led one Coptic Christian leader to vow that the Copts would resist to the point of martyrdom.

"There is no compulsion in religion," certainly. Non-Muslims are not forced to become Muslim. But under the stipulations of traditional Islamic law, failure to convert would make their lives so miserable that they do convert simply to be able to live life with some dignity and hope. When Muslim forces conquered Egypt in the seventh century, it was 99 percent Christian; now, 1,400 years later, it is around 10 percent Christian. The Christians of Egypt did not emigrate; they are the ancestors of the Muslims of Egypt. Though most were not forced at sword point, over the centuries most of Egypt's population converted to Islam to escape the institutionalized discrimination of dhimmitude. And so it was with non-Muslim populations all over the Islamic world.

That the thirty-eight scholars who wrote to the pope do not mention this, but rather give the impression that Islam allows for the freedom of conscience and for non-Muslims to practice their religions freely and unhindered, does not speak well of their sincerity. And unfortunately, this was by no means the only instance of disingenuousness in their letter.

Allah as absolute will?

The scholars disparaged the pope's reference to Ibn Hazm dismissing him as a marginal figure in Islamic thought, and asserting "to conclude that Muslims believe in a capricious God who might or might not command us to evil is to forget that God says in the Quran, "*Lo! God enjoins justice and kindness, and giving to kinsfolk, and forbids lewdness and abomination and wickedness. He exhorts you in order that ye may take heed* (al-Nahl, 16:90)."

Yet what Ibn Hazm said was not exactly that Allah might command the Muslims to do evil. The pope characterized his views thusly at Regensburg: "Were it God's will, we would even have to practice idolatry." This would not be to command evil; it is, rather, a complete nominalism in which the appellations "good" and "evil" are applied arbitrarily and have nothing to do with the nature of the things to which they are applied. In Islam, as we have seen again and again, what is good is not a matter of the intrinsic nature of a thing; what makes something good is Allah's fiat. The premier example of this is the exaltation of Muhammad as the "excellent example" (Qur'an 33:21) for believers. Although in a few places in the Qur'an Allah upbraids Muhammad for his sin, and Islamic tradition regards only Jesus and Mary as sinless, nevertheless all the sects and schools of Islam hold Muhammad in such high esteem that essentially if he did something, it is good to do, and Muslims must imitate him. This is not so much to say that Muhammad, or Allah, might command something that is against the absolute moral law; it is to say that there is no absolute moral law, save what Allah commands or Muhammad exemplifies.

The same rejection of absolutes occurs in Islamic cosmology. The twelfth-century Jewish philosopher Moses Maimonides described the Islamic thinkers with whom he was in contact as rejecting absolutes as illegitimately binding upon Allah's will:

> Human intellect does not perceive any reason why a body should be in a certain place instead of being in another. In the same manner [the Muslim philosophers] say that reason admits the possibility that an existing being should be larger or smaller than it really is, or that it should be different in form and position from what it really is; e.g., a man might have the height of a mountain, might have several heads, and fly in the air; or an elephant might be as small as an insect, or an insect as huge as an elephant.
>
> This method of admitting possibilities is applied to the whole Universe. Whenever they affirm that a thing belongs to this class of admitted possibilities, they say that it can have this form and that it is also possible that it be found differently, and that the one form is not more

possible than the other; but they do not ask whether the reality confirms their assumption.

[They say] fire causes heat, water causes cold, in accordance with a certain habit; but it is logically not impossible that a deviation from this habit should occur, namely, that fire should cause cold, move downward, and still be fire; that the water should cause heat, move upward, and still be water. On this foundation their whole [intellectual] fabric is constructed.[191]

The abandonment of reason

In the scholars' critique of the pope's remarks about the importance of reason, they insisted that "the Islamic tradition is rich in its explorations of the nature of human intelligence and its relation to God's Nature and His Will, including questions of what is self-evident and what is not," and that "Muslims have come to terms with the power and limits of human intelligence in their own way, acknowledging a hierarchy of knowledge of which reason is a crucial part." They said that Islamic tradition has ably avoided two extremes: "one is to make the analytical mind the ultimate arbiter of truth, and the other is to deny the power of human understanding to address ultimate questions."

The outcomes of two controversies, however—the defeat of the Mu'tazilites at the hands of those who held that the Qur'an was eternal and uncreated, and al-Ghazali's undoing of the philosophers for their reliance on reason rather than the Qur'an—demonstrate that reason has not always enjoyed the respect in the Islamic world that these scholars suggest. An apocryphal story about the caliph Umar sums up an attitude that has always been prevalent in the Islamic world. Umar, after conquering Egypt, is said to have ordered the burning of the fabled Library of Alexandria. When asked why, he responded: "If the books in it agree with the Qur'an, they are superfluous. If they disagree with the Qur'an, they are heretical." Only one book was needed.

The Italian journalist Oriana Fallaci wrote forcefully about the all-too-common Muslim tendency to reject reason:

> Islam has always persecuted and silenced its intelligent men. I remind you of Averroes who for his distinction between Faith and Reason was accused of heterodoxy by the caliphs and forced to flee. Then, imprisoned like a criminal. Then, confined to his home and humiliated to such a degree that when rehabilitated he no longer had any desire to live and died within a few months. Not without good reason, in his famous lecture held in 1883 at the Sorbonne, Ernest Renan said that attributing the merits of Averroes to Islam would be like attributing the merits of Galileo to the Inquisition.[192]

Here again, the scholars were not to be expected to have said, "Yes, Holy Father, the Islamic faith disparages and denigrates human reason," but they would have inspired more confidence in the genuineness of their appeal to him had they at least acknowledged that his statements were not actually "errors" at all but reasonable and accurate summations of genuine tendencies within Islamic thought.

Jihad and the unbelievers

The same problem recurs in the scholars' discussion of jihad, about which they accused the pope of contradicting his own faith: "It is noteworthy that Manuel II Paleologus says that 'violence' goes against God's nature, since Christ himself used violence against the money-changers in the temple, and said 'Do not think that I came to bring peace on the earth; I did not come to bring peace, but a sword' (Matt. 10:34-36). When God drowned Pharaoh, was He going against His own Nature? Perhaps the emperor meant to say that cruelty, brutality, and aggression are against God's Will, in which case the classical and traditional law of *jihad* in Islam would bear him out completely."

They summarize "the authoritative and traditional Islamic rules of war" as including the principle that "religious belief alone does not make anyone the object of attack" and that "the original Muslim community was fighting against pagans who had also expelled them from their homes, persecuted, tortured, and murdered them. Thereafter, the Islamic conquests were political in nature." They insist that "Muslims can and should live peacefully with their neighbors," although "this does not exclude legitimate self-defense and maintenance of sovereignty."

That all sounds so . . . reasonable. Unfortunately, it doesn't jibe either with Islamic texts or with Islamic law.

The Qur'an contains numerous exhortations to fight against the infidels, as do all the *hadith* collections of Muhammad's words and deeds. It directs Muslims to "fight those who believe not in God and the Last Day and do not forbid what God and His Messenger have forbidden—such men as practice not the religion of truth, being of those who have been given the Book—until they pay the tribute out of hand and have been humbled" (9:29), which sounds as if *religious belief alone* makes these people the object of attack. Nor does Muhammad mention any other pretext for an attack when he expands upon this passage with more detailed instructions on fighting against unbelievers:

Fight in the name of Allah and in the way of Allah. Fight against those who disbelieve in Allah. Make a holy war;

do not embezzle the spoils; do not break your pledge; and do not mutilate (the dead) bodies; do not kill the children. When you meet your enemies who are polytheists, invite them to three courses of action. If they respond to any one of these you also accept it and withhold yourself from doing them any harm. Invite them to (accept) Islam; if they respond to you, accept it from them and desist from fighting against them. . . . If they refuse to accept Islam, demand from them the *jizya*. If they agree to pay, accept it from them and hold off your hands. If they refuse to pay the tax, seek Allah's help and fight them.[193]

This triple imperative of conversion, subjugation, or death is reinforced in Islamic law. One manual of Islamic law that some of Sunni Islam's foremost authorities have certified as conforming to the "practice and faith of the orthodox Sunni community" states flatly that the "lesser jihad" means "war against non-Muslims."[194] The Muslim community is directed to make war "upon Jews, Christians, and Zoroastrians . . . until they become Muslim or pay the non-Muslim poll tax."[195]

Most Muslims are Sunnis. There are four schools of Sunni Muslim jurisprudence: the Shafi'i, Hanafi, Hanbali, and Maliki. The legal manual quoted above originated with the Shafi'i school; a Hanafi authority, meanwhile, directly contradicts the scholars, specifically explaining jihad as a religious war. The infidels must first be called to embrace Islam, "because the Prophet so instructed his commanders, directing them to call the infidels to the faith." It states that Muslims must not wage jihad in order to enrich themselves but only for the cause of Islam. And when the infidels hear the call to Islam, they "will hence perceive that they are attacked for the sake of religion, and not for the sake of taking their property, or making slaves of their children, and on this consideration it is possible that they may be induced to agree to the call, in order to save themselves from the troubles of war."[196]

However, things will go badly for the non-Muslims who choose not to convert or pay the tax. Muslims must "make war upon them, because God is the assistant of those who serve Him, and the destroyer of His enemies, the infidels, and it is necessary to implore His aid upon every occasion; the Prophet, moreover, commands us so to do."[197]

Ibn Khaldun (1332-1406), a Maliki jurist as well as a pioneering historian and philosopher who authored one of the first works of historiography, likewise notes "in the Muslim community, the holy war is a religious duty, because of the universalism of the Muslim mission and (the obligation to) convert everybody to Islam either by persuasion or by force." Islam is "under obligation to gain power over other nations."[198] And the Hanbali jurist Ibn Taymiyya (1263-1328) directed that "since lawful warfare is essentially jihad and since its aim is that the religion is God's entirely and God's word is uppermost, therefore according to all Muslims, those who stand in the way of this aim must be fought."[199]

These are old authorities, but none of these Sunni schools of jurisprudence have ever reformed or rejected these directives. For the scholars not to mention any of this, and to represent jihad warfare solely as a matter of "legitimate self-defense and maintenance of sovereignty," is hard to see as anything but deceptive.

Nonetheless, the scholars declared that they share the pope's "desire for frank and sincere dialogue." They expressed a wish to "build peaceful and friendly relationships based upon mutual respect, justice, and what is common in essence in our shared Abrahamic tradition, particularly 'the two greatest commandments' in Mark 12:29-31 (and, in varying form, in Matthew 22:37-40), that *the Lord our God is One Lord; / And thou shalt love the Lord thy God with all thy heart, and with all thy soul, and with all thy understanding, and with all thy strength: this is the first commandment. / And the second commandment is like, namely this, Thou shalt love thy neighbor as thyself. There is none other commandment greater than these."*

It is odd that the scholars should cite the commandment to "love your neighbor as yourself" as part of a shared tradition with Christianity, since nowhere does that commandment appear in Islam. Rather, as we have seen, the Qur'an says, "Muhammad is the Messenger of God, and those who are with him are hard against the unbelievers, merciful one to another." This dichotomy runs through the entirety of Islam. One may be merciful to one's fellow Muslims. But toward those outside, the believer must behave quite differently: "O believers, fight the unbelievers who are near to you; and let them find in you a harshness" (9:123).

A Common Word

A year after this flawed and arguably deceptive letter appeared, 138 Muslim leaders and scholars from all over the globe issued a more extensive appeal to Christians for mutual understanding, entitled *A Common Word Between Us and You.* The "Common Word" initiative is quite extensive, with ongoing conferences and other mutual endeavors between Muslims and Catholics, as well as between Muslims and other Christian groups. The Common Word website describes the project in enthusiastic terms: "Never before have Muslims delivered this kind of definitive consensus statement on Christianity. Rather than engage in polemic, the signatories have adopted the traditional and mainstream Islamic position of respecting the Christian scripture and calling Christians to be more, not less, faithful to it."[200]

Following the pattern set by the earlier document, data contradicting the assertions in *A Common Word Between Us and You* are not addressed and refuted but simply ignored. Nothing is said, for example, about the Islamic claim that the Christian Scripture has been corrupted. While claiming they want to respect Christian Scripture and build on common ground, the Muslim scholars (despite copious Qur'an quotes) never mention Qur'an 5:17, which says that those who believe in the divinity of Christ are unbelievers; or 4:171, which says that Jesus was not crucified; or 9:30, which says that those who believe that Jesus is the Son of God are accursed; or 9:29, which mandates warfare against and the subjugation of Jews and Christians. Why should they mention these unpleasant passages in the midst of trying to build bridges? Because they are precisely the obstacles to such bridges. For there to be any true and honest dialogue, verses like these must be addressed in some way, even if only to give them a benign interpretation.

When Blessed John Paul II died, the *Washington Post* reminded its readers how "during his long reign, Pope John Paul II apologized to Muslims for the Crusades, to Jews for anti-Semitism, to Orthodox Christians for the sacking of Constantinople, to Italians for the Vatican's associations with the Mafia and to scientists for the persecution of Galileo."[201] In reality, he never apologized for the Crusades; the closest he came was on March 12, 2000, the "Day of Pardon," when he said, "[W]e cannot fail to recognize *the infidelities to the Gospel committed by some of our brethren,* especially during the second millennium. Let us ask pardon for the divisions which have occurred among Christians, for the violence some have used in the service of the truth and for the distrustful and hostile attitudes sometimes taken towards the followers of other religions."[202]

Though it's hardly an "apology for the Crusades," none-theless one would be hard pressed to find a similar state-ment from any Muslim leader, still less one of the pope's su-preme stature, acknowledging any wrongdoing on the part of Muslims individually or of any Islamic state. The idea of a Muslim asking pardon and forgiveness from a non-Muslim is anathema to Islamic theology. But some kind of reciproc-ity of this kind would seem necessary for genuine dialogue.

Reading the entire Qur'anic verse from which the phrase "a common word between us and you" was taken makes clear the Common Word initiative's agenda: "Say: 'People of the Book! Come now to a word common between us and you, that we serve none but God, and that we associate not aught with Him, and do not some of us take others as Lords, apart from God.' And if they turn their backs, say: 'Bear witness that we are Muslims'" (3:64). Since Muslims consider the Christian confession of the divinity of Christ to be an unacceptable association of a partner with God, this verse is saying that the "common word" that Muslims and the People of the Book should agree on is that Christians should discard one of the central tenets of their faith and es-sentially become Muslims.

Not a promising basis for an honest and mutually re-spectful dialogue of equals. The *Common Word* document's explanation for this was disingenuous, not mentioning that according to the mainstream Islamic understanding of what it means to "ascribe a partner to God," the Christians were guilty of this sin:

> The words: *we shall ascribe no partner unto Him* relate to the Unity of God, and the words: *worship none but God*, relate to being totally devoted to God. Hence they all relate to the *First and Greatest Commandment*. According to one of the

oldest and most authoritative commentaries on the Holy
Qur'an the words: *that none of us shall take others for lords
beside God*, mean "that none of us should obey the other in
disobedience to what God has commanded." This relates
to the Second Commandment because justice and freedom
of religion are a crucial part of love of the neighbour.

"Being totally devoted to God" is a drastically inadequate
summation of what Islam's understanding of monotheism
really is, and how it relates to Christianity. Islam may preach
"total submission of the human will to the divine will," to
use Kreeft's phrase,[203] but Jesus said, "I no longer call you
servants, because a servant does not know his master's busi-
ness. Instead, I have called you friends, for everything that I
learned from my Father I have made known to you" (John
15:15). Catholics do indeed submit to God, but as a child
does to a loving father, not as a slave does to a capricious
and angry master. Christian submission is to a God who is
good, and who—with no implied limitations on his power
or freedom—is not the author of evil.

Christians who believe that they and Muslims share a
common aspiration to be "totally devoted to God" are not
guilty of deception. But they have been deceived.

The Common Word document suggests its true intentions
in its Qur'anic epigraph: *"Call unto the way of thy Lord with wisdom and fair exhortation, and contend with them in the fairest way.
Lo! thy Lord is Best Aware of him who strayeth from His way, and He
is Best Aware of those who go aright."* This verse (16:125) is a curious choice to head up a document that is ostensibly devoted
to finding common ground for dialogue and mutual cooperation—unless the intention is actually only to proselytize.

The use of this epigraph recalls the words of the Egyptian Islamic supremacist writer Sayyid Qutb (1906-1966),

the great theorist of the Muslim Brotherhood: "The chasm
between Islam and Jahiliyyah [the society of unbelievers]
is great, and a bridge is not to be built across it so that the
people on the two sides may mix with each other, but only
so that the people of Jahiliyyah may come over to Islam."[204]
Muslims in the U.S. and Europe often term their outreach
to non-Muslims "bridge-building," but to Muslims this expression has a very different meaning.

A further explanation of the "common word" passage
from the Qur'an makes it clear that building a bridge only so
that Catholics may convert to Islam is indeed the objective of
the "Common Word" document and initiative as a whole.

> Clearly, the blessed words: *we shall ascribe no partner unto
> Him* relate to the Unity of God. Clearly also, worshipping
> *none but God*, relates to being totally devoted to God and
> hence to the *First and Greatest Commandment*. According
> to one of the oldest and most authoritative commentar-
> ies (*tafsir*) on the Holy Qur'an . . . *that none of us shall take
> others for lords beside God* means "that none of us should
> obey in disobedience to what God has commanded, nor
> glorify them by prostrating to them in the same way as
> they prostrate to God." In other words, that Muslims,
> Christians, and Jews should be free to each follow what
> God commanded them, and not have "to prostrate before
> kings and the like"; for God says elsewhere in the Holy
> Qur'an: *Let there be no compulsion in religion. . . . (Al-Baqa-
> rah*, 2:256). This clearly relates to the Second Command-
> ment and to love of the neighbour of which justice and
> freedom of religion are a crucial part.

In this there is nothing to which Christians could object,
but the reference to prostrating before others besides God

becomes more pointed when, immediately following it, the Muslim leaders "as Muslims invite Christians to remember Jesus' words in the Gospel (Mark 12:29-31)":

> "The LORD our God, the LORD is one. /And you shall love the LORD your God with all your heart, with all your soul, with all your mind, and with all your strength." This is the first commandment. / And the second, like it, is this: "You shall love your neighbour as yourself." There is no other commandment greater than these.

The juxtaposition is striking. This passage from the Common Word document speaks not only of the two Great Commandments but of worshipping none but God alone. Then we have Jesus enunciating the two Great Commandments beginning with the affirmation that "the LORD our God, the LORD is one." The framers of the Common Word document, undoubtedly familiar with the Qur'an's anti-Trinitarian passages, here are subtly using Jesus' words to argue against the doctrine of the Trinity even as they pretend to be seeking points of agreement.

In closing, the Common Word document adds another indictment of Christian theology veiled as an invitation to cooperation: "Finally, as Muslims, and in obedience to the Holy Qur'an, we ask Christians to come together with us on the common essentials of our two religions . . . *that we shall worship none but God, and that we shall ascribe no partner unto Him, and that none of us shall take others for lords beside God.*"

Anyone acquainted with Islam's view of the Christian doctrine of the divinity of Christ cannot fail to see this as a call to abandon orthodox Christianity. Nonetheless, in some quarters the response to the Common Word document was enthusiastic. Noting the Muslim scholars' declaration that "the future of the world depends on peace between Muslims and Christians," the headline in the British newspaper the *Telegraph* depicted the document, in language that was typical of the international coverage, as "Muslim scholars' olive branch to Christians."[205] Reuters wrote excitedly about an "Unprecedented Muslim call for peace with Christians."[206] Dinesh D'Souza praised the 138 authors of the document: "Certainly some relief was in order, because Muslims who seek common cause with the West, or at least with the Christian West, are far preferable to those who seek to destroy us."[207]

Rowan Williams, then the archbishop of Canterbury and head of the Anglican Communion worldwide, exulted: "The appearance of the *A Common Word* [Open Letter] of 2007 was a landmark in Muslim-Christian relations and it has a unique role in stimulating a discussion at the deepest level across the world."[208] Even Pope Benedict XVI, during his May 2009 visit to Jordan, hailed such initiatives as having "achieved much good in furthering an alliance of civilizations between the West and the Muslim world, confounding the predictions of those who consider violence and conflict inevitable."[209] However, his other statements made this appear more to be an expression of hope than a statement of fact. The next day he observed, during his visit to the King Hussein Mosque in Amman, Jordan, that the *Common Word* letter "echoed a theme consonant with my first encyclical: the unbreakable bond between love of God and love of neighbor, and the fundamental contradiction of resorting to violence or exclusion in the name of God (cf. *Deus Caritas Est*, 16)."[210]

In that same 2009 address, Pope Benedict also gingerly brought up the Muslim persecution of Christians in Iraq:

> Before I leave you this morning I would like to acknowledge in a special way the presence among us of His Beatitude

Emmanuel III Delly, Patriarch of Baghdad, whom I greet most warmly. His presence brings to mind the people of neighboring Iraq many of whom have found welcome refuge here in Jordan. The international community's efforts to promote peace and reconciliation, together with those of the local leaders, must continue in order to bear fruit in the lives of Iraqis. I wish to express my appreciation for all those who are assisting in the endeavors to deepen trust and to rebuild the institutions and infrastructure essential to the well-being of that society. And once again, I urge diplomats and the international community they represent together with local political and religious leaders to do everything possible to ensure the ancient Christian community of that noble land its fundamental right to peaceful coexistence with their fellow citizens.[211]

This was an extraordinarily important moment, for true dialogue and mutual respect do not advance by papering over or ignoring significant differences, and certainly not by slyly appealing for conversion under the guise of respectful discussion, but by frankly and honestly confronting serious issues and offering to discuss them in a respectful manner. Even if the Common Word appeal were entirely sincere, the escalating Muslim persecution of Christians in Muslim lands, perpetrated by Muslims acting in accord with mainstream understandings of Qur'anic teaching and Islamic law, indicates that all too many Muslims do not share the desire for peaceful and respectful coexistence professed by the authors and signers of the Common Word document.

The leaders of the Common Word initiative have never publicized any attempts to establish any kind of dialogue with their coreligionists, to try to bring them to a more positive view of Christians.

That is telling. And it is essentially all there is to go on. There are many friendly, non-violent Muslims in the world, and many have Christian friends. But although it is relatively easy to find Muslims who have no intention ever of acting upon the Islamic texts and teachings that jihadists use to justify violence, it is significantly harder to find Muslims who will actively repudiate those teachings and reinterpret those texts. Muslim spokesmen in the West generally deny that there are any violent teachings in Islam, or practice moral equivalence when confronted with them, claiming that Christianity is just as violent or even more so, as if that is a sufficient answer to the problem of Islam-inspired violence around the world today. Deception is not reform, although among Muslim spokesmen today there is considerable confusion between the two.

Conclusion

Not Peace but a Sword

*"They have healed the wound of my people lightly, saying,
'Peace, peace,' when there is no peace."*
— Jeremiah 6:14

It is hard for modern Westerners to believe that there could exist a group with which they could not reach some peaceful accord, some framework for friendly coexistence as equals on a sustainable basis. It seems inconceivable to many Catholics, looking for allies against secularism and the culture of death, to believe that their gestures of goodwill towards Islam would not be reciprocated and would even be regarded with contempt.

Yet, despite the peaceful overtures of Muslims such as those involved in the Common Ground initiative—even when sincere—that is exactly the attitude built into the heart of Islam. It teaches its followers to regard non-Muslims—especially those among the "People of the Book" who have rejected Muhammad, the Qur'an, and Islam—as "the worst of creatures" (Qur'an 98:6). They have no compelling interest to have good relations with them except so as to protect Muslim communities in non-Muslim countries. The Islamic imperative remains to make them Muslims or else make them "pay the tribute out of hand" and be "humbled" (Qur'an 9:29).

What, then, is to be done? Are we condemned to perpetual hostility between Catholicism and Islam, punctuated by attempts at "outreach" featuring smiling, disingenuous Muslims and credulous, well-meaning Catholics? Do there exist *any* true boundaries for peaceful coexistence, even cooperation?

Any attempt at legitimate and peaceful dialogue must proceed not by ignoring, denying, or glossing over differences but by confronting them honestly and charitably. And Catholics should be aware of Muhammad's dictum that "war is deceit" and enter into such dialogue shrewdly aware of the fullness of Islam's teachings about itself, about Christianity, and about warfare against unbelievers (as well as the role that deception plays in that warfare).

We can enter into dialogue, but we must do so with our eyes open. We can work together on ventures of common interest, but we must do so knowing that the Muslim party will never regard Catholics as equal partners or consider the partnership lastingly viable.

The title of this book is not a call to war any more than it was when the Lord Jesus said, "Do not think that I have come to bring peace on earth; I have not come to bring peace, but a sword" (Matt. 10:34). It *is* a call to Catholics to take up a sword—not the sword of conquest and subjugation, but what St. Paul called the "sword of the Spirit, which is the word of God" (Eph. 6:17): To bear witness to Jesus Christ in word and deed, standing firm on the truth without compromise or dissembling in the interests of getting along with a group that will never—barring a massive transformation of Islamic doctrine—regard Catholics as anything but renegades from the true faith that the Muslim prophet Jesus taught. But such a massive transformation is extraordinarily unlikely.

For one thing, there is no single unifying authority, no pope of Islam, who can oversee and guide an Islamic "reformation." Further stymying the possibility of reform is the belief that the Qur'an was dictated by Allah word for word, miraculously protected from scribal error, and contains no human element whatsoever. Then there is the high value placed upon juridical consensus in Islam; a matter upon which the various schools of Islamic jurisprudence have agreed is considered no longer open to question, since Muhammad promised that his community would not agree on an error. Since jihad warfare against unbelievers and their subjugation is rooted in the Qur'anic text and sealed by juridical consensus, it is unlikely in the extreme that it will ever be revisited on a large scale in the Islamic world.

★★★

Secularism is encroaching upon the West, making it ever more difficult to hold fast to the fullness of the Faith in a culture that is daily growing more hostile to it. In such a world it is always good to have allies. Pope Benedict XVI enunciated a noble aspiration in September 2012 when he said to young Muslims and Christians in Beirut: "It is vital that the Middle East in general, looking at you, should understand that Muslims and Christians, Islam and Christianity, can live side by side without hatred, with respect for the beliefs of each person, so as to build together a free and humane society."[212] It is indeed up to Muslims worldwide, particularly in Pakistan and Egypt, where Muslims are persecuting Christians with increasing ferocity, to demonstrate that that harmony is possible.

Yet a true ally is not one who is likely to turn and join one's enemies in the struggle, or to initiate new hostilities within the alliance once the battle is won. The doctrines of Islam that inculcate among all too many Muslims hatred and suspicion of Christianity and Christians have never been reformed or rejected by any Islamic sect. Catholics who believe that their Muslim dialogue partners desire to establish a lasting friendship, or who trust Muslims to be faithful brothers-in-arms in the culture war, should proceed with full awareness of the contents of Islamic doctrine, and with an awareness of the many pitfalls involved.

Ultimately, the requirements of charity do not include the denial of the truth. We may want to believe that Islam is a spiritual cousin and a moral partner, and that idea may be greatly comforting; but its comforts will one day evanesce before the sword that the complacently self-deceived had thought they had staved off forever.

Is the Only Good Muslim a Bad Muslim?
The Kreeft/Spencer Debate

On November 4, 2010, Robert Spencer and Peter Kreeft debated the proposition "The Only Good Muslim Is a Bad Muslim" at The Thomas More College of Liberal Arts, in Merrimack, New Hampshire. Moderating was John Zmirak, a professor at the college. This transcript is presented with Dr. Kreeft's consent.

Professor Zmirak: I'm very proud to have with me the most distinguished writers in their fields alive, the most distinguished Catholic philosophical writer in English, Dr. Peter Kreeft, and the leading expert on jihad and political Islam, Mr. Robert Spencer. Dr. Kreeft has written a book called *Between Allah and Jesus* exploring the interface and the interactions and the commonalities and divergences between Christianity and Islam. Dr. Kreeft is also a professor of philosophy at Boston College and has written more than forty-five books; I've read a large percentage of them and enjoyed them immensely. I'm very honored and proud he was able to make it. Mr. Spencer is author of ten books and he's also the editor of JihadWatch.com.

Our topic is "Resolved: that the only good Muslim is a bad Muslim." Mr. Spencer will be speaking first, in the affirmative, for twenty minutes, then Dr. Kreeft responds for twenty minutes, then there will be twenty minutes of them asking each other questions. Then I'll pose a few questions. There will be opportunities for questions from the audience. So Mr. Spencer, if you would like to lead off . . .

Mr. Spencer: Thank you very much. Thank you all for coming and thank you to everyone at Thomas More College for hosting this. I think this is a discussion that needs to be had in the public square and is all too often ignored and not held where it should be, and so I hope that this will perhaps bring some needed attention to these questions. It's a great honor for me to be appearing with Dr. Kreeft, who was my professor many hundreds of years ago.

Dr. Kreeft's book *Between Allah and Jesus* is one that I read with great interest, and I certainly see what is the motive behind what he's trying to do in it, insofar as I understand it correctly and why he would want to portray Islam in this manner. Now the question before us is somewhat uncomfortable; it even seems kind of insulting to say that the only good Muslim is a bad Muslim—especially in a context where we have a Catholic college hosting a debate and it's as if one of the debate participants, namely myself, is saying that religious people of a certain kind should be discouraged from holding to their religion. It seems like something that other religious people should not be in the position of saying, and certainly it seems like something that most religious people would reject out of hand on the face of it and say, "Obviously this is not true, because we all know that the people who are committing violence in the name of Islam are twisting and hijacking the religion. If they only go back to the tenets of the Qur'an and of Muhammad, the Prophet of Islam, then this problem and attendant problems of terrorism and Islamic supremacism would evanesce."

And I think it's in that spirit that Dr. Kreeft wrote his book. It is something devoutly to be wished that people of good will of all faiths could find some common accord and work on that common accord for their shared values. We have even seen that happen between the Catholic Church and Islamic countries at the United Nations against various anti-life initiatives. And so this is something many people have great hope for. The great danger in holding such a hope is that many people fall into and project upon other religious people values which we ourselves may hold, and that therefore we assume that people of other religious traditions must also hold—when actually that's not the case. And unfortunately I must say, with regret, that I did find a great deal of that kind of thing in this particular book. The idea, for example, is posited several times in the book by the Muslim character, who I think it's fair to say is the hero of the story. Many times he says that jihad is an interior spiritual struggle. Now that is something that does exist in Islamic tradition. But tonight we are asking: Should Muslim piety be encouraged?

Should Muslim people be encouraged to be more rigorous and more devout and more fervent in their religious observance? So we have to go back to the wellsprings, to the teachings of Islam in the Qur'an and Muhammad, the Prophet of Islam, who is held up in the Qur'an—as in chapter 33, verse 21, which calls him *uswa hasana*, or the Excellent Example of conduct. In Islamic tradition he is even exalted in many places as *al-insan al-kamil*, the Perfect Man. And in practice, in Islamic tradition, even though Muhammad is rebuked several times in the Qur'an (notably in chapter 80) for his sinfulness, in practice, in Islamic tradition, Muhammad is essentially the touchstone of all behavior, and if he did it, then it's good and right and ought to be imitated. Now, that's important for the present question, because when we have the Muslim character saying, "Jihad is an interior spiritual struggle," he is in fact putting himself in the position of contradicting the words and example of Muhammad and the words of the Qur'an itself. There's an entire chapter of the Qur'an, chapter eight, called *al-Anfal*: the spoils of war. There are no spoils of war in an interior spiritual struggle. There is no booty to be captured, there are no slave girls to be distributed among the warriors, and yet that chapter of the Qur'an and others contain instruction for doing just that kind of thing. And a fifth of the spoils are reserved for the Prophet himself; he took part in these wars, he actually fought seventy-eight battles during his career as the Prophet, and seventy-seven were offensive in nature. The Qur'an does not teach that jihad is an interior spiritual struggle.

The Qur'an almost unanimously when it speaks of jihad—and when it uses the Arabic word *jihad* in its various forms—means "struggle." Of course in Arabic the word *struggle* has just as many connotations as *struggle* does in English: You can struggle to quit smoking, you can struggle to lose weight, you can struggle against Communism or have states struggling against one another. So it is also in Islam. But the primary meaning of the word *jihad* in the Qur'an is unmistakably *warfare*. The Muslim hero of Dr. Kreeft's book further says that Muhammad never fought against Christians and Jews unless he did so in a defensive manner. That, unfortunately, is factually false. As a matter of fact, in the last battle of his career, right before he died, Muhammad went to Tabuk, which was a Byzantine imperial outpost, to fight a Christian garrison there. He didn't actually find them there. They had left.

In chapter nine of the Qur'an are numerous teachings—which of course are portrayed as divine revelation which cannot be questioned and have to be obeyed by any pious and observant Muslim. These are instructions to wage offensive warfare against Jews and Christians—particularly in chapter nine, verse twenty-nine, which tells Muslims to fight against those who do not obey Allah and his messenger and do not forbid that which he has forbidden (in other words, don't follow the strictures of Islamic law), even if

they are the People of the Book, which is the Qur'anic designation for primarily Jews and Christians, until they pay
the *jizya* (which is a tax) with *willing submission* and *feel themselves subdued.*

That verse became the foundation of an elaborate super-
structure of laws that are still part of Islamic jurisprudence
and of Islamic political law that Islamists, that jihad terrorists, that any Islamic supremacist wants to impose over the
world today. These laws mandate that non-Muslims, the
People of the Book, must pay a special tax from which Muslims are exempt. As a matter of fact, you can pretty much
correlate in Islamic history the strength and aggression and
rise of the great Islamic empires of the past with the size
of the Jewish and Christian communities that were subjugated within those empires and were paying for that imperial expansion. When those communities were exhausted
economically, then the Islamic empires went into decline.
This is an absolute correlation that recurs again and again
and again. The Christians and Jews in Muslim lands were
subjugated in accord with that section of the verse, that last
part where they must 'pay the *jizya* with willing submission
and feel themselves subdued.' They never enjoyed equality
of rights with Muslims. They were denied the right to build
new houses of worship or to repair old ones; they were denied the right to hold authority over Muslims so that Jews
and Christians were relegated to the most menial and de-
grading jobs in the society. They were subject to various
other humiliating and discriminatory regulations.

Now this is, as I cannot emphasize enough, *still part of
Islamic law.* This is not one sect or one school or one group
that's heretical that has made this part of their teaching.
This is universal among all sects and schools of jurisprudence that are recognized as mainstream and orthodox by

fellow Muslims. They all teach—you cannot find one that
does not teach—the necessity to wage wars against unbelievers and to subjugate them under the rule of Islamic law.
In fact, Hamas, in Gaza, has announced its intention, once
it's fully consolidated its power, to impose this system of
dhimmitude and subjugate the Christians that remain there
under institutionalized forms of discrimination. Gangs in
Baghdad, without government authority to be sure, terrorized the Christian community—which I'm sure you know
is terrorized on a more or less daily basis. There was just another massacre in a church in Baghdad the other day—they
were knocking on doors in Baghdad last year and demanding payment of the *jizya*, this tax that amounts to protection
money. You pay it and you don't get killed. But you don't
pay it, or you transgress some of the other laws that are set
out for these subjugated peoples, and then your life is forfeit.
   These things are still part of the agenda for Islamic jihadists today. The Islamic jihadists routinely portray themselves
in the Muslim community worldwide and among peaceful Muslims, as being the most pious, most observant—in
other words, the best Muslims available. They are, in other
words, the Muslims who present themselves as being the
true, the pure Muslims. As a matter of fact, the worldwide
Salafi movement is dedicated to restoring the purity of Islam
as they see it. Hasan al-Banna founded the Muslim Brotherhood in 1928 after Kemal Ataturk abolished the caliphate
in 1924, which was the symbol of the supranational unity
of the Muslims that transcended all national boundaries.
Ataturk abolished the caliphate in 1924. Hasan al-Banna established the Muslim Brotherhood in 1928 in Egypt as a direct reaction, because he believed that without the political
aspects of Islam—that have never been considered separable
from the religious individual aspects of spiritual observance

in any Islamic tradition—without the political aspect of Islam that had been damaged by the abolition of the caliphate, Islam was not being fully observed in the world.

He dedicated the Muslim Brotherhood—which is the direct forefather of Hamas and Al Qaeda and other terrorist groups, as well as many pseudo-moderate groups in the United States today like the Council on American Islamic Relations—to what he saw as the fullness of Islamic observance, the true observance of Islamic piety, which involved the subjugation of unbelievers, violence against them if they resisted, and the establishment of Muslims as a special class that would enjoy certain rights and privileges that the other classes would not enjoy. These things are represented around the world today, in the Islamic world and in Muslim communities in the West as well, as being part of what it means to be a good Muslim. They make their appeal to peaceful Muslims. They justify their own actions of terror or supremacism and they make recruits among peaceful Muslims by representing themselves as being the embodiment of authentic Muslim observance.

Now, obviously, there are Muslims who do not consider acts of terrorism or violence, or the supremacist attempts to impose Islamic law over non-Muslims, part of their Islamic piety. And certainly I applaud them and wish there were more of them insofar as they're sincere. They are, however, universally worldwide on the defensive today. They are represented as the bad Muslims by their fellow Muslims who are pointing to the texts of the Qur'an and the teachings of Muhammad. And so the Muslims who we could look to with hopes of reform, the Muslims who we would look to in hopes of their being our allies, they are the ones who are considered to be the bad Muslims generally in the Islamic community. Now it must also be further stated, unfortu-

nately, that there is no theological system in Islam, there is
no sect, there is no group within Islam that has formulated
a comeback, a construction of Islamic theology based on the
Qur'an that makes a case to reject violence and supremacism
and the subjugation of unbelievers. It doesn't exist. There
are many individuals who are working against it, but there
is no group that we can point to and say "Ah, they're the
ones we need to work with!" In other words, they have not
formulated any kind of convincing comeback. The texts are
not on their side.

There are peaceful, pacifistic texts in the Qur'an. Dr.
Kreeft quotes many of them in his book. He does not, unfortunately, quote the violent ones to which I alluded before.
I mentioned one of them specifically—chapter eight, verse
sixty, part of that *al-Anfal* (spoils of war chapter) that directs
Muslims to "strike terror into the hearts of the enemies of
Allah." Now you can say "Well, that doesn't have anything
to do with modern terrorism, that's terror in a much broader sense," but unfortunately, modern terrorists can and do
point to that verse and say, "That's what we're doing! That's
why we're doing what we're doing. We're striking terror
into the hearts of the enemies of Allah."

The peaceful passages, according to mainstream Islamic
theologians, and to the preponderance of Islamic theological tradition, do not take precedence over the violent passages. The peaceful passages generally were revealed earlier
in Muhammad's career. He was a prophet for twenty-three
years, and over those twenty-three years he received revelations from God, which were collected in the Qur'an. Early
in his career when he was in Mecca he had a small band of
followers facing a very powerful pagan Arab establishment
of his own tribe, the Quraysh, in Mecca. That's when he
was saying, "Say to the unbelievers that you have your reli-

gion and we have ours; you don't worship what we worship and we don't worship what you worship," and essentially, "Let's just leave each other alone." That's chapter 109 of the Qur'an. The unfortunate fact is that when he later moved in the *hijra* to Medina and became for the first time a political and military leader, the tenor of the Qur'anic revelations began to change and the violence began to be taught and carried out by Muhammad himself.

Now, mainstream Islamic theologians and the preponderance of Islamic theological tradition teaches that if there is a disagreement between two passages in the Qur'an, then one of the chief ways to see which one takes precedence in our own day is, which one came later chronologically in Muhammad's career. Unfortunately for us, the violence comes later, and thus is considered under the principles of *al-nasikhwal-mansukh* (or abrogation) to cancel out the peaceful passages. Or the peaceful passages only apply when Muslims are a small group, as the Meccan Muslims were in the first stage of Muhammad's career. So in other words, when they're a small group, when they're powerless, then they teach tolerance and non-violence. But later, gaining in power and numbers, the other parts begin to kick in, and the violence and the supremacism apply.

I believe right now we're in the state of transition in the United States where we're moving from one to the other. There's a great deal more aggression and a great deal more assertiveness in Islamic communities and by Islamic jihadists against the United States, because they see that we are at a tipping point so they can move away from tolerance. Over a third of the attacks or attempted jihad attacks against the United States that have happened since 9/11 *have happened in the past year*, which means there's been a sharp uptick in the last year. And so this indicates that we are dealing with

a group that considers itself to be acting in complete accord
with the dictates of Islamic teaching, and thus to say that we
want to encourage Islamic piety is only to encourage, ultimately, the cutting of our own throat: culturally, politically,
societally. Thank you.

Professor Kreeft: I find myself in some difficulties here.
I love debates, but I usually debate pro-choice people or
atheists. And that's a knock-'em-down-drag-'em-off debate
between me and my enemy. Bob's a good friend, a fellow
Catholic, not my enemy, so I view this more as a discussion than a debate: a kind of in-house theological exploration between friends. Bob knows much more about Islam
than I do. It is a minor interest of mine and usually when I
say something about minor interests, even when it's true, I
get in trouble. Especially about controversial issues, like the
sexual revolution or homosexuality or Islam! My final difficulty is I agree with almost everything Bob said tonight.

(Audience laughs.)

Professor Kreeft: Except! Except one more little question in the spirit of Columbo or Socrates, "one last little
question." Almost all your premises are true, but do they
really entail your conclusion? It seems to me you have two
conclusions, two main points, and I disagree with both of
them. First is that the only good Muslim is a bad Muslim;
the second is that Islam is a greater threat to us than the Enlightenment, so those are the two things I'd like to focus on.

I'd like to make very clear that my standards of judgment
are exactly the same as Bob's. First of all, the magisterium of
the Catholic Church; secondly, basic human reason; thirdly,
the facts of history and experience, which can't be denied.
Since my ultimate standards of judgment are Catholic, I
would like to start not with my own opinion but with the
"opinion" of the Catholic Church. For the first time in 450

years, the Church has issued a universal Catechism. There is a paragraph in it especially about Islam—just one—but I think this quotation is just about the most important one we can use about Islam. It says, paragraph eight, verse forty-one, "The Church's relationship with the Muslims: The plan of salvation also includes those who acknowledge the Creator, in the first place amongst whom are the Muslims. These profess to hold the faith of Abraham and together with us they adore the One Merciful God, mankind's judge on the Last Day."

Now, I think Bob would agree with that. First of all, he's a Catholic; secondly, nothing he said contradicted that; but I would like to add to what Bob said rather than contradict it, because that's a half-truth. I don't think he uttered any lies, and I don't think he uttered any false judgment except for his conclusions, but there are a lot of other things to say. First of all, "The only good Muslim is a bad Muslim." I know that's not true because I've met some good Muslims who are good. I've also met some bad ones. The only good Muslim is a bad Muslim means, quote unquote, a "good Muslim" is a self-contradiction.

Somebody completely faithful to the teachings of Islam and the Qur'an—and there are many different interpretations of it, not just one Islam as there is one Catholicism, as you know there's no magisterium for all the Muslims in the world, they're like Protestants, they're all over the place—

(Laughter)

Professor Kreeft: Well, not quite as bad as that, there are not 28,000 different sects and denominations. But just as all Protestants believe the Bible, all Muslims believe the Qur'an: It's a textual unity rather than a magisterial unity. Let's say there are three different levels of Islam that we have to distinguish: First of all, there's the level of terrorist activ-

ity, which none of us here supports in the least—we abomi-
nate that, there's absolutely no excuse for that. Secondly,
there's "Islamism," there's the imposition of sharia law over
everyone, there's a refusal to make a distinction between the
church and the state, there's the identification of religion
with politics, which all good Muslims share. Not all good
Muslims justify terrorism; in fact, most Muslims in the West
profess not to, but I have never met a Muslim who believed
in the separation of church and state. Therefore universal,
equal human rights for people of all religions is not the ideal
of any Muslim in the world, including good, pious Muslims
who I am defending. So I thoroughly disagree with them on
those two levels.

But there's a third level—namely, personal piety—and on
that level I think we can learn a lot from Muslims. I think
they can sometimes put us to shame. Especially the Sufis
who, although they're not mainline Muslims and although
they're labeled by most Muslims as unorthodox, are pretty
universally respected for their piety. And if you read some of
the writings of the Sufis you find, among some flaky stuff,
some very profound stuff. So it is simply not true that the
only good Muslim is a bad Muslim. Let me tell you a story
about a good Muslim, based on some combination of ideal-
ized features of Muslims I've met or read about and my own
imagination. One of them was a student at Boston College
who I had in a course about comparative religions, and he
always sat next to a Jewish student who I think was Orthodox, because he had a beard and a yarmulke and dreadlocks
and they fought all the time over Palestine. They almost
came to blows, but they sat in the front row and asked most
of the difficult questions, and I loved them for it—because
I love troublemakers as long as they don't use physical violence, and they didn't quite use physical violence, though

they shouted a bit. And the rest of the students, about twenty-four of them, were Catholics, at least nominally and some stage of dissent or assent—you know, Boston College.

(Laughter)

Professor Kreeft: It used to be a Catholic college, now it's a Jesuit college.

(Laughter)

Professor Kreeft: Actually, they're not so much non-Catholics that think they're Catholics, they're really Hindus who think they're Catholics, you know, they're all pantheists who think God is everything, that's the surprising result of questionnaires. You find out amazing things from your students from questionnaires. Anyway, it was time for the break, and we learn more during the break than in my lectures, so I gave them a long break. And we were munching on potato chips and drinking Coke, and the Jewish student, whose name was Zvai, noticed that behind my head, on the cinderblock wall, there was a faint cross painted there, so he said, "Is that supposed to be a cross?" I turned around and looked and realized that that was where the crucifixes used to be before they were taken down. So I turned around and I was about to, in a shamed-faced sort of way, try to give some lame explanation for the fact that the Jesuits took the crucifixes down—when the Holy Spirit closed my mouth and opened the mouth of the student next to Zvai and said, "Oh, that's where we used to have the crucifixes before we took them down," in a very proud and self-satisfied sort of way. And I thought Zvai was going to say, "Why did you take them down?" But he said, "*When* did you take them down?" So I said, "Why is he saying *when*?"

So the student scratched her head and said, "Last semester, I think." "What month?" "February, I think." "Aha!" said Zvai, "it was the Bundy money." "What's that?" Well, Zvai explained that McGeorge Bundy was the Secretary of State under either Johnson or Carter, one of the presidents, and there was a case that was going to come before the Supreme Court as to whether it violated the separation of church and state for Catholic schools to receive government grants. And the president didn't want that case to come before the Supreme Court for some reason or other, so he had his Secretary of State negotiate an out-of-court settlement, if the school was not sectarian, divisive, or exclusionary, whatever that meant (it was vague enough to satisfy everybody). Zvai pointed out that in the semester following the ruling, every single one of the twenty-one Jesuit colleges and universities in America took down their crucifixes. "Is that a coincidence?" he said. So, none of the Catholic students knew that and they were kind of embarrassed and one said, "We wouldn't do that for money."And Zvai smiled wickedly and said, "Of course not, but I hope you got more than thirty pieces of silver."

(Laughter)

Professor Kreeft: Half the students didn't get it.

(Laughter)

Professor Kreeft: They're biblically illiterate. They're not Protestants, they don't read the Bible.

(Laughter)

Professor Kreeft: So Zvai turned to them and said, "You see, the first Catholic to accept a government grant was Bishop Judas Iscariot."

(Laughter)

Professor Kreeft: So they kept saying, "No! We didn't do that for money, we did that to be ecumenical." At this point, the Muslim chimed in and said, "What's the meaning of ecumenical?" directing the question to me; I was the expert. So I opened my mouth and for the second time was about to utter some sort of answer to his reasonable question, when again, the Holy Spirit interrupted me, closed my mouth, and opened the mouth of the student next to him, another Catholic student who gave a really stupid answer to the question: "'Ecumenical' means we all love each other and we're all equal and here comes everybody and we won't offend others," or something like that. So the Muslim said, "Oh, others, you mean like me, the Muslim, and my friend, the Jew?" Now they were friends. Now, as soon as the two words, *Muslim* and *Jew*, were pronounced, everybody got very quiet, as if a blasphemy or an obscenity had been uttered. Those are very concrete words. They have teeth in them. So the Catholic student said, "Yeah!"

So the Muslim student said, "Well you *have* offended me." "What?" "Yes, you have offended me by taking down your crucifixes." "Why have we offended you, you're a Muslim! You don't believe Jesus died on the cross." The Muslim said, "You took down your crucifixes to avoid offending me; you have insulted me." "Why have we insulted you?" "Suppose you came to my country." I think it was Iran. Not even sure. "Suppose you enrolled in a Muslim university knowing that it was a Muslim university. Now, we don't have pictures of saints or statues. We think that's idolatry, but when you are at a Muslim university, you know you are at a Muslim university. You may see quotations from the Qur'an. Would you be offended at seeing a Muslim symbol in a Muslim university?" "Of course not!" said the Catholic. "Who would? Only a bigot, correct?" "Yes." "Now, you expect me to be offended at seeing a Catholic symbol in a Catholic university so you expect me to be a bigot. I am highly offended." They were very quiet; I could smell the wood burning.

(Laughter)

Professor Kreeft: Then comes the important part. He didn't stop at that, he turned around and faced the class like a fundamentalist preacher and he said, "How many of you believe that Jesus Christ is the Son of God?" I said to myself, "Who is this? Jerry Falwell in disguise—? This guy's a Muslim? Is he from central casting or something?" So they gradually put their hands up in a very embarrassed sort of way, and he said, "Well, I don't believe that. I'm a Muslim. The Qur'an says that's blasphemy, that's ridiculous, that's absurd, it's awful, 'Allah has a Son: the very mountains cover their ears before such blasphemy,' and so on. But as a Muslim, I love Jesus. We don't call him the Son of God. We call him one of the greatest men who ever lived. And the Qur'an says nothing bad about him, it says that he performed miracles, that he raised the dead, he was virgin-born, the Qur'an even has Allah rebuke Muhammad and say, 'You must repent of your sins.' It doesn't say that about Jesus. And the Qur'an also says that Jesus will come at the end of the world to administrate the Last Judgment. So we Muslims have a deep love for the prophet Jesus, blessed be his Name. And, like Muhammad, we never say his name without 'blessed be he' or 'peace be upon him.'

"Now, if we had pictures of the prophet Jesus in our classroom, we would never take them down, not for anything. Not for money, not for prestige, not even if soldiers came into our classroom with fixed bayonets and said, 'There has been [a] regime change; there's a new law: you must take down pictures of your prophet Jesus.' Every good Muslim in that class would get out of his seat, go to the front of the picture of the prophet Jesus, and say, "You take down the picture of our beloved prophet Jesus over our dead body. We would be glad to be a martyr for his honor." And now you take down pictures of your beloved prophet Jesus simply to get money from the government. So I think perhaps we are better Christians than you are."

(Laughter)

Professor Kreeft: I was the only one smiling. I said, "Thank you, Holy Spirit, for sending a prophet outside Israel to our midst." Now, in the Old Testament, God does that very frequently. He sends pagans, either to be prophets or to be wise men or, more often, to be military generals who smash the Jews and teach them a lesson. They are agents of God. I think, therefore, since I believe everything in the Bible, that it is quite likely—I know Bob will disagree with this—it is quite likely that one of the reasons why Islam is growing so fast, especially in Europe and Canada and America—that is, in what used to be called Christendom, which is now apostate Christendom or Western Civilization—is that God fulfills his promises.

And one of the promises he made in the Bible is that he will bless everyone who obeys his laws, and he will not bless anyone who disobeys his laws. Now, there's one law through history that Muslims have disobeyed very badly: Thou shalt not kill. And Christians have a mixed track record there, and while it's not a track record to be proud of, it's certainly not as bad as the Muslim track record. But if you look at all the other commandments, especially the one that characterizes our society the most—Thou shalt not commit adultery—I think you can see why the Muslims are being blessed. Why are they conquering Europe? They tried to do it by force of arms for a thousand years and they couldn't do it; now they're doing it, why? Well, because they found a weapon much stronger than swords: It's called mothers. They are having children. They are deferring gratification, they are paying forward, they are respecting families, and we aren't. There's the fruit of the Enlightenment, of rationalism, individualism, secularism. If I had to choose, therefore, between a Muslim and a secular humanist defender-of-the-sexual-revolution Enlightenment person—for instance, a Boston College theologian...

(Laughter)

Professor Kreeft: ...I would certainly choose the Muslim. To say that Islam is more our enemy than the Enlightenment is to say that people who believe in, love, and worship the One True God, even though in ways that are defective and very seriously defective, are worse than people who don't believe in God at all: That doesn't make sense.

Our primary enemies are not Muslims. Our primary enemies are demons, according to Jesus Christ. According to St. Paul, we wrestle "not against flesh and blood but principalities and powers." Throughout our history we've forgotten that, and we have confused who our enemies are, whether it's Protestants or Communists or Muslims or whoever, we have tried to convert souls by killing bodies. Now, we don't do that anymore, and that's good. But what we've substituted for that—we used to act more like Muslims, that is—what we've substituted for that, unfortunately, is a kind of indifferentism and, "Oh, c'mon, let's just get along" and "It's not really that important," which I think is worse.

Indifferentism means you don't even play the game; you don't even take religious truth seriously. That's different from playing the game on the wrong side, believing a religion that has very bad things in it as well as very good things in it, a heretical religion—which is all religions other than Christianity; every religion has some very good things in it and very bad things in it. (Buddhism for instance: They have a wonderful sense of peace and mind control and a terrible theology with no God at all or a pantheistic pudding.) To say that our fundamental enemies are people who, on a very deep level, believe in love and worship and try to obey the same God although in a much more primitive and a much more barbaric way and through a heretical communications network, but ones who've borrowed enough from Judaism and Christianity so that the attributes of Allah, the ninety-nine names of Allah, are all found in the Bible—to say that they are more our enemies than our own apostates, that strikes me as absurd. I debated an atheist once at the University of New Hampshire; they didn't know who I was, and the atheist was one of those analytical philosophers who thought that the word *God* was meaningless, so we didn't get to debate whether God exists till the last fifteen minutes. We spent most of the time trying to defend the meaning of the word *God* and describing what God's attributes were, so I thought it was a bad debate. Afterwards, though, a Muslim came up to me and said, "You teach at Boston College?"

(Laughter)

Professor Kreeft: He said, "You're a Muslim, aren't you?" I said, "No. I'm a Catholic." "Oh, oh, I was confused." "Why were you confused?" "Well, your theology is perfect, you know Allah exactly." Now, at that point I'd never even read the Qur'an. It is obvious the *Catechism* is right: We worship the same God in very different ways. And there are very serious differences between Christianity and Islam, and I don't want to minimize them at all, therefore I agree with almost everything Bob said. But let's get a sense of perspective. Who is Jesus' real enemy? Is it Caesar? Is it the Roman soldiers? Or is it Judas Iscariot? Once we get the Judas Iscariots out of the Church, I think we may be able to convert Muslims, and I would love nothing better than to convert Muslims. But the way you convert people is by holiness, by sanctity. Now, if we could meet on a fair battlefield here, in which the weapons were not swords but hearts, if we could

send saints to Muslim countries and they send their saints
to our country and we tried to convert each other by the
power of sanctity—that would be a wonderful battle, because nobody would lose. And I think we'd win more hearts
than they would.

    Professor Zmirak: Thank you.

    (Applause)

    Mr. Spencer: Well, I understand, Dr. Kreeft, your point
that the Enlightenment is a greater enemy and we need to
have some kind of a convergence or a cooperation between
people with a shared morality. So I suppose what I would
ask you is: How can we find an accord when there are elements of Islamic morality itself that are so deeply problematic? For example, Muhammad, when he was fifty-four,
consummated a marriage with a nine-year-old girl. As he is
the "excellent example" of conduct, that is something that
is considered normative, such that the Ayatollah Khomeini,
when he took power in Iran, lowered the legal marriageable age of girls to nine; when the aid workers went into
the refugee camps in Afghanistan in 2003, they found that
half the second-grade-age girls were already married and
virtually all the girls older than that were already married.
So this is something that is essentially rampant and very hard
to eradicate. You mentioned also adultery. I think about Islamic marriage law, and the fact that a man can have four
wives, all he has to do is say *talaq*, "You are divorced," and
she's gone and he can get another—as well as sex slaves he's
conquered in battle, which is specifically allowed for in the
Qur'an (chapter four, verse three). And so there's kind of
an appearance of morality that I'm not sure really squares
with the morality we might want. I remember the great
Oriana Fallaci—who was an Italian journalist internationally famous, and a great hero for freedom and human rights.

I had the great privilege of knowing her towards the end of her life, and she told me that when she did a very famous interview with the Ayatollah Khomeini, she was preparing with the translator in a room in Tehran before they went to meet Khomeini. And suddenly a mullah burst in and said, "It's a scandal! It's terrible! You're sharing a room and you're not married! And you're in a room alone with a man!" And so he forced her to marry the translator. They have in Shi'ite Islam temporary marriage, which is essentially, usually—not in Fallaci's case—but usually prostitution: a marriage contract with a deadline. You can marry somebody for an hour, or for a weekend, and then it expires and you're not married anymore. So there's no adultery, sure! Why should there be?

(Laughter)

Mr. Spencer: But it's not really anything that I would say is really preferable, even to Enlightenment "anything-goes" morality, which is a corruption of Judeo-Christian standards. How can we square that with the idea that there should be some kind of an accord between moral people?

Professor Kreeft: We can't. However, I don't think most Muslims would defend that. Although that may be wrong, I think it's parallel to our attitude toward the Mormons. Can we tolerate polygamy? Certainly not, but most Mormons don't like polygamy anymore, either. And most Muslims don't in fact, especially those in the West, have more than one wife, either. Can we tolerate African Animism? No. Can we tolerate polygamy in Africa? No, the Church has a big problem with that. Nevertheless, we can still learn something from the Mormons; we can learn something from the Africans, and we can learn something from the Muslims. George Weigel says that the Catholic Church could get its social agenda through Congress if it just did

one thing: kick out every single Roman Catholic and replace them with a Mormon or a Muslim. In some areas, they
are better than we are at preaching and practicing morality;
in other areas they're horrible. But we can still learn something from them, and the thing that I try to point out in this
book that we can learn from them—it's a difficult concept,
it's not formulatable in just one concept, really, it's a set of
concepts—I call it the primitive. Certainly Muslims have a
more primitive concept of God. It's not a God of Love, it's
not a Trinitarian God, it's not a God who has a Son or who
does an Incarnation or who saves you, it's a very early Old
Testament God. But if we repudiate those roots entirely, as
the Enlightenment does, we don't really have a God at all.

Here's a passage from Chesterton, from *Saint Thomas
Aquinas*—and this I think we can learn from Muslims—and
we'd better, because we've forgotten it. It's a defense of the
fear of God as the beginning of all wisdom, which most
religious teachers say is a very bad thing and the beginning
of all foolishness. But it doesn't say that fear of God is the
whole story, just the beginning of the story.

(Reading aloud:) "The Fear of the Lord: that is the beginning of wisdom and therefore it belongs to the beginnings
and is felt in the first cold hours before the dawn of civilization; the power that comes out of the wilderness and rides
on the whirlwind and breaks the gods of stone, the power
before which the Eastern nations are prostrate like the pave-
ment, the power before which the primitive prophets run
naked and shouting, at once proclaiming and escaping from
their God. The fear that is rightly rooted in the beginning
of every religion true or false, the fear of the Lord: that is the
beginning of wisdom. But it is not the end."

Now, religion is an organic thing, like a tree, and if this
primitive fear of God is its roots, and if we have detached

from our own roots, and if a religion like Islam is clearer and stronger about those roots even though it has corrupt branches, we can learn to our own use some things from Islam about those roots. We can learn the same thing from primitive Africans.

Mr. Spencer: There are certainly things we can learn from any given individual. There are certainly wise people in all religious traditions. That's really, I think, not at issue here; the question before us is, "Is the only good Muslim a bad Muslim?" and you mentioned earlier that you know that there are good Muslims who are good Muslims because you've met them. And I think, "Well, sure, I know good Catholics who contracept," and yet they will tell you that they are perfectly good Catholics and they're completely observant. This is, of course, in defiance of Catholic Church teaching, and there are other people who would say, "Well, no, you're not actually good Catholics." And how is one to determine that? You go to the sources; you go to the teaching of the Church. And so I would submit that you only know whether a Muslim is a good Muslim or not by Islamic standards, and we have to look at what their own texts and teachings say.

And so, for example, that very charming story you told about the crucifix and the pictures and the Muslim student—there are several very notable things that I think ought to be added for our edification tonight. One is that, in Islamic tradition, Jesus will indeed come back at the end of the world, not Muhammad. But Jesus will return at the end of the world and he will break all the crosses: that's Islamic tradition. In other words, he will destroy Christianity, which is believed to be a perversion of the true teachings of Jesus. And so he will break all the crosses, kill the pigs— because of course the Christians are the ones who eat the pork—and abolish the *jizya*, the tax that I mentioned before. In other words, He will destroy Christianity and Islamize the world; that's obviously one of those people St. Paul mentions in Corinthians when somebody comes to you with another Jesus, "other than the One we have preached to you," you receive him readily enough, but it is not remotely the Jesus of the New Testament. And further, in regard to the pictures, while I applaud and appreciate this gentleman saying that he would protect a picture of who he terms as the Prophet Jesus and would revere in other words these religious figures, actually, unfortunately, his co-religionists in the Balkans in particular, in Serbia, Croatia, Bosnia-Herzegovina, there are videotapes—you can find the tapes on YouTube—of them going into churches, going into Orthodox and Byzantine Catholic churches and kicking down the icons of Jesus and of his Mother and burning the church, pulling down the cross off the top, destroying any representational art. Now, which one of these is really the good Muslim? Well, Islam does teach that representational art, particularly of prophets and religious figures, is a blasphemy and ought rightly be destroyed. And thus, the people who are actually being the pious, good Muslims were the ones who were destroying the icons of Jesus and his Mother in the churches in the Balkans.

Professor Kreeft: This is true, this is true. But my Muslim student would not deny that, but he said, "*If* we had pictures, which we don't because they are blasphemous and idolatrous, *if* we had pictures we would defend them to the death." Now, here's my question for you: What do you think of this? This same student once asked to go to Mass with me. I was surprised, and he said, "Don't get me wrong, I have absolutely no intention of becoming a Catholic or anything or that I'm even interested in this—it's pure curiosity, but I promise to be respectful." So we went to Mass together and he just sat there like a stone, he wouldn't move, he wouldn't rise, or kneel, or in any way cooperate, but he was very quiet and respectful and afterwards I said to him, "What did you think?"

And he said two things that impressed me. The first was—this was in St. Mary's Chapel, which was a beautiful little stone Gothic chapel on B.C. [Boston College] campus—he said, "How old is this building?" I said, "Well, it's over a hundred years old, it's the oldest building on the B.C. campus back in nineteenth century." And he said, "How old are the words that the priest uttered?" And I said, "Well, half of those were his own interpolations—

(Laughter)

Professor Kreeft: "—and half of them were a sort of revision of the Church's liturgy which was translated a couple of years ago. But the structure of the Mass goes back to the beginning, while the actual words are fairly modern words." He said, "I thought so." I said, "Why?" I knew he knew nothing about Catholic tradition. He said, "Well, when I looked at the building, the stones brought my spirit closer to Heaven, but when I listened to the words, they were rather like shallow, babbling brooks moving on the surface of the Earth." I thought that was rather perceptive.

And then, then he said, "Do you Christians really believe that Jesus is literally the Son of God?" I said, "Yes, the orthodox ones do, the modernists don't, the liberals don't, but both Protestants and Catholics believe that." And he said, "And the difference between Protestants and Catholics is you Catholics also believe that when that priest holds up that little round piece of bread, that really turns into Jesus, literally?" I said, "Yes." He said, "And that's why everybody got very quiet then?" I said, "Yes, that was worship; that was adoration." And I said, "I know you think that's blasphemous and ridiculous, and Protestants do, too, except for Anglicans and Lutherans, who believe in the Real Presence."

(By the way, one of the things that made me a Catholic—I was born and brought up as a Calvinist—was reading the Church Fathers and how they never questioned the Real Presence for a thousand years. I said, "How could God allow such an error to exist in the Church for a thousand years? I mean, bowing down and worshipping bread and wine thinking it's God? That's really bad!")

So he said, "So you Catholics believe that that is really Jesus and that Jesus is really Allah, fully divine?" I said, "Yes." And he said, "Oh, I don't think so."

And I said, "Well, I don't expect you to believe it, it's a difficult thing to believe, but of course you're a Muslim, you don't believe that." He said, "That's not what I mean. I—I—I don't want to tell you what I mean, it's too embarrassing." So I tried to be nice and said, "Well, I suppose you mean you can't ever imagine doing what the other people did, the other Catholics, namely, getting down on your knees before what merely seemed to be a piece of bread."

He said, "No, that's not what I mean." He said, "I try to imagine myself believing that—which I of course never would, it's blasphemous—but I don't really think that you believe it." "Why not?" "Well—" And he stopped again, saying, "I don't want to insult you." I said, "I have thick skin, try." So I said, "You can't imagine yourself ever getting down on your knees?" And he said, "No, I can't imagine myself, if I believed that, ever getting up off my knees again."

Now there's seriousness there. There's something there, directed to a wrong object and a wrong religion, which I think we can learn some profound lessons from.

Mr. Spencer: Well, that's actually the question before us, then. The question is not really, "Are there pious Muslims?"

or "Are there pious people who are Muslims?" That's manifest, that's obvious, that's easy. The question before us, as far as I understand it, is whether Islamic piety really is something in accord with the best elements of the human spirit and whether it exalts it or whether it degrades it ultimately, if somebody follows it out.

Professor Kreeft: Wouldn't you agree that the answer to that question has to be neither a simple yes nor a simple no, because there are obviously ingredients in Muslim piety which no Christian can rightly agree with, and other ingredients in Muslim piety, equally important and equally orthodox, which every Christian must agree with?

Mr. Spencer: Well, I guess what I would say to that is—

Professor Kreeft: That's the heart and soul of Islam itself: total surrender and submission to God, which is the formula for a saint.

Mr. Spencer: Yes, absolutely, and as you very ably pointed out in your book, that's something that is common to Judaism and Christianity. It's not something that was originated in Islam, and so I find myself agreeing, I must say, with the Byzantine Emperor Manuel Palaiologos, who was quoted so famously by Pope Benedict XVI a few years back, touching off worldwide riots and murders of innocent people when he quoted him saying: "There was nothing that was new or original that Muhammad brought that was not evil and inhuman." There's plenty of good in the Qur'an that's taken from Judaism and Christianity. Where it becomes problematic is where it departs from that. Now, we can see that, because we're standing outside it and we understand—probably most of the people in this room know a great deal about Christianity and some of you about Judaism as well, and of course Judaism and Christianity come from the same wellsprings and are very similar in many important ways. Now, that is something we know then when we see these elements of Islam: that they are separable conceptually from the rest, but for Muslims these things are all a whole. Like you mentioned for an example the Sufis, that the Sufis have a wonderful spirituality. They do have a wonderful spirituality and in my first book, *Islam Unveiled*, I quote in its entirety a poem written by the Ayatollah Khomeini, who was very deeply influenced by Sufism. Now, the Ayatollah Khomeini also said, "I spit on the foolish souls" who believe that Islam is a religion of peace. He didn't have any trouble having these mystical flights that exalted his soul and also thinking that it was part of the Muslim's responsibility to take up arms against unbelievers. And there was no separation: It was all considered to be part of the devoutness of his observance. The Sufis for several hundred years have been at the forefront of the armed jihad warfare in Chechnya against the Russians. Hasan al-Banna, the founder of the Muslim Brotherhood, who I mentioned before, was very influenced by the Sufis, and as he was establishing this violent arm of political Islam he prescribed various Sufi exercises for members of the Brotherhood. Also al-Ghazali, one of the foremost Sufis in history, is very, very clear that Jews and Christians must be fought against and subjugated. He had no trouble seeing these two things together. So once again I have to come back to the topic: The only good Muslim is a bad Muslim. It's perhaps a little coarse and insulting way to put it, as I explained before—but nonetheless, it contains a truth, that there are elements of Islamic piety that are not separable from the rest, that are deeply embedded within the religion itself, within the core teachings of the Qur'an and of Muhammad, that lead one not toward God nor any authentic spirituality but toward absolute evil.

Professor Kreeft: Would you agree, though, at least that there are things in Islam that they have learned from Jews and Christians—not new things, the Emperor is perfectly right—that we have forgotten and that therefore we can relearn from them?

Mr. Spencer: Insofar as they are the Jewish and Christian traditions, then certainly, we should look to any pious people and say that piety is a good thing and ought to be fostered; I'm not sure we need to go to them to rediscover that kind of thing. There's plenty within our own traditions that would do that for us if we would simply recover those.

Professor Kreeft: Yes, okay. I don't think we disagree about very much.

Professor Zmirak: Mr. Spencer, you say that the only good Muslim is a bad Muslim. Presumably you mean "good" for us as Christians living in the West—in other words, "good," as to our benefit, to our safety, promoting our freedom, our ability to worship, evangelize, live in peace. But if you hope that Muslims are not true to their own religion and are not true to their own conscience, then aren't you hoping that they are disobeying the voice of conscience and therefore damning their own souls? Isn't that a perverse thing for us to hope for, and isn't it a little crass to hope that Muslims go to hell just because it makes them less likely to kill us?

(Laughter)

Mr. Spencer: It's a wonderful question, but I think there's a bit of sophistry there. I don't think that God, that the true, living, existing God who is God of all creation, would ever condemn someone to hell for doing evil that he thought was the right thing or doing the right thing that he thought was evil. There is absolute good and absolute evil. These things are clear; these things are actually relatively universal across religious traditions, with the notable exception of Islam. In *The Abolition of Man*, C. S. Lewis's book, he has an appendix, a listing of various quotations establishing what he calls the

Tao, the Way. What he is explaining are universally held moral principles among Christians, Jews, Buddhists, Hindus, etc. Very notably absent are quotations from the Qur'an and from the teachings of Muhammad that would support these otherwise universal moral principles: "Thou shalt not kill, thou shalt not steal," and so on and so on. Islam does uphold those things, but for Muslims only. Pretty much, all the [positive] things the media says about Islam are true if you add "for Muslims" at the end. "Islam is a religion of peace 'for Muslims.'" "Islam is a religion of tolerance 'for Muslims,'" and so on. So the point is that when we're talking about people following their conscience, there's a great danger, I think, the great danger of hellfire for anyone, the great danger is to become convinced that to do evil is good. And thus we should do everything we can to show them that that is a demonic deception.

Professor Kreeft: I think it is very probable indeed that it is a demonic deception, and I think it is very probable that the Qur'an is a mixture of three things. It claims to be a divine revelation; it could conceivably come from three and only three sources: the human, the demonic, or the divine. In the Catholic tradition, private revelations are not infallible; the devil loves to mess up private revelations to confuse even the saints to get whatever falsehood he can in with truths. It seems to me in the Qur'an you have a mixture of divine revelation at least influenced by, if not totally derived from, Judaism and Christianity, but maybe, maybe God sent an angel to Muhammad to get some messages through, and maybe a few of them got through, I don't know.

Mr. Spencer: So are you saying that Islam is on par with private revelation like Fatima?

Professor Kreeft: No, no, I'm saying that there may be some supernatural good as well as supernatural evil in the experience that Muhammad claims to have had in that cave mixed with Muhammad's own very human proclivities to a mixture of good and evil. Which would explain the mixture.

Mr. Spencer: Well, I don't know. I go back to the cave, and the very earliest *hadith*, the very earliest traditions about Muhammad, are all about what happened to him in that cave. It's very fascinating, because if you were a Muslim going to Muslim school to learn about Islam, then you would learn that Muhammad was praying in a cave, and the angel Gabriel appeared to him and told him to recite, and he recited. That's what 'Qur'an' means, recitation. And over the next twenty-three years he was given recitations to recite that were the words of God, the word of God, the perfect and eternal word of God that had existed forever with God in Paradise and was then being transmitted to Earth through Gabriel to Muhammad. Now, that's a very nice story, that's sort of the Sunday-school version, or, we could say, the Friday-school version.

But in the actual *hadith* about the incident, the angel is not named as an angel or as Gabriel. He is some sort of spiritual being who then presses Muhammad very hard on his chest so that he thought he was going to die and tells him to recite. And he says, "I can't, I can't read!" because he was thinking he would have to go get a printed text or written text and then recite it. And he presses him even harder and all the breath is going out of him! He's like a cosmic thug pressing on Muhammad, forcing him and saying, "Recite!" And finally Muhammad says "OK, OK!" and he goes home, and he's shaking with fear, and he says to his wife, "Cover me with a blanket," because he's shivering, and he says, "Woe is me, either poet or possessed." By poet he didn't mean Rod McKuen, he meant like someone who is receiving ecstatic demonic visions. And so, is that really the kind of story we would expect if it was Gabriel, the one who appeared to the Blessed Mother in the Gospel of Luke and tells her she's going to be the Mother of Jesus? It's a very different kind of story; it's a very different character of story. And I think that, in itself, is very telling and revealing.

Professor Kreeft: It sounds suspiciously like some of the disturbing stories in some of the early parts of the Old Testament.

Mr. Spencer: I don't know that there's any comparable story in the Old Testament. I appreciate the—

Professor Kreeft: Jacob wrestling with the angel?

Mr. Spencer: But what does the angel do to Jacob that would terrify him to thinking he's demon possessed?

Professor Kreeft: He breaks his hipbone.

Mr. Spencer: Jacob doesn't go home and say, "I think I've just been demon possessed!," does he?

Professor Zmirak: Dr. Kreeft, couldn't we learn what we need to learn from Muslims by reading their books—but nevertheless energetically fighting their attempts to assert themselves in American society, restricting their entrance into our countries and just generally fighting political Islam and protecting our own religious freedom and our own political freedom by aggressively imposing our own values on our own societies? In other words, not permitting them polygamy, not permitting them honor killing or wife beating or any of the other aspects of *sharia* that they claim to be asserting and in some cases are trying to assert in the legal system as in Great Britain; couldn't we get all this from your book? Your book tells us what we need to gain from Islam and so, "OK, fine, they can go home now."

(Laughter)

Professor Kreeft: The long and complete and nuanced version of my answer to your question is yes.

(Laughter)

Professor Zmirak: We might actually agree more than I realized.

Mr. Spencer: Yes.

(Laughter)

Professor Kreeft: On the other hand, on the other hand, I would not necessarily condemn the idea of a foundation which arose and came up with this flaky proposal. The Clash of Civilizations, Islam vs. the West, could be at least mitigated if not overcome if we simply spent some millions of dollars buying a fleet of planes and using them for a kind of double-transportation system. Let's take all our pop psychologists and put them in Muslim countries, and let's tell them to send us some fiery mullahs to give us some spine.

(Laughter)

Professor Zmirak: I like that idea better than the one [Israeli] Prime Minister [Benjamin] Netanyahu once expressed in the Knesset, that they should translate *Sex and the City* into Persian and drop the DVDs all across Iran.

(Laughter)

Mr. Spencer: What the mullahs would do if they were imported here—I mean, we're already seeing what's happening, so I don't think that that really would necessarily be a good idea. But it's interesting to note also in terms of secularism and Islam that a lot of people have the idea that—and this is absolutely germane to the point of tonight's discussion that the only good Muslim is a bad Muslim—it might not even be so that a bad Muslim is a good Muslim. Because secularism has often been posited as an antidote to all this as in, "Well, they're so pious, and their piety leads them into dangerous and violent directions, so therefore we have to make them less pious, so we'll airlift *Sex and the City* into Iran or whatever." But actually, you know, American culture is already there. And there is plenty of *Sex and the*

City all over the Islamic world, make no mistake. Charles Glass was an American journalist who wrote a very fascinating book called *Tribes with Flags* in the '80s; the book *Tribes with Flags* is an account of his crazy decision to walk from Antioch in southern Turkey to Cairo, down Lebanon into Israel all the way down. And of course in Lebanon he was kidnapped by Hezbollah and held as a hostage. And while he was there, he found that his captors were listening to Michael Jackson records and Madonna. They would come up to him and they would say, "Do you think American girls would find me attractive?"

(Laughter)

Mr. Spencer: And meanwhile they're holding the Kalashnikovs on him! And they would go and pray and *"Allahu Akbar,"* and they were going to slit his throat. It's a very straight journalistic account of what happened, but then at the end it gets very interesting because [Glass] starts having visions of the Virgin Mary who tells him how to escape from his captivity, and he does follow her directions and escapes.

Professor Kreeft: I have been told by numerous missionaries, most of them Protestants, that something is happening in the Islamic world in the last few decades that has never happened before: Conversions to Christianity are happening and almost every single one of them has to do with a vision of the Blessed Virgin Mary.

Mr. Spencer: Yes. Yes. There are visions of Mary that have appeared and been seen by really many thousands of people; it's a phenomenon.

Professor Kreeft: Zeitoun! More people saw that miracle than saw any other miracle in the entire history of the world.

Mr. Spencer: Yes.

Professor Kreeft: Two million.

Mr. Spencer: In Cairo, standing on top of a church.

Professor Kreeft: Muslims and Christians together saw the Blessed Virgin Mary.

Mr. Spencer: So, yes, something is happening.

Professor Kreeft: And she, unlike you, was making peace signs.

(Laughter)

Mr. Spencer: Oh, I'm all for peace! But I think that peace without a realistic appraisal of the situation is just naïve, and could be suicidally naïve.

Professor Kreeft: I agree, I totally agree.

(Applause)

Professor Kreeft: The only thing you've said tonight, other than your conclusions that I disagree with, I think it was just a slip of the tongue, was you spoke of absolute good and absolute evil. Now, God is certainly absolutely good, but even the devil is not absolutely evil, because God created him. So how could Islam be worse than the devil?

Mr. Spencer: I don't want to speak about the devil, he doesn't interest me. But chapter ninety-one, verse seven of the Qur'an says that God "places evil within the heart of man," which is markedly different from the Christian idea that evil is the absence of God's presence in the soul, and evil is a rejection of God, not something that God actively encourages.

Professor Kreeft: But the Bible also says, "I create good and evil," evil there being death and suffering, not moral evil.

Mr. Spencer: That's a different kind.

Professor Kreeft: Maybe the Qur'an means that.

Mr. Spencer: Well we could trade verses all night —

Professor Zmirak: Wait, are you referring to the question of free will in Islam?

Mr. Spencer: Yeah, that's just where I was going to go. In chapter thirty-two, verse thirteen of the Qur'an, Allah says "We" (he always speaks in the royal "we" even though he's an absolute unity). He says, "If We had willed, We could have guided all men to the truth. But instead We will fill Hell with djinns (genies) and men." So this is the god of Islam speaking, saying, "I could have brought everyone to a knowledge of the truth, but I just want to fill up Hell."

Professor Kreeft: But, like Augustine, most Muslims also claim to believe in free will as well as infallible predestination.

Mr. Spencer: I don't know where you're finding them, because actually the Qur'an decisively rejects the idea of free will. It says repeatedly that Allah "leads astray those who he wills," does not "allow to go astray" but he "leads astray those whom he wills and guides those whom he wills." And this verse I just quoted to you is also echoed in chapter seven, verse one-seventy-nine, which also says, "I will fill Hell with men." He could have decided to do otherwise, but he has decided to condemn people to a very luridly, lovingly, lavishly described vision of Hell in the Qur'an, and he's sending them there because he wants to.

Professor Zmirak: Perhaps, Dr. Kreeft, I can ask you this, as a former Calvinist. In the Regensburg Address, Pope Benedict was talking about commonalities between Islam and Calvinism in their rejection of the idea that we can reason about God, because analogy does not apply to God. If we cannot reason about God, there can be no theology. Pope Benedict was talking about this as the beginning of the secularization of the Western mind. It seems to me that when the Muslims rejected the Mu'tazilite option, when they rejected philosophy, they rejected Avicenna, they rejected Averroes, at the same time Thomas Aquinas was taking these thinkers and trying to reconcile faith and reason. The Muslims saw an irreparable divide, an insuperable divide, and they chose faith as opposed to reason. Pope Benedict seemed to be saying that with Calvinism and with the

Reformation, the long process began of the West rejecting faith and only accepting reason. So is there some sense in which Islam and the secular West are kind of mirror images of each other? Two broken pieces of a puzzle?

Professor Kreeft: Yes! That's very profound.

Professor Zmirak: Thank you.

(Laughter)

Professor Kreeft: Well, he didn't make it up, the pope made it up.

Professor Zmirak: I'm proud of myself for remembering it.

(Laughter)

Professor Kreeft: Robert Reilly's recent book, *The Closing of the Muslim Mind*, is very enlightening on that. It is a desperate philosophical mistake. It's nominalism.

Mr. Spencer: Yes.

Professor Zmirak: All right, are there questions from the audience?

Questioner No. 1: I'm seeing a parallel with the Sufis and their piety—which you were lauding them for—and the Pharisees and their piety, which was really dirty rags because the inside was corrupt. So that's what I put to you is the Sufis' piety.

Professor Kreeft: Even the Gospel writers didn't say that the only good Pharisee is a bad Pharisee. In fact, there were good Pharisees: Nicodemus was one of them, Joseph of Arimathea was one of them, Gamaliel was one of them, and he was St. Paul's teacher. Here you have very good Pharisees, although many of the Pharisees were wicked people.

Questioner No. 2: This is one for Mr. Spencer. Since politics is a practical art that brings together strange bedfellows, factions, and coalitions of people and persons that normally would be opposed to each other, from a purely practical standpoint, couldn't we say that the Christian West and Is-

lam, individuals or political groups or nations, we can make
a deal with the devil so to speak and cooperate with them in
the United Nations on the global front to fight the kind of
evils that Dr. Kreeft was talking about?

Mr. Spencer: Well, I don't have any objection to doing
that. Obviously, it worked in Beijing, and I think the only
hazard of it is that people don't recognize the limitations of
it. Here again, I'm all for peace, but we need to go into such
things with open eyes and understand that we're dealing
with a group that will never regard non-Muslims as their
equals and will not regard us as any more their friends because we have cooperated on these various ventures than
they would if we had not cooperated. I think, for example,
the American military's idea of going and handing out can-
dy on the streets of Baghdad and Kabul and basketballs and
going in and building hospitals and schools and roads and all
that, it's all great, but it's predicated on the idea that we will
win over their hearts and minds by doing that—as if, for
example, they hate us because we aren't being nice to them.
Or they hate us because of our immorality, or they hate us
for whatever other reason, when actually if you go back to
the Qur'an it says, "Fight against the Jews and Christians,"
not just the "immoral Jews and Christians" or "the Jews and
Christians whose foreign policy you dislike" or something
like that. Just, "Fight against the Jews and Christians." So
for a Muslim who takes that seriously, ultimately no accord
is possible unless we submit or convert.

Questioner No. 3: We often find here in the media when
there's an event such as the Christmas Day Bomber or Fort
Hood, that the Muslim has been radicalized—either one or
both. What is it that radicalized them?

Professor Kreeft: Well, I know how Bob's going to answer that question: "They haven't been radicalized because

Islam is essentially radical. They haven't been turned into radicals from being moderate Muslims, rather moderate Muslims probably began by being more radical Muslims and then softened their religion." And that's probably historically true. But we certainly can hope for a softening of Muslims as has happened before in history; it can happen again, because Islam is like Protestantism. It has a Bible, but there are so many different interpretations of it possible without an infallible magisterium that there are no preset limits on emphases or interpretations that could be in the future. I don't personally hold much hope for a moderate and liberal Islam suddenly arising in our lifetime, but it's not intrinsically impossible, so I think we should encourage any movement in that direction.

Mr. Spencer: What radicalizes Muslims? It's generally an appeal to Qur'anic texts and teachings; it's generally a call, saying, "You are not being a good Muslim unless you do this." Chapter nine, verse 111 of the Qur'an guarantees Paradise to those who "kill and are killed for Allah." And this is used today by suicide bombing recruiters to get people to strap bombs on themselves. They go kill some infidels, they get killed in the process, they're guaranteed a place in Paradise. And that's a very powerful inducement if you really believe that this is how things work. Now, what would soften these things—I wouldn't say it's impossible, but Islam, we should know in the first place, is not really like Protestantism at all. Protestantism, as far as I understand it, operates on the principle of, "The Bible alone is the authority," and so anybody can read it and come to a different view, because no book interprets itself. But in Islam, there are authorities. There are the *ulama* of various countries, the religious scholars who issue *fatawa*, which are considered binding upon those within the jurisdiction. There are the schools of jurisprudence, the *mad-*

hhahib. There are nine of those. Incidentally, eight of those nine do admit to utility of artificial contraception, and so that's something that they differ [on] from the teaching of the Catholic Church. The teaching authority of those schools of jurisprudence is considered to be binding upon the Muslims who adhere to one or the other of the schools, although it's not a matter of conversion or some kind of rupture if one moves from one to the other. They're regionally distributed, and generally, if you grow up in one area then you interpret the Qur'an according to the teachings of these various schools. As I said before, there is no sect or school that doesn't teach the necessity to wage war on unbelievers and subjugate them. Could there arise some kind of Islam in the future that didn't teach that or actively rejected it? I suppose anything is possible, but it would have to come with a wholesale rejection of Qur'anic literalism, and they would have to be considered by traditional and mainstream Muslims to be bad Muslims.

Professor Zmirak: They would have to be like Jesuits at Boston College?

Professor Kreeft: Exactly!

(Laughter)

Professor Zmirak: Maybe the Jesuits can help soften up the Muslims.

Questioner No. 4: Isn't the real problem with the fact that Europe doesn't have enough young men—they can't replace themselves—and the fact that Europe will be Muslim in thirty years and Germany will be totally Muslim in fifty years, is that the real problem? It seems to me that with what Peter Kreeft said, "I bring the student here and he understands, he's respectful," then I think about what happened two days ago or three days ago in Iraq.

Professor Zmirak: The slaughter in the Catholic Church in Baghdad?

Questioner No. 4: With Peter Kreeft, isn't it possible he could be back—he might even have been in the church two days ago! They're schizophrenic. Here in the United States they're perfectly—it's part of the faith that says when you're outnumbered to be a pacifist. When they're amongst themselves, when they're in a group, they seem to lose control. So how do we handle that? What is our philosophy? How do we address that practical problem?

Mr. Spencer: I would like to amplify just a bit a couple of these points, because Dr. Kreeft said earlier that most Muslims don't practice polygamy, don't practice these other elements of the faith that we would consider to be noxious and I think are objectively so. Actually, that's not entirely true. Actually, even by most recent accounts—I believe, was it 20,000 or 30,000 polygamous families in the United States that are Muslim. It was very noteworthy, that Ibrahim Hooper of the Council on American-Islamic Relations—which is a Hamas-linked Muslim Brotherhood front group that masquerades as a moderate organization—actually said in response to that news item: "Yes, there is polygamy among Muslims in the United States, and Islamic scholars differ as to whether it's permissible." Notice, he didn't say anything about American law making it illegal. He didn't seem to care about that at all, it was only "Islamic scholars." And also, just today in San Diego, there was an Islamic cleric, a preacher of nonviolence and tolerance well regarded in his community named Mohamed MohamedMohamud, I'm not making that up.

(Laughter)

Mr. Spencer: And Mohamed MohamedMohamud was arrested today for aiding the jihad in Somalia. And so what are we to do about this? The first thing we would have to do is assess it realistically and understand that, really, anybody who professes the Islamic faith, if he delves into the teachings of his own religion, is somebody who could end up being very dangerous to us. Now, that doesn't mean that people should be rounded up and put into camps or any of this nonsense, but we need to enforce our own laws about sedition and to formulate some sane immigration policies and recognize this as an ideological conflict and not some sort of a problem with "racism" or all these things that usually cloud these issues.

Professor Kreeft: May I ask you a question?

Mr. Spencer: Certainly.

Professor Kreeft: Which do you think is worse in the Eyes of God: Muslim polygamy or the fruit of the Enlightenment by which we say that a man can marry a man?

Mr. Spencer: You know, it's very interesting that in Dr. Kreeft's book, he has a chapter about marriage and writes very movingly, as he can do so well, about the nature of marriage. And he has the Muslim expatiating upon the nature of marriage and the respect that a husband should have for his wife and the respect that a wife should have for her husband and so on. The interesting thing to note, however, is that is not the concept of Islamic marriage at all. In Islamic marriage, the woman is essentially chattel, and actually the word for marriage in Islam is an obscenity in Arabic. I'm not making this up, but the theological term for marriage in Islam is a word that people don't say in polite company. And it's because it's really a degraded idea. And so when you ask me "Which one is worse?" I think that both are deviations from the kind of mutual respect and mutual self-giving that the Catholic Church envisions as a marriage.

Professor Kreeft: But doesn't the Qur'an also say that you can have four wives, but only if you can respect all of them and do justice to all of them?

Mr. Spencer: It doesn't say respect all of them, it says you can have four wives—I happen to have it right here—it says you can have four wives if you can treat them all equally. In other words, if you treat them all the same, if you're beastly to all of them—

(Laughter)

Mr. Spencer: —then you can have them. It doesn't say anything about respect.

Questioner No. 5: First of all, I'd like to say that it's nice to be at a college where we can have a debate on Islam where the faculty and students are not outside shouting obscenities.

(Applause)

Mr. Spencer: I was at Temple University in Philadelphia just last month and there were protestors outside shouting about racism and how I was such a terrible person and we could barely hear ourselves in there.

Questioner No. 5: So what I would like to address is this growing allegiance between right-wing Islam and not only the American Left but the global Left on an ideological level. And a recent example is when Bill O'Reilly went on *The View*, a left-of-center show, and he mentioned that we were attacked by Muslims on 9/11, Joy Behar got up and walked out. And right after that, Juan Williams was fired from NPR for saying he gets nervous when he sees Muslims getting on an airplane. So I'm sure it's something most of us innately feel, and so I'm trying to figure out if you guys have any thoughts on this growing—because I feel browbeaten any time I want to speak about Islam in public, and sometimes I feel like my life might be in danger because of it. So why the alliance?

Professor Zmirak: Well, I'd like to point out that Al-Qaeda has issued a *fatwa* against Mr. Spencer, and he's number four on their list of targeted Americans. That's why he has a bodyguard here tonight. I would like both of you to be able to respond to that: Why would the Left feel an affinity with Islam? It seems bizarre to us. Do you have any insight, Professor Kreeft?

Professor Kreeft: Yeah: because the Left wants to feel an affinity with everybody.

(Laughter)

Mr. Spencer: Except us.

Professor Kreeft: Absolutely right, except us.

(Laughter)

Mr. Spencer: The Left hates America, and because the Left hates America and because they see the Islamic jihadists hate America, they see a friend there. They see someone they can cooperate with. And also the Left doesn't understand religion, doesn't take religion seriously and thinks, "Well, yes, they're nutty religious people, but we can control that. We'll take care of that after we've defeated the real enemy."

Professor Kreeft: Dinesh D'Souza wrote a book called *The Enemy at Home*, one of the best books I've ever read—

Mr. Spencer: One of the worst books I've ever read.

(Laughter)

Professor Zmirak: All right, you guys can duke it out now.

Professor Kreeft: I heard Dinesh debate Alan Wolfe at Boston College, and it was the most one-sided thing I've ever seen, the most embarrassing debate I've ever heard, and Boston College since the debate refused to put the transcript out because Dinesh totally demolished Alan Wolfe, who was a classic Liberal who says, "We're all equal, why can't we just get along?"

Mr. Spencer: Well, certainly I wasn't at the debate. I have debated Dinesh myself, you can see the debate on YouTube if you're interested, we were debating because Dinesh contends in his book, *The Enemy at Home*, that essentially Britney Spears caused 9/11.

(Laughter)

Professor Kreeft: That's not that far off!

Mr. Spencer: That the American pop culture going into the Islamic world made these straitlaced moral people rise up and strike back against us. That, of course, completely ignores—and I don't think Dinesh is even aware of—the fact that they were fighting jihads against us before pop culture was immoral. As a matter of fact, it's noteworthy, Sayyid Qutb, one of the key theorists of the Muslim Brotherhood, came to the United States in 1948 and spent two years here in Colorado. And he wrote about his experiences in America and how they hardened his understanding that America had to be destroyed and it was this deeply immoral principality. And in 1948, Doris Day was on top of the pop charts. The idea that that kind of thing was immoral actually betrays the fact that if you look back even in Crusader literature, you find that the Islamic world generally always thinks of the Christian world as immoral. And the immorality is ultimately beside the point because, as I said before, the teachings of Islam say, "Fight the Jews and Christians." It doesn't say, "Leave the moral ones alone and only fight the immoral ones." It says, "Fight the Jews and Christians."

Professor Kreeft: Is the difference, then, between the Muslims and the Christians [is] that during the Crusades, Muslims put chastity belts on their men and it said, "Make war, not love?"

Questioner No. 6: I was wondering, what difference [is] there between our concept, the Christian concept, of the ultimate beatitude, heaven, and the Muslim concept of that, and what effect that may have on motivations like you mentioned earlier, "to lose your life" or "take a life for Allah"?

Mr. Spencer: Charles de Foucauld, who is a blessed now, lived in North Africa and was killed by jihadis there. Earlier in his life, before he dedicated himself to that kind of life in North Africa, he essentially was a libertine. And when he looked at the Islamic idea of Paradise, when he first encountered Muslims and the Qur'anic teaching about Paradise and the afterlife, he said he had tasted those pleasures and he knew they were not the ultimate good and not the ultimate joy and not the ultimate happiness, and so he knew that Islam was not the true faith, because he knew that the soul needed something else. But the Islamic vision of Paradise is, just as you may already have heard, it's essentially what you might expect a 14-year-old boy to dream up as being the highest good.

(Laughter)

Mr. Spencer: Lots of girls, lots of cool breezes, lots to drink, it's a pleasure palace!

Professor Kreeft: It sounds like Boston College!

(Laughter)

Professor Zmirak: I wonder why they don't go to Vegas?

Mr. Spencer: You could start a successful nightclub and call it 'Muslim Paradise.' It'd be very pious.

(Laughter)

Professor Kreeft: I think when the pious Muslim gets to Paradise he will indeed find forty virgins, but they will be nuns.

(Laughter)

Questioner No. 7: I'm curious to hear from both of the panelists what our public policy should look like with respect to Muslim practice in the United States.

Professor Kreeft: No question: even-handed equal protection, equal rights, no privileges, nothing special. Here is American law: it is not Muslim or anti-Muslim; it is not Christian or anti-Christian. It's based on universal human rights. If they don't like it, too bad!

Mr. Spencer: I'm all for that.

Questioner No. 7: Well, there were jokes about enforcing sedition laws and—

Professor Kreeft: I will support the right of Muslims to build a mosque or Muslim center by 9/11; I would also support the right of an anti-Muslim or Jewish organization to put something right next to it.

Audience member: In Saudi Arabia?

Professor Kreeft: Yes.

Mr. Spencer: I believe absolutely in human rights and in the United States Constitution and that Muslims should be accorded all those rights. That doesn't mean, however, that the supremacists' initiatives, including the triumphal mosque at Ground Zero, should be allowed; that's not really a religious freedom issue at all. It's a question of whether a mosque like the Dome of the Rock (built on the site of the Jewish Temple) or like the Hagia Sophia (converted from the grandest church in Christendom) should be allowed to mark the victory of Muslims on 9/11—which is how it will be understood in the Islamic world.

But that's a side issue: What should we do in terms of public policy? Dr. Kreeft is right: Enforce our laws and not accord any special rights, which Muslims are pressing for today in all kinds of ways, to Muslims or anyone else. And if we did that, then a lot of this problem would be solved. There's also an example, I think, for us in how the MacArthur occupation government in Japan after World War II treated state Shinto. Shintoism was the militaristic fuel that fueled the Japanese war machine; the militaristic ideology. And after World War II, when MacArthur was in charge in Japan, he said, "Shintoism as an individual religious faith should not be interfered with at all, but Shintoism will have no place in the government or in making public policy with preference over any other group.

Questioner No. 7: Well, wasn't a major crux of your argument that orthodox Muslim practice encourages this bad behavior?

Mr. Spencer: Yeah. And so what you have here is a situation where we have to understand that there are elements of orthodox Muslim practice that Muslims are going to have to give up in the United States because they are not in accord with American law. And that is not something that is without precedent, and it is not something that's against the First Amendment. Look at Mormon polygamy, which has come up already. The United States government did not hesitate to outlaw polygamy, even though it was a religious tenet of the Church of Jesus Christ of Latter-day Saints. And this was considered to be something within the national interest. I don't think it's the least incompatible with the First Amendment to understand that there are certain elements of Islam which Muslims must not practice in the United States because they are against the national interest and in contradiction to the freedoms guaranteed to us by the U.S. Constitution.

(Applause)

Questioner No. 8: I was wondering if you could answer this. I'm sure you're probably at least familiar with the supremacy clause in the Qur'an that says that in order to honor Allah you must kill all the infidels, first the Saturdays and then the Sundays. So how is it that you would justify that statement that it is easier to work with the Enlightenmentists [sic] when their view, the Muslim's view, is inherently contradictory to Judeo-Christian values, where the Enlightenment's view is not?

Professor Zmirak: OK, first, you had a clarification?

Mr. Spencer: Yeah, I did, I wanted to point out that the Qur'an does *not* say to kill all the infidels, it says actually to kill the *mushrikeen*, which are the polytheists, those who commit *shirk*, which is the association of partners with Allah. Usually, but not universally, Jews and Christians are not considered to be *mushrikun*, they are considered to be "People of the Book." And the People of the Book have a third option; they don't have to be killed or converted. They can be subjugated as *dhimmis*. Ultimately, however, there is a *hadith* that is very pernicious where Muhammad says, "The end times will not come until Muslims kill Jews. And the Jews hide behind trees and the trees cry out and say, 'O Muslim, there is a Jew hiding behind me, come and kill him.'" Now that is an authenticated *hadith*, that is, one that is considered to be part of Islamic doctrine. And so it is considered to be a laudable practice for a Muslim to kill a Jew, because it is something that hastens the coming of the end times, in which all things will be consummated. But anyway, it's not specifically in the Qur'an like that, that's all.

Professor Zmirak: Did you want to respond?

Professor Kreeft: Well, most Muslims in the West do not believe or practice that. And I suppose Bob must be right in saying that if everything in the Qur'an must be accepted literally and practiced, then these are bad Muslims. So in that sense I agree with him that the best Muslim is a bad Muslim.

Appendix

Some Fundamental Differences Between Islam and Christianity

I. The Nature of God

Islam: One single person, an absolute unity.

Christianity: Three persons, Father, Son, and Holy Spirit.

Islam: Creator and master of all, but not a father. Human beings are his slaves.

Christianity: Father of all creation.

Islam: No free will. Allah chooses to send people to hell rather than guide them to the truth.

Christianity: Free will. God desires all people to be saved and come to the knowledge of the truth.

Islam: Allah places inclinations to both good and evil within the soul.

Christianity: God is good and created man good; evil is the rejection of God.

Islam: No limits can be placed upon the sovereignty of Allah, the absolute monarch, including even consistency.

Christianity: God is good and consistent in his actions.

II. Jesus

Islam: Jesus is a Muslim prophet, and a human being like any other.

Christianity: Jesus is the Son of God, both divine and human.

Islam: Jesus was not crucified, but it seemed to the Jews as if he was. He did not die on the cross and so did not rise from the dead and is not anyone's Savior.

Christianity: Jesus was crucified for our sins and rose from the dead to save us from our sins.

Islam: Jesus is a human prophet, the nephew of Moses.

Christianity: Jesus is the divine Son, and foster-son of St. Joseph.

Islam: Jesus announces that Muhammad will come after him and guide mankind to all truth.

Christianity: Jesus announces that the Holy Spirit will come after him and guide mankind to all truth.

Islam: Jesus will return at the end of the world, destroy Christianity, and Islamize the world.

Christianity: Jesus will return at the end of the world to initiate the divine judgment.

III. Divine Revelation

Islam: The biblical prophets were all Muslims who taught Islam. Their messages were twisted and hijacked to create what we know as Judaism and Christianity.

Christianity: The biblical prophets were all Jews who were preparing the way for the coming of Christ.

IV. The Moral Law

Islam: There are no moral absolutes beyond what is good for the advance and defense of Islam.

Christianity: There are moral absolutes; e.g., those delineated in the Ten Commandments and the precepts derived therefrom.

Islam: Deception of unbelievers is allowed when believers are at war or under other kinds of pressure.

Christianity: Mental reservation allowed in extreme cases, but never outright deception.

Islam: The goods of the unbelievers may be taken as the spoils of war, and unbelievers subjugated under Islamic rule must pay a special tax from which Muslims are exempt.

Christianity: Theft, like any intrinsically immoral act, is never justified.

Islam: Muslims' lives are more valuable than those of non-Muslims.

Christianity: All human beings are equal in dignity before God.

Islam: Virtue is enforced in society by the threat of draconian punishments.

Christianity: Virtue involves the free choice of the good.

Islam: Many Islamic scholars find no Islamic prohibition for artificial contraception.

Christianity: Artificial contraception is a sin against the purposes of marriage.

Islam: Abortion is permitted through the first trimester and, according to some scholars, beyond that point.

Christianity: Abortion is murder.

Islam: A man may marry up to four wives.

Christianity: A man cleaves to his wife and they become one flesh.

Islam: A man may divorce his wife by saying, "You are divorced."

Christianity: "What God has joined together, let no man put asunder."

Islam: A man may buy sex slaves and keep them in addition to his wives.

Christianity: Slavery of any kind is contrary to the dignity of the human person.

Islam: In Shi'ite Islam, a man may enter into a temporary marriage, a marriage with a specified ending point.

Christianity: Marriage is indissoluble.

About the author

Robert Spencer is the director of Jihad Watch (www.ji-hadwatch.org), a program of the David Horowitz Freedom Center, and the author of twelve books, including two *New York Times* best sellers, *The Truth about Muhammad* and *The Politically Incorrect Guide to Islam (and the Crusades)*. Spencer, a Melkite Greek Catholic, has led seminars on Islam and ji-had for the United States Central Command, United States Army Command and General Staff College, the U.S. Army's Asymmetric Warfare Group, the FBI, the Joint Terrorism Task Force, and the U.S. intelligence community.

Endnotes

1   Quotations from the Qur'an are taken from A. J. Arberry, *The Koran Interpreted* (London: George Allen & Unwin Ltd., 1955).

2   Peter Kreeft, *Ecumenical Jihad* (San Francisco, Ignatius Press, 1996), 26.

3   Ibid., 30.

4   "Religion and Ethics in Global Women's Issues," Santa Clara University, November 6, 2009. http://www.scu.edu/ethics-center/world-affairs/systems/WomensIssues.cfm

5   Barbara Crossette, "Vatican Drops Fight Against U.N. Population Document," *New York Times*, September 10, 1994.

6   Donna Lee Bowen, "Abortion, Islam, and the 1994 Cairo Population Conference," *International Journal of Middle East Studies* 29(2), 1997, 161.

7   Jeff Schogol, "McChrystal denies claims of secret military crusade against Islam," *Stars and Stripes*, January 21, 2011.

8   "Priest says Muslim extremists want to rid Middle East of Christians," Catholic News Agency, December 19, 2010.

9   "6 dead in religion-torn central Nigerian region," Associated Press, January 24, 2011.

10   Aid to the Church in Need, "Religious Freedom in the Majority Islamic Countries 1998 Report: Iraq." http://www.alleanzacattolica.org/acs/acs_english/report_98/iraq.htm.

11   Bridget Johnson, "Bipartisan effort pressures Obama to help Iraq's Christians," *The Hill*, December 25, 2010.

12   "Baghdad church hostage drama ends in bloodbath," BBC, November 1, 2010.

13   "Death toll in Egypt church bomb blast rises to 22," Press Trust of India, January 3, 2011.

14   "Egypt on alert as Copts gather for Christmas Eve," BBC, January 6, 2011.

15   "Sunni Islam's al-Azhar freezes talks with the Vatican," Deutsche Presse Agentur, January 20, 2011.

16   "Al-Azhar asks Coptic Church to denounce US religious discrimination claims," Al Masry Al Youm, November 26, 2010.

17   "Egypt recalls Vatican envoy over pope remarks," Agence France-Presse, January 11, 2011.

18   Rick Westhead, "Some Christians in Pakistan convert fear into safety," *Toronto Star*, January 20, 2011.

19   "Punjab governor Salman Taseer assassinated in Islamabad," BBC, January 4, 2011.

20   "Pope insults Muslims, say MPs," *The Times*, January 12, 2011.

21   "Pakistan: Islamists criticise Pope's anti-blasphemy law comments," Adn Kronos International, January 11, 2011.

22   Muhammed Ibn Ismaiel Al-Bukhari, *Sahih al-Bukhari: The Translation of the Meanings*, translated by Muhammad M. Khan, Darussalam, 1997, vol. 9, book 84, no. 57.

23   *Reliance of the Traveller*, o8.1, o8.4.

24   IslamOnline.net, April 2006. www.islamonline.net/English/contemporary/2006/04/article01c.shtml##top3. This article has been removed from the IslamOnline site, but is quoted in Robert Spencer, "Death to the Apostates," FrontPageMagazine.com, October 24, 2006.

25   "One-legged Afghan Red Cross worker set to be hanged after converting to Christianity," *Daily Mail*, February 7, 2011; Sayed Salahuddin, "Man faces death over Christianity," Reuters, March 19, 2006.

26   Afghanistan Constitution, Adopted by Grand Council on January 4, 2004. http://
      www.servat.unibe.ch/law/icl/af00000_.html.

27   Tim Albone, "Anger over Christian convert in Kabul who faces death," *The Times*,
      March 21, 2006.

28   Maggie Michael, "Threats force Egyptian convert to hide," Associated Press, August
      12, 2007.

29   Abdallah Daher, Sarah Pollak & Dale Hurd, "Ex-Muslim on the Run for Conversion,"
      CBN News, March 27, 2008.

30   David Pryce-Jones, *The Closed Circle: An Interpretation of the Arabs* (Chicago: Ivan R.
      Dee, 2002), 31-2.

31   Stephen Farrell and Rana Sabbagh Gargour, "'All my staff at the church have been
      killed—they disappeared,'" *The Times*, December 23, 2006.

32   Middle East Media Research Institute (MEMRI), "Islamist Leader in London: No
      Universal Jihad As Long As There is No Caliphate," MEMRI Special Dispatch No.
      435, October 30, 2002.

33   Jonathan Adelman and Agota Kuperman, "Christian Exodus from the Middle East,"
      Foundation for the Defense of Democracies, December 19, 2001. Reprinted at www.
      defenddemocracy.org/publications/publications_show.htm?doc_id=155713.

34   Middle East Media Research Institute (MEMRI), "Friday Sermons in Saudi Mosques:
      Review and Analysis," MEMRI Special Report No. 10, September 26, 2002. www.
      memri.org. This sermon is undated, but it recently appeared on the Saudi website
      www.alminbar.net.

35   Sonia Verma, "First Catholic Church Opens in Qatar, Sparking Fear of Backlash
      Against Christians," Fox News, March 14, 2008.

36   Carmel Crimmins, "Philippines' Islamic city proud to be different," Reuters, March
      17, 2008.

37   This sermon is undated. Like the others quoted here, it was posted at the Saudi website
      Al-Minbar (www.alminbar.net).

38   Etgar Lefkovits, "Expert: 'Christian groups in PA to disappear,'" *Jerusalem Post*, De-
      cember 4, 2007.

39   Amnesty International Report 2007: Egypt. http://thereport.amnesty.org/eng/Re-
      gions/Middle-East-and-North-Africa/Egypt.

40   "Sectarian tensions flare in Egypt," BBC News, April 16, 2006.

41   Amnesty International Report 2007: Indonesia. http://thereport.amnesty.org/eng/
      Regions/Asia-Pacific/Indonesia.

42   "We Are the Church of Islam," Interview with the patriarch of Antioch Grégoire III
      Laham by Gianni Valente, *30 Days*, April 2006.

43   Mohammed Zaatari, "Sidon archdiocese reopens following refurbishment," *Daily Star*,
      December 6, 2010.

44   Amin Maalouf, *The Crusades Through Arab Eyes* (New York: Schocken Books, 1984), 179.

45   Quoted in Thomas Madden, *The New Concise History of the Crusades* (Lanham, Mary-
      land: Rowman & Littlefield, 2005), 76.

46   Ibid., 78.

47   Ibn Kathir, *Tafsir Ibn Kathir* (Abridged) (Riyadh: Darussalam, 2000), vol. 4, 133.

48   Muhammad Aashiq Ilahi Bulandshahri, *Illuminating Discourses on the Noble Qur'an*
      (*Tafsir Anwarul Bayan*), translated by Afzal Hussain Elias and Muhammad Arshad
      Fakhri (Karachi: Darul-Ishaat, 2005), vol. 2, 291.

49   Will Lester, "Poll: Fewer People Link Islam, Violence," Associated Press, July 26, 2005.

50 Ibn Kathir, *Tafsir Ibn Kathir* (Abridged), vol. 1, Darussalam, 2000, 87.

51 *The Navarre Bible: The Pentateuch* (Princeton: Scepter Publishers, 1999), 48.

52 Sahih Muslim 6325.

53 "Ask the Religion Experts: Are people inherently sinful?" *Ottawa Citizen*, February 19, 2012.

54 www.whitehouse.gov/the-press-office/2011/11/05/statement-president-hajj-and-eid-al-adha.

55 George W. Bush, Message on the observance of Eid al-Adha, January 8, 2007.

56 Jalalu'd-Din al-Mahalli and Jalalu'd-Din as-Suyuti, *Tafsir al-Jalalayn*, translated by Aisha Bewley (London: Dar Al Taqwa Ltd., 2007), 1194.

57 *Ecumenical Jihad*, 30.

58 Gregory VII, Letter to Anzir, King of Mauritania (1076), in J. Neuner and J. Dupuis, *The Christian Faith in the Doctrinal Documents of the Catholic Church* (New York: Alba House, 1996), 380.

59 Nicole Winfield, "Pope marks 50th anniversary of Vatican II, seeks to correct errors that emerged," Associated Press, October 11, 2012.

60 Pope Benedict XIV, *Quod Provinciale*, Aug. 1, 1754, in *The Papal Encyclicals*, edited by Claudia Carlen (Ypsilanti, Michigan, Pierian Press, 1981), vol. 1 (1740-1878), 49-50.

61 Von Pastor, *History of the Popes*, II, 346; quoted in Warren H. Carroll, *A History of Christendom*, vol. 3, *The Glory of Christendom* (Front Royal, Virginia: Christendom Press, 1993), 571.

62 Jalalu'd-Din al-Mahalli and Jalalu'd-Din as-Suyuti, *Tafsir al-Jalalayn*, translated by Aisha Bewley (London: Dar Al Taqwa Ltd., 2007), 524.

63 "Ask the Religion Experts: Are people inherently sinful?," *Ottawa Citizen*, February 19, 2012.

64 Ibn Kathir, vol. 1, 120.

65 *Tafsir al-Jalalayn*, 941.

66 *Tanwir al-Miqbas min Tafsiribn Abbas*, translated by Mokrane Guezzou, 36:9. www.al-tafsir.com.

67 Ibn Kathir, vol. 8, 171.

68 Ibn Kathir, vol. 8, 172.

69 Ignaz Goldziher, *Introduction to Islamic Theology and Law*, translated by Andras and Ruth Hamori (Princeton: Princeton University Press, 1981), 82.

70 G. F. Haddad, "The Qadariyya, Mu'tazila, and Shi'a," *Living Islam*, www.livingislam.org/n/qms_e.html.

71 Sayyid Abul A'la Maududi, *Towards Understanding the Qur'an*, translated and edited by Zafar Ishaq Ansari (Leicester: The Islamic Foundation, 2008), 955.

72 St. Thomas Aquinas, *Summa Contra Gentiles*, Book Two: Creation, translated by James F. Anderson. (Notre Dame, Indiana: University of Notre Dame Press, 1975), ch. 25, sec. 14.

73 Rodney Stark, *The Victory of Reason* (New York: Random House, 2005), 22-23.

74 Stanley L. Jaki, *Chance or Reality and Other Essays* (Lanham, Maryland and London: University Press of America; BrynMawr, Pa.: The Intercollegiate Studies Inc., 1986), 242.

75 Abu Hamid al-Ghazali, *The Incoherence of the Philosophers*, translated by Michael E. Marmura. (Provo, Utah: Brigham Young University Press, 2000), 2.

76 Ibid., 8.

77 Tilman Nagel, *The History of Islamic Theology from Muhammad to the Present*, translated by Thomas Thornton, (Princeton: Markus Wiener Publishers, 2000), 211.

78 Al-Ghazali, 226. Emphasis added.

79   Stanley Jaki, *The Savior of Science* (Washington, D.C.: Regnery Gateway, 1988), 43.

80   Rodney Stark, *The Victory of Reason* (New York: Random House, 2005), 20-21.

81   Stanley Jaki, *The Savior of Science* (Washington, D.C.: Regnery Gateway, 1988), 56.

82   Ibrahim Hooper, "Love for Jesus can bring Christians, Muslims together," *Washington Post*, December 17, 2010.

83   "Muslims Publish 'Jesus' Ad," *World Net Daily*, March 24, 2004.

84   "The Second Treatise of the Great Seth," translated by Roger A. Bullard and Joseph A. Gibbons, in *The Nag Hammadi Library*, James M. Robinson, general editor (Leiden: E.J. Brill, 1988), 365.

85   Bulandshahri, vol. 2, 8.

86   Ibn Kathir, vol. 3, 26-27.

87   For example, the Qu'ran says the Jews "had disbelieved the signs of God and slain the Prophets unrightfully" (2:61; cf. 3:21, 3:112). Allah tells Muhammad to ask them: "Why then were you slaying the Prophets of God in former time, if you were believers?" (2:91).

88   Tanwîr al-Miqbâs min Tafsîr Ibn'Abbâs for 19:33. www.altafsir.com.

89   *Sahih Muslim*, translated by Abdul Hamid Siddiqi (New Delhi: Kitab Bhavan, revised edition 2000), book 25, no. 5326.

90   *Tafsir al-Jalalayn*, 130.

91   Christoph Luxenberg, "Christmas in the Koran," translated by Ibn Warraq. Unpublished. An abridged version of this article was first published in German in *Imprimatur*, No. 1, March 2003, 13-17.

92   Samir Khalil Samir, "The Theological Christian Influence On the Qur'an," in *The Qur'an in Its Historical Context*, Gabriel Said Reynolds, editor (New York: Routledge, 2008), 35-36.

93   *Tanwir al-Miqbas min Tafsiribn Abbas*, translated by Mokrane Guezzou, 3:45. www.al-tafsir.com.

94   Ibn Kathir, vol. 2, 160.

95   "Gospel of Thomas Greek Text A," from *The Apocryphal New Testament*, translated by M.R. James (Oxford: Clarendon Press, 1924). http://wesley.nnu.edu/biblical_studies/noncanon/gospels/inftoma.htm.

96   Abdullah Yusuf Ali, *The Meaning of The Holy Qur'an* (Beltsville, Maryland: Amana Publications, 1999), 1461.

97   Ibn Ishaq, *The Life of Muhammad: A Translation of Ibn Ishaq's Sirat Rasul Allah*, translated by Alfred Guillaume (Oxford: Oxford University Press, 1955), 410.

98   Ibn Ishaq, 402-403.

99   "Friday Sermons in Saudi Mosques: Review and Analysis," *Middle East Media Research Institute*, Special Report No. 10, September 26, 2002.

100   Muhammed Ibn Ismail Al-Bukhari, *Sahih al-Bukhari: The Translation of the Meanings*, trans. Muhammad M. Khan (Riyadh: Darussalam, 1997), vol. 3, book 46, no. 2476.

101   Ibn Kathir, vol. 3, 32.

102   Abdullah Yusuf Ali, "On the *Injil*," *The Meaning of the Holy Qur'an* (Beltsville, Maryland: Amana Publications, 1999), 291.

103   Reza Kahlili, "Iran: Discovery Will Collapse Christianity," World Net Daily, May 23, 2012.

104   "How the Gospel of Barnabas Survived," March 23, 2008, *The Gospel of Barnabas*, www.barnabas.net/how-the-gospel-of-barnabas-survived.html.

105   Lonsdale and Laura Ragg, *The Gospel of Barnabas* (New Delhi: Islamic Book Service, n.d.), 103-104.

106 *The Gospel of Barnabas*, 104.

107 Ibid., 106.

108 Peter Kreeft, *Between Allah and Jesus* (Downers Grove, Illinois: IVP Books, 2010), 11-12.

109 Dinesh D'Souza, *The Enemy At Home* (New York: Doubleday, 2007), 15.

110 Sharia states base their entire criminal code upon Islamic law, criminalizing sins such as adultery, apostasy, and blasphemy, and prescribing for them the punishments that are mandated in the Qur'an and Sunnah. The most notable Sharia states today are Saudi Arabia and Iran.

111 Saeed Kamali Dehghan, "Necklace ban for men as Tehran's 'moral police' enforce dress code," *The Guardian*, June 14, 2011.

112 John Geoghegan, "Widow of suicide bomber is arrested by terror squad on suspicion of helping husband plan attack on Christmas shoppers," *Daily Mail*, September 15, 2011.

113 Ibn Ishaq, 287-288.

114 Ibid., 288.

115 For example, 2 Corinthians 6:14: "Do not be mismated with unbelievers. For what partnership have righteousness and iniquity?"

116 Sahih Muslim, book 32, no. 6309.

117 Bukhari, vol. 4, book 56, no. 3030; Muslim, vol. 4, book 32, no. 6303.

118 Ibn Kathir, vol. 2, 141-42.

119 Ibn Kathir, vol. 5, 530.

120 Maududi, *Towards Understanding the Qur'an*, 72.

121 *Catholic Encyclopedia*, "Mental Reservation." www.newadvent.org/cathen/10195b.htm.

122 IbnSa'd, *Kitab Al-Tabaqat Al-Kabir*, vol. I, S. MoinulHaqand H K. Ghazanfar, translators (New Delhi: KitabBhavan, n.d.), vol. I, 328.

123 Ibn Sa'd, vol. I, 328-329.

124 Bukhari, vol. 4, book 58, no. 3162.

125 "Muslims Forcing Christian Assyrians in Baghdad Neighborhood to Pay 'Protection Tax,'" Assyrian International News Agency, March 18, 2007.

126 "Egyptian Salafi Leader Yassir Al-Burhami Compares the Christians of Egypt to the Jews of Al-Medina," Middle East Media Research Institute, December 3, 2011.

127 "Yohanna Qulta, Deputy Patriarch of the Coptic Catholic Church in Egypt: If the Salafis Come to Power and Instate the Jizya Poll Tax, We Will Oppose This to the Point of Martyrdom," Middle East Media Research Institute, December 10, 2011.

128 Bruce Bawer, *While Europe Slept* (New York: Doubleday, 2006), 30.

129 Faraz Rabbani, "Zakat Cannot Be Given to Non-Muslims," Qibla, n.d. http://qa.sunnipath.com/issue_view.asp?HD=1&ID=1527&CATE=5.

130 *Reliance of the Traveller*, 4.9. This manual of Islamic law is certified by one of the highest authorities in Sunni Islam as conforming to the practice and faith of the orthodox Sunni community.

131 Sultanhussein Tabandeh, *A Muslim Commentary on the Universal Declaration of Human Rights*, translated by F. J. Goulding (London: F. T. Goulding and Co., 1970), 18.

132 Bulandshahri, vol. 1, 235.

133 Pope Benedict XVI, Post-Synodal Apostolic Exhortation *Ecclesia In Media Oriente*, September 14, 2012. www.vatican.va/holy_father/benedict_xvi/apost_exhortations/documents/hf_ben-xvi_exh_20120914_ecclesia-in-medio-oriente_en.html.

134 "Hilali in hot water again," *The Age*, January 11, 2007.

135 Bukhari, vol. 6, book 65, no. 4556.

136 As-Suyuti, *Al-Itqanfii Ulum al-Qur'an*, p. 524, in Gilchrist.

137 Bukhari, vol. 8, book 82, no. 816.

138 Quoted in Amir Taheri, *Holy Terror: Inside the World of Islamic Terrorism* (Bethesda, Maryland: Adler & Adler, 1987), 241-3.

139 "Gunmen attack night club Mombasa," *Telegraph*, May 15, 2012; "Bomb in south Lebanon restaurant injures five," Reuters, April 23, 2012.

140 "Officials: Islamic extremist planned to bomb Florida sites," WKMG ClickOrlando.com, January 9, 2012.

141 Mohamed Saadouni, "Rabat Salafists assault woman over dress," *Magharebia*, May 11, 2012.

142 Dinesh D'Souza, "Land of the Free: The Islamic critique cuts deep, but there is an answer," *National Review*, July 2, 2004.

143 Jamie Glazov, Interview with Dinesh D'Souza, "Did the Cultural Left Cause 9/11?," FrontPageMagazine.com, January 25, 2007.

144 "Islamic Rulings on Contraception," Islamic Learning Materials, http://islamiclearningmaterials.com/islam-birth-control.

145 Sahih Bukhari, vol. 3, book 34, no. 2229.

146 Malik's Muwatta, translated by 'A'isha'Abdarahman at-Tarjumana and Ya'qub Johnson, vol. 29, book 32, no. 98. Center for Muslim-Jewish Engagement. www.cmje.org/religious-texts/*hadith*/muwatta.

147 Sahih Muslim, book 8, no. 3377.

148 Sunan Abu Dawud, translated by Ahmad Hasan, book 11, no. 2166. Center for Muslim-Jewish Engagement. www.cmje.org/religious-texts/*hadith*/abudawud.

149 Sahih Muslim, book 8, no. 3388.

150 Malik's Muwatta, vol. 29, book 32, no. 100.

151 Sa'diyya Shaikh, "Family planning, Contraception and Abortion in Islam: Undertaking Khilafah: Moral Agency, Justice and Compassion," in *Sacred Choices: The Case for Contraception and Abortion in World Religions*, edited by D. Maguire (Oxford: Oxford University Press, 2003).

152 S. M. Rizvi, "Marriage and Morals in Islam." www.al-islam.org/m_morals/chap4.htm.

153 SayyidSabiq, *Fiqhu'l-Sunnah*, special edition, vol. 2, (Cairo: ShirkahManar al-Dawliyyah, 1997), p. 334. Quoted http://al-mawrid.org/pages/questions_english_detail.php?qid=374&cid=227#_ftn3.

154 Tom Ehrlich, "Where does God stand on abortion?," *USA Today*, August 13, 2006.

155 Sherman Jackson, *Islam and the Blackamerican: looking toward the third resurrection* (Oxford: Oxford University Press, 2005), 151.

156 Barbara Crossette, "Vatican Drops Fight Against U.N. Population Document," *New York Times*, September 10, 1994.

157 Nina Bernstein, "In Secret, Polygamy Follows Africans to N.Y.," *New York Times*, March 23, 2007.

158 Nicholas Hellen, "Muslim second wives may get a tax break," *The Times of London*, December 26, 2004; www.muslimparliament.org.uk/about.htm.

159 "Two wives," *Jerusalem Post*, July 12, 2005.

160 Maryclaire Dale, "Pa. bigamist slain hours before trip," Associated Press, August 8, 2007.

161 There have been a few notable exceptions. See, for example, Lornet Turnbull, "Opponents of gay-marriage law get unexpected aid: from Muslims," *Seattle Times*, May 24, 2012.

162 Some Muslim sources render this as "I divorce you."

163 Bukhari, vol. 7, book 67, no. 5206.

164 Bukhari, vol. 5, book 63, no. 3894.

165 Bukhari, vol. 5, book 63, no. 3896; cf. Bukhari, vol. 7, book 67, no. 5158.

166 "Islamist leader threatens of waging Jihad," Weekly Blitz, April 20, 2011.

167 "Fatwa: 'It Is Permissible to Have Sexual Intercourse with a Prepubescent Girl,'" *Translating Jihad*, January 14, 2011.

168 Amir Taheri, *The Spirit of Allah: Khomeini and the Islamic Revolution* (Adler and Adler, 1986), 35.

169 Lisa Beyer, "The Women of Islam," Time, November 25, 2001.

170 "Yemen: Ban on Child Brides Is Imperiled," Associated Press, March 22, 2010.

171 "Human Rights Watch urges Yemen to ban child marriage, details plight of country's child brides," Associated Press, December 8, 2011.

172 "Outcry in The Hague over 'pedo imam,'" Radio Netherlands Worldwide, December 6, 2011.

173 "Calls to end child marriages rejected," *Straits Times*, December 8, 2010.

174 Pavan Amara, "Islington girls forced into marriage at the age of nine," *Islington Tribune*, January 27, 2012.

175 "Flerahundra fall avbarnäktenskapi Sverige," *Dagen*, April 20, 2011. Translated as "Several hundred cases of child marriages in Sweden," translated by Nicolai Sennels, Jihad Watch, June 13, 2011.

176 Hilary Andersson, "Born to be a slave in Niger, *BBC News*, February 11, 2005.

177 *Reliance of the Traveller*, o9.13.

178 "Egyptian Shaykh: Jihad Is Solution to Muslims' Financial Problems," *Translating Jihad*, May 31, 2011.

179 "Video: Shaykh al-Huwayni: 'When I want a sex slave, I just go to the market and choose the woman I like and purchase her,'" *Translating Jihad*, June 11, 2011.

180 "Video: Kuwaiti Activist: 'I Hope that Kuwait Will Enact a Law for . . . Sex Slaves,'" *Translating Jihad*, June 22, 2011.

181 Raymond Ibrahim, "Muslim Woman Seeks to Revive Institution of Sex-Slavery," FrontPage Magazine.com, June 6, 2011.

182 Graham Smith and Damien Gayle, "Grooming gang found GUILTY: Nine men shared girls aged 13 to 15 for sex and raped one up to twenty times a day," Daily Mail, May 8, 2012; Dominic Casciani, "More than 2,000 children 'victims of sex grooming,'" BBC News, June 29, 2011; James Tozer, "Police 'hid' abuse of 60 girls by Asian takeaway workers linked to murder of 14-year-old," Daily Mail, April 8, 2011.

183 Brandon Gee, "Sex trafficking trial unusual in scope: As many as 23 will face jury simultaneously," *Tennessean*, February 28, 2012.

184 Najafi Quchani, *Siyahat-e Sharq* (Tehran, 1984), 399-401. Quoted in BaqerMoin, *Khomeini: Life of the Ayatollah* (New York: St. Martin's Press, 1999), 30.

185 Benedict XVI, "Faith, reason and the university: memories and reflections," Papal Address at University of Regensburg, September 12, 2006.

186 Khaled Abu Toameh, "Gazans warn pope to accept Islam," *Jerusalem Post*, September 18, 2006.

187 "Open Letter to Pope Benedict XVI," *Islamica Magazine*, issue 18, 25, October 13, 2006. http://islamicamagazine.com/?p=634.

188 "Sheikh Ahmad Abu Quddum of Jordan's Tahrir Party Discusses Jihad Against Germany, Pledges to Impose 'Jizya' Poll Tax on Non-Muslims, and Vows to Annihilate Israel," Middle East Media Research Institute, December 12, 2011.

189 "Jordanian Sheik Nader Tamimi, Mufti of the Palestinian Liberation Army, to the West: We Will Restore the Caliphate and You Will Pay the Jizya 'or Else We Will Bring the

Sword to Your Necks,'" Middle East Media Research Institute, December 15, 2011.

190 Sandro Magister, "The Mayor of Bethlehem Is Christian, But It's Hamas That's in Charge," Chiesa, December 29, 2005.

191 Moses Maimonides, *The Guide for the Perplexed*, M. Friedländer, trans. (New York: Barnes & Noble, 2004), 220-221.

192 Quoted in Pamela Geller, "'Rediscovered' Another Museum Exhibit of Muslim Lies," AtlasShrugs.com, February 21, 2012.

193 *Sahih Muslim*, book 19, no. 4294.

194 *Reliance of the Traveller*, o9.0.

195 *Reliance of the Traveller*, o9.8.

196 *Al-Hidayah*, vol. Ii. P. 140, quoted in Thomas P. Hughes, *A Dictionary of Islam* (W.H. Allen, 1895), "Jihad," 243-248.

197 *Al-Hidayah*, vol. Ii. P.140, in Thomas P. Hughes, "Jihad," in *A Dictionary of Islam*, (London: W.H. Allen, 1895), 243-248.

198 IbnKhaldun, *The Muqaddimah: An Introduction to History*, translated by Franz Rosenthal; edited and abridged by N. J. Dawood (Princeton: Princeton University Press, 1967), 183.

199 Ibn Taymiyya, "Jihad," in Rudolph Peters, *Jihad in Classical and Modern Islam* (Princeton: Markus Wiener Publishers, 1996), 49.

200 "A Common Word between Us and You (Summary and Abridgement)," A Common Word, www.acommonword.com/index.php?lang=en&page=option1.

201 Alan Cooperman, "For Victims, Strong Words Were Not Enough," *Washington Post*, April 3, 2005.

202 Pope John Paul II, "Homily of the Holy Father: 'Day of Pardon,'" March 12, 2000. www.vatican.va/holy_father/john_paul_ii/homilies/2000/documents/hf_jp-ii_hom_20000312_pardon_en.html.

203 *Ecumenical Jihad*, 30.

204 Sayyid Qutb, *Milestones*, Mother Mosque Foundation, n.d., 263.

205 "Muslim scholars' olive branch to Christians," *Telegraph*, October 12, 2007.

206 Peter Graff, "Unprecedented Muslim call for peace with Christians," Reuters, October 11, 2007.

207 Dinesh D'Souza, "Muslims Who Renounce Violence," AOL.com, February 20, 2008.

208 "Declaration on Interfaith and Intercultural Dialogue," *Jordan Times*, December 17, 2010.

209 Benedict XVI, Address at Queen Alia International Airport of Amman, May 8, 2009. www.vatican.va/holy_father/benedict_xvi/speeches/2009/may/documents/hf_ben-xvi_spe_20090508_welcome-amman_en.html.

210 Benedict XVI, Address at the King Hussein Mosque in Amman, Jordan, May 9, 2009.

211 Benedict XVI, Address at the King Hussein Mosque in Amman, Jordan, May 9, 2009.

212 David Kerr, "Pope calls Lebanese youth to 'revolution of love,'" Catholic News Agency, September 15, 2012.